Who is WRITING ACTIVE l for?

Beginners AND advanced w to engage readers from page on get there.

Writers who want to understand hooks and how to use them. You want to create more compelling stories, stories that readers just can't put down. (the kind you stay up all night to finish!)

You want to enhance up your current story, but more than that, you want to understand exactly how hooks can help set the pace of a story, in any genre.

You're also busy with a job, family, or other obligations so while you want more than a prompt you'd LOVE to find clear, actionable steps that you can start implementing immediately.

Who are the Writing Active Setting books NOT for?

"Just give me the prompt" writers. These books assume you want to grow as a writer and not simply find a quick, one answer description that fits all novels.

Writers who aren't really interested in improving in their craft. Do you write for fun, but don't really care if anyone sees your work? Do you want a quick answer but don't want to understand how to make a difference long term in your writing? These books are created specifically to help you grow as a writer by powering up your ability to show not tell setting descriptions. So if that doesn't sound like you, these books are probably not the best fit for you.

"The Writing Active series takes an all too often overlooked technique, and elevates it to a next-level game changer for powerful fiction."

~ **Cathy Yardley,** author of *Rock Your Plot*

"WRITING ACTIVE HOOKS is a powerful combination of fresh insights, practical examples, and how-to advice on the often overlooked but critical element of Hooks…written in a quick-to-read and easy to understand style, and packed with useful application exercises."

~ **Kelly L. Stone,** author of THINKING WRITE: The Secret to Freeing Your Creative Mind

**Writing Active Hooks:**

**The Complete How-to Guide**

Published by
Cantwell Publishing LLC
162 Taylor Blvd
Sequim, WA 98382
USA

ISBN: 978-1-939210-19-7

Cover design by
THE KILLION GROUP, INC.
www.thekilliongroupinc.com

## Table of Contents

# HOOKS

## INTRODUCTION

If you've read the shorter e-books in this series—*WRITING ACTIVE HOOKS: Book 1 and WRITING ACTIVE HOOKS: Book 2*—thank you! For those of you who have, and haven't, I'll clarify the differences between those versions and this one.

In *WRITING ACTIVE HOOKS: Book 1*, I examined the five most common hooks writers can use—Action/Danger, Overpowering Emotion, Surprising Situation, Totally Unexpected and Question(s) Raised Hooks—and gave some information on where using those hooks can really pay off for the writer in terms of pacing and guiding a reader deeper into your novel.

In *WRITING ACTIVE HOOKS: Book 2* we looked at an additional four hooks—the Unique Character Hook, the Evocative Hook, the Foreshadowing with or without Warning Hook and the Surprising or Shocking Dialogue Hook and went into detail about hook placement throughout your novel and why specific placement matters.

In this version, *WRITING ACTIVE HOOKS: Book 3: All Ten Universal Hooks plus more,* you will receive everything from the smaller e-books PLUS an additional hook—the Humor Hook—with even more examples from a variety of genres to dig deep into why these ten hooks are so powerful regardless of what you write.

As a writing craft instructor I've found that it's important to repeat salient points in as many ways as possible to introduce and anchor the concepts, especially if most of the information is new to you.

Hooks are a vital tool to engage readers, and to keep them engaged, as they read deeper into your story. They are used to raise questions for—and elicit responses from—a reader to compel them to read a little further.

It's that simple. And that hard.

Let's be clear about this last point. In any book there are always story hooks—the premise, or implied promise—depending on your specific story and the readers' expectations. If you are writing a mystery, romance, sci-fi, thriller, or any genre/commercial fiction type of book, your implied promise is to find justice, discover love, save a species or planet, or stop a threat. Yes, there are nuances to these promises, but the reader picks up these novels knowing that, by the end of the story, certain expectations will be met. The killer is found and justice balanced. The hero and heroine (or hero/hero; heroine/heroine; etc.,) will find love or the strong possibility of love. A planet, people, remaining hope of a species, etc., will survive an external threat, or that the race to stop something bad from happening will resolve squarely in the fact that the good—or mostly good—guys will overcome the threat.

If you are writing literary fiction, there still remains a story premise. The reader will finish the novel with a change in their understanding of what the human condition means and how we function. There are no clear happy-ever-after endings; in fact, it's often just the opposite. The promise to the reader in a literary novel is that they will be compelled to rethink their assumptions and expand their understanding of whatever issue is the glue that holds the story together: survivor's guilt, abandonment, betrayal, abuse, or whatever other issue is being explored.

**NOTE:** Writers can write anywhere along the continuum between strong literary and strong commercial fiction or they can lean toward one end of the continuum or the other.

The following definition might help:

*Commercial fiction derives from myths and fairy tales, and is often called "genre fiction". It is based on the readers' belief that if they try hard enough they can achieve something and make a change in their world for the better. Romances, mysteries, suspense, thrillers, science fiction (often called "sci-fi"), fantasy, etc., are commercial fiction genres.*

*. . .Literary Fiction is based on the readers' belief system that they cannot change their world, but they can understand it better. The plot structure of literary fiction does not move toward a specific goal but involves peeling away the emotions and dark secrets of the human condition in an attempt to better understand. The protagonist in literary fiction need not grow or change over the course of the story.*

—Mary Buckham and Dianna Love—*Break Into Fiction*®

If you don't know what it is you are writing—and many writers don't until they've been writing for a while—go to a brick-and-mortar store and walk down the aisles. Look at the selections and consider where your novel might fit best. If it doesn't fit under one of the Section headings—Mysteries, Romance, Sci-Fi/Fantasy, Westerns, etc., —you have a 50/50 chance of writing more literary than commercial fiction. Keep in mind that this is an approximation, as some modern commercial fiction doesn't fit cleanly into those categories, such as paranormal, urban fantasy, speculative fiction, which may be shelved under romance, mysteries, sci-fi or in general fiction.

Look in the general fiction or fiction area and see what blurbs and story descriptions resonate with your story. If at the end of the story the protagonist grows or changes, you'll most likely be writing commercial fiction.

Unfortunately, there are exceptions to every assumption. Since this is not a book about understanding commercial versus literary fiction and the nuances in between, I won't go into more detail. What's important to note is that hooks are applicable no matter what you write. It's also important to know what you are writing and what types of hooks are used most often for YOUR type of novel.

The placement of the hooks we'll be discussing will be the same regardless of your type of story. The number and type of hooks used will vary depending on the type of story you are crafting and, when applicable, I'll explain those differences.

That's an important distinction to make, and I'll guide you into discovering how to know what hooks you might want to use and how many, depending on the genre of novel you're writing.

First, we have to understand in greater depth what a hook does for the reader.

Hooks, or more specifically, the questions raised by hooks, help guide your reader deeper and deeper into your book like a map. Hooks are the road signs that intentionally entice and direct them to turn the page and keep reading. Yes, it's that straightforward. By strategically using hooks you are giving your readers strong incentives to read just a little more.

The intention of the first line of your book is to get the second line read. The intention of the second line is to compel the reader to read until the end of the first paragraph and so on. Good hooks pull the reader, step by step, into and through your story.

You know a strong sentence or paragraph has hooked you if you continue to turn the page when you had intended to stop. This is why hooks are used in key locations — to encourage the reader to turn that page. Understanding how to do that with the ten hooks detailed in this book, as well as their placement, will help you reach that goal.

**NOTE:** The strongest hooks raise questions or reactions in a reader.

A reaction, whether overt or reluctant, is subconsciously elicited, which makes the reader want to discover more. We're not talking about a question or questions raised that will take the reader all the way to the end of the book to discover the answers, though some hooks may have elements of that included. For the most part, it's smaller increments of curiosity we, as writers, raise with our word choices and strategic use of hooks. We're seeking the kinds of responses that pay off for both reader and author.

We'll spend a fair amount of time examining ten specific types of hooks in one of the most important places to position your hooks — your opening sentence. Why? Usually if readers don't read past this line, they won't read the first paragraph or the first page. If they don't get to the bottom of the page and turn it, they usually won't buy or read your book at all. Unless they have another compelling reason to do so — the book club is reading it, it's required for a class assignment, or everybody and their second cousin is talking about this book so they have to find out why.

Those are exceptions, and they'll always occur. What we want to focus on more importantly is why these ten universal hooks work and where they work the hardest.

**NOTE:** Be aware that *not* all hooks will resonate as strongly, and in the same way, with every reader.

Hooks, by their very nature, are subjective, which means what catches your attention strongly may not work for another reader. That's okay, because as we examine these ten hooks, one by one, and why a particular hook works, we'll also look at how to combine each specific hook with other hooks.

In the key places to use hooks, including that opening sentence and paragraph, we rarely trust ourselves with one hook only. Why? The subjective issue — if your chosen hook doesn't resonate as strongly with a reader — which is what an editor or agent is, also — then an additional hook makes sure that your reader is engaged and remains engaged.

**NOTE:** Some hooks work better in some types of stories, whereas other hooks will not work as well, so study the type of story or stories you want to write in order to learn which hooks are most common and which hooks are rare.

One other issue to consider as we dig further into hooks is to be aware of your intention and what your readers expect, given the types of books they are reading and you are writing. Using too many hooks in an opening for a story that's not meant to be fast-paced, or conversely, too few hooks in a story that's meant to jump you into the events at a breakneck speed, will put you, the author, in conflict with a reader's expectations.

A cozy mystery, a literary novel, or women's fiction for example, are not paced at the speed of a thriller or romantic suspense or action-adventure novel, so keep your hooks appropriate to what you're writing.

**NOTE:** As you apply hooks be conscious of what you are writing, based on your readers' expectations.

Be prepared to experience a certain degree of awkwardness when you first start playing with hooks. That's natural and to be expected. When any instructor stops your current process temporarily to adjust your mechanics, there can be a period of resistance, whether you are learning to write, swing a club or drive a motorcycle. You might need to slow down your writing or revising to pay attention so that you are writing with intention. Initially, that may feel labor intensive and unnatural, but eventually, your writing process becomes easier and your writing improves.

The oral telling of a story is one thing; writing a story so readers experience what the writer intends them to experience is based on the craft of writing. There are no every-book-follows-the-same formulas in crafting a great story—no one way to use a hook—no hard and fast rules. Hooks are tools added to your craft toolbox, and what makes a professional writer is the understanding of how and when to use a specific tool in a fresh way and with intention. Focusing on hooks forces you, as the writer, to write with intention.

Don't worry if you don't include hooks in your first (or rough) draft. That's what the revision process is all about—looking for opportunities to strengthen your writing. Use hooks whenever the opportunities present themselves, and you'll go a long way toward accomplishing your goal of creating stronger stories.

Also keep in mind that the hooks as presented here are in numeric order, only to make it easier to access them. The order in no way reflects the importance of a hook or which hooks you must study most, that depends on what you are writing and what hooks you need to explore most.

## SECTION 1: UNDERSTANDING HOOKS

## HOOK 1: ACTION OR DANGER HOOKS:

Action is more than movement. Think James Bond action vs. a Jane Austen amble along the lane. Think strong verbs. Think of the type of movement that, were you to see it out of the corner of your eye, would snag and hold your attention. A person walking—not so much. A person running—more so, unless you are in a situation where running is expected. A person running full stop, gasping for breath, creates the strongest Action/Danger Hook possible because it is out of the ordinary; it's what we as readers don't expect to see on a daily basis (unless you're a coach on a high school track team or are training for a sporting event).

**NOTE:** Think: At this point in your story, based on the action or danger you are showing, would the average reader have a question raised in their minds as to what's happening and why?

If you can answer yes to the above question, you most likely have an Action/Danger Hook. If that answer focuses on strong action, not simply movement of a character on the page, then the hook applies. Think, too, of the action in the context of your story. Are you writing Women's Fiction? Then you might not find the Action/Danger Hook used as often because these stories are not usually involving a lot of intense physical action or physical danger. Emotional danger, yes, but since that's often internal, it's not as obvious to a passerby.

Either that or the Overpowering Emotion Hook applies, which we'll examine in a bit.

Danger oftentimes is associated with strong action, which is why these two words create the same kind of hook and can help give you a clue as to whether there really is an Action/Danger Hook on your page. There's danger in a runaway car, whereas a car simply moving doesn't contain that same degree of possible harm.

Danger can be to the POV (point of view) character, another character, inherent in the situation, or implied. Ask yourself: is someone in danger here? Could someone be in danger? Is the situation dangerous?

A man defusing a bomb or rappelling down a mountain is in an inherently dangerous situation, so the hook applies. A car driving down the road—not so much. (Unless there's a sixteen year old male at the wheel with a driver's license in his pocket that's so new the plastic hasn't set yet.) If you are the parent of a new driver, and are at that key stage where you're on hyper vigilance or have experienced firsthand the ramifications of a vehicle accident that came out of the blue, then car movement can ratchet up your sense of danger. But these are the exceptions, the small minority of your readers. Write to the larger set of readers who read what you are writing, not the exceptions.

A man carving a wooden toy is not so dangerous. Sure, he's doing an action, but not something that would draw attention because of that action. It's more a movement. Any danger in that same situation? Not really, as carving can be a common enough activity that most people could do it without thinking this is a dangerous action.

**NOTE:** Action is not movement on the page. Ask yourself, if you saw this action in real life, would it snag your attention until you could find out what exactly is happening?

Always keep in mind where you're using this hook, because deeper into your story the reader might have expectations based upon what you've set up earlier. Think of an action/adventure, or suspense/thriller story, where there's been non-stop action throughout, and you use the same type of action to end chapter twenty or forty that you used in chapter three or five. The Action/Danger Hook used in this context will not have as strong an impact on the reader because they expect your character to continue doing what they've been doing.

For example, let's say in chapter three, you ended with your character defusing a bomb as part of their routine job. The Danger Hook (minus the Action element) applies because, duh, there's a bomb. If twenty chapters later this same character is still doing his everyday job and attempts to defuse a bomb, the reader knows this is expected given what the character does, and he or she survived the first time around, so it's most likely they are going to survive now. So the Danger Hook has been decreased.

However, if you add in an additional risk — the character just had a terrible fight with his/her spouse and isn't one hundred percent focused on the job; this bomb is described as a trickier, more deadly bomb; the POV character must dangle off a tall building to diffuse the bomb — all of these types of issues mean a different form of danger has been injected into the scenario, which will keep the Action/Danger Hook strong.

Let's now look at the Action/Danger Hook in more detail.

### EXAMPLES OF ACTION OR DANGER HOOKS:

*The missile hit without warning.*
–DJ MacHale–*The Soldiers of Halla*

Not knowing anything else about the story, does the above first line of a story imply danger to someone? If you can say yes, even if you as a reader don't yet feel the immediacy of this danger, then you have the Danger Hook without the Action element.

**NOTE:** Danger is relative to your character and the situation, as well as to you as the reader.

There is little action in the line above, but there is danger. Sometimes action goes hand-in-hand with danger, and at other times, one or the other aspects of the hook—action or danger—applies. It's still one hook. Not two.

What if the author, MacHale wrote a rough first draft without hooks?

ROUGH DRAFT: *Missiles had been hitting near the headquarters for some time.*

Notice how the above draft creates a more passive statement. It's a statement of fact and, without any further information; the reader might assume this was being accepted as the normal state of events. Using the past tense decreases the emotional impact of the Action/Danger Hook. The sense of urgency that something bad could happen at any moment has been watered down so the hook no longer applies. The danger, or threat, of the missile is past, so the hook is not as strong as it could be.

The Action/Danger Hook can most often be seen in mysteries, but not all of them. When we talk about mysteries, there are a number of different types of mysteries, or subgenres, and reader expectations can vary between them. Mysteries can be cozy, amateur sleuth, police procedural, legal, medical, private eye, historical, suspense, thriller, crime caper, and more. Again, think of the continuum within the mystery genre. You can have those stories that are not tense and those stories that are very tense. Our next example is from a historical mystery. In historicals, because the writer must set the stage, building awareness for the reader about the time and place; these types of stories often warrant a slower pacing sensibility.

This mystery example is of a passage in an opening scene that is a little over a third of the way into the story. Opening and ending of scenes and chapters can build to a hook using a few sentences, versus one sentence. The keyword is can. They do not always need to, but it is something to keep in mind as you're writing — hooks can be created in one sentence or, once you're past the opening sentence, can be built hook by hook through several sentences. In this example the protagonist is helping a friend named Conrad, who has become embroiled deeper and deeper into a messy and dangerous situation. The author may have written something like this as an early draft:

FIRST DRAFT: *I was sure Conrad was going to get into more trouble so I decided to leave him on the side of the road so it'd take him a long time to walk home.*

This is straight telling, which keeps the reader at arm's length, so decreases the tension of the Action/Danger Hook. Let's see how Walter Mosley incorporated the Action/Danger Hook to encourage the reader to keep reading in his draft:

*I had a knotty problem. There was a semiconscious killer wedged into Conrad's bathroom. The killer now hated me more than he did Conrad. I couldn't let him see me or question Conrad about my identity. On the other hand, if I left Conrad at his house, he might have shot the gangster through the door or window. One way I'd be a target of a killer. The other I'd be an accessory to murder.*
— Walter Mosley — *Bad Boy Brawley Brown*

Can you see how Mosley raises a question in the reader's mind, enough to want to find out what will happen next? The next example comes from a suspense mystery, and is a great example of action, combined with potential danger to create the Action/Danger Hook. First, let's look at a rough draft version. The protagonist normally works behind the scenes in a police investigation in this particular series. In this case, the bottom of the page in chapter twenty-nine in a thirty-six chapter book, the author might have written:

ROUGH DRAFT: *I hopped into the car with the police officer Woolsey and went chasing after the suspect.*

This tell vs. show approach is appropriate if the author wants no focus on the action of a chase scene, or the movement between one place and another is simply to transition the reader to the next scene. But in this case, the author wanted to ramp up the tension by showing that the risks to the protagonist were increasing, and the more risk you show the reader the more tension and the faster the pacing. Here's the example from the author:

*Woolsey hammered up the block and took the corner in a tire-screaming turn. I braced between the door handle and dash. Another hard turn and we were boogying down an alley. Gravel flew from our tires and pinged off dumpsters and rusting car chassis moored at angles to our right and left.*
— Kathy Reichs — *Bare Bones*

Let's look a little closer to see how the author built her Action/Danger Hooks.

The key words to keep in mind in Kathy Reich's example are in bold so they stand out.

*Woolsey **hammered** up the block and took the corner in a **tire-screaming** turn. I **braced** between the door handle and dash. Another **hard** turn and we were **boogying** down an alley. Gravel **flew** from our tires and **pinged** off dumpsters and rusting car chassis moored at angles to our right and left.*

If the author wanted to decrease the tension, keep the movement, but eliminate the Action/Danger Hook, she might have written:

Woolsey drove quickly up the block and turned the corner. Another turn and we were headed down a gravel alley. Dumpsters and rusting car chassis were at angles to our right and left.

Totally different feel isn't it? Watch your power verbs and your descriptive terms in applying the Action/Danger Hook.

Let's examine an Action/Danger Hook from deeper into a story. In this case, the second to the last lines of the prologue of a Fantasy novel:

*Long elegant hands brushed his cheek, then tightened around his throat.*

—George R.R. Martin—*A Game of Thrones*


In this example, can you answer in the affirmative the question: would you feel danger if you were the individual in this situation? If the answer is yes, then the Action/Danger Hook applies even though there is no overt action.

What if Martin wrote:

ROUGH DRAFT: *The man was killed by strangulation.*

Is the immediacy of danger now present? For some readers, any hint of violence creates danger. Remember, you are not writing to the outliers—the readers who don't normally pick up and read your kind of story, because it's outside their comfort zone. You are writing to your core target audience first.

You have to think whether they—your core target audience of readers—would feel danger or action as a result of this line to have it qualify as an Action/Danger Hook. With that criterion, it's clearer that the rough draft version is more passive than immediate.

**NOTE:** End of scenes or chapters can use several sentences or the last paragraph to build additional hooks to engage the reader. Opening lines of a story (whether it's the prologue or the first chapter) require hooks in the first sentence with only a few exceptions—a short sentence that leads to the hooks in the second sentence, a one-hook opening that builds on that a little deeper into the first paragraph, or a writer who doesn't care if they sell their work on a regular basis.

Here's another example of a Danger Hook deeper into a suspense novel. At this point of the story, we know we're in a police procedural, a novel where the protagonist, or in this case, dual protagonists, are involved in a crime scene investigation in an official capacity. The main protagonists, Detective Rizolli and Chief Medical Examiner Dr. Maura Isles, have not yet been introduced, but this story is twelve books into the Rizolli and Isles series.

This particular story does not open in either of the protagonists' points of view but in that of a secondary character, a woman who is in her home, afraid, expecting a threat at any time from a stalker who's been relentless. She is alone and trying to protect her daughter. This situation, at the end of the first chapter, implies danger—a vigilant woman with her vulnerable sleeping daughter, facing an intruder.

Before we move along to how Tess Gerritsen opens the second chapter, keep in mind the last chapter ended on these lines:

*There is no screen over the window. Where is the screen?*
*Only then do I sense the malevolent presence. While I stood lovingly watching my daughter, it was watching me. It has always been watching, biding its time, waiting for its chance to spring. Now it has found us.*
*I turn and face the evil.*
—Tess Gerritsen—*The Keepsake*

This example does a great job of using the Danger (without Action) Hook. The average reader, whether woman or man, would feel the threat and get a visceral response that would compel us to discover more of what happened or was about to happen. The next chapter opens like this:

*Dr. Maura Isles could not decide whether to stay or to flee.*
—Tess Gerritsen—*The Keepsake*

What happened above is we shifted point of view from a woman in danger to one of the series' protagonists. We know this by the specific use of her name, but know nothing else about what is happening. However, coming off the ending of the previous chapter, this chapter opening continues the Danger Hook. The reader is set up from the end of one chapter to the beginning of the next to read just a smidge more to find out if Dr. Maura Isles is indeed in danger, what's threatening her and if she will be all right.

**NOTE:** The danger does not need to go on indefinitely in the scene or the chapter to work as a hook. An initial Danger Hook line can be clarified almost immediately, or prolonged deeper into the scene, chapter or story.

Let's look at another example; this one is from a light, sexy romantic suspense novel.

*Detective Chase Kelly stared into the nose of a .45 semiautomatic, his mind desperately seeking a way out.*
–Christie Craig–*Divorced, Desperate, and Delicious*

The author clearly understands her target audience by using a Danger Hook but not an OMG he's-going-to-die-any-second version.

The key words Craig uses to keep this opening line on the light side include: *his mind* (filtering words which allow the reader to step away from the immediacy of the situation); *desperately* (the reader is told what emotions the character is feeling vs. shown by sweat beading his forehead, the kick start of his heart rate, his muscles locking in a freeze or fight response); *seeking a way out*; these type of longer phrases slow the momentum. The more words used, the easier it can be to soften the immediacy, which again downplays the threat level.

**NOTE:** Burying the danger or action in the middle of a longer sentence with less intense word choices is an effective way to tone down the Action/Danger Hook. The hook still applies, but it's not as intense.

Look what happens if we rewrite the example above — for mystery readers of a police procedural on the darker side — a different core reader audience.

> *Detective Chase Kelly stared into the blunt and ugly nose of a .45 semiautomatic pistol.*

Notice how adding three key words and eliminating the last phrase of the original sentence changes the intention of this opening line. Do you, as a reader, feel the immediacy of the danger more here? Does the character feel in a dangerous situation without anything else being known about the story? If you can say yes to one, or both, of these questions, then you've crafted a strong Danger Hook.

**NOTE:** Within any genre, stories can run a continuum between less tense to very tense, falling anywhere on the spectrum. The differences are created because of the authors' word choices, voice, intentions, pacing sensibilities, tension created, etc.

Let's try a different version of the original sentence. This one is for literary readers:

> *Highly decorated Detective Chase Kelly gazed into a .45 semiautomatic, not for the first time and probably not for the last time, but today there was a difference.*

In this example, the focus is shifted off the danger by bracketing it with more information, watering down the intention of an immediate threat, and changing the situation more into an intellectual conundrum.

The phrase *but today there was a difference* is the strongest hook here. This Question(s) Raised Hook (which we'll get into in more detail deeper into this book), is appropriate for those who want to read more about the character's reactions and responses to bad things that have happened *than* if they wanted to read about the bad things *about* to happen.

The readers of the darker police procedural want the emotional response of the situation as it's being experienced by the POV character. They want to be in the character's skin and emotions as he is facing danger, not just in his head. Understanding hooks is not enough. You must also understand what your readers expect from them. How? You were a reader first, before you became a writer. Now become a reader who takes their reading one step further by learning to analyze/understand what you're reading. Read a novel or story the first time for sheer pleasure or escapism or whatever reason you want. Then return to read a second time to learn how to replicate (or avoid) your personal experiences in reading.

Back to another Action/Danger Hook example:

> *One minute before the explosion, the square at Sensasie was at peace.*
> –Ken Follett–*Jackdaws*

This example is a very subtle use of the Action/Danger Hook because Follett sets up the reader to expect a catastrophic event to happen in less than sixty seconds and compares it to the current situation and the potential loss of life. There are a number of hooks in the above example but we want to focus on just the Action/Danger Hook here.

What if Follett was not such a master of his craft? What if he trusted, or assumed, that the reader would keep reading without giving them a strong reason to do so? What if he was a debut or mid-list author who had not learned to treat every new reader as the important people they are? Without them, and without their willingness to take a risk on an unknown-to-them author and talk about that book after they've read it, authors could not make a living and continue to write.

So let's examine how Follett could have approached his opening sentence.

FIRST DRAFT: *The square at Sensasie was at peace.*

No hooks are present at all. No sense of immediate danger. No sense of violence and loss of innocent lives. Nothing. The reader is kept waiting for something more to engage them. They must continue to read to find a hook.

Most readers will not continue reading, especially if the author is new to them or unless they are engaged for a totally different reason than the writing/story—subject matter, a friend strongly recommended the book to them, or perhaps everyone is talking about the story. If you as a writer have none of these factors on your side, you'd better hook a reader based on your specific word choices and hold them based on the strength and execution of your writing.

SECOND DRAFT: *Before the explosion, the square at Sensasie was at peace.*

This is a stronger sentence that does raise a question for the reader but not the Action/Danger Hook, not without that sense of immediate threat created by the key phrase—*One minute before the explosion.* The reader is left aware there will be an explosion, but the tension is decreased because we don't know if this is happening now, tomorrow, or five years from now. We're being told about danger in an abstract sense, as if we're reading a history book and not in the middle of something horrible that's about to happen.

NOTE: Always ask yourself, would you, in the situation you've written, feel in danger based on this particular line or paragraph? If your answer is based on what's going to happen later on the page, or in the story, you do not have the Action/Danger Hook present.

Here's another example, this one from an amateur sleuth mystery series. Look specifically at how the author includes danger without the danger being immediate. Here we have a situation that can create fear, which often implies danger, and a body language description that enforces that danger may be present, but the character is not in a dangerous situation.

> *A sudden banging on the front door sent a chill down my neck and into my chest.*
> — Walter Mosley — *Fear Itself*

Let's pull apart this opening line of Mosley's novel to see how he creates an Action/Danger Hook that is very appropriate for a mystery, but one less intense than some, while more intense than others.

*A sudden banging on the front door* – by putting yourself in this position, and knowing nothing else about the story, answer this question; would a sudden banging on the front door spike your adrenaline enough to make you have to know more? If your answer is yes, the danger is present if implied. The key word is *banging*, which is a stronger verb than knocking, which would not hint at danger or a threat at all. Now look at . . . *sent a chill down my neck and into my chest.* Here is a visceral reaction our bodies feel when faced with danger or fear. Since this is a universal response, it implies there may be a threat, and thus danger, beyond that door. If the implied danger proves to not be dangerous at all in a few sentences or paragraphs, the hook still works. This applies to all hooks. Remember, the hook is only meant to keep a reader reading. Once the question created by the specific hook — in this situation, is there something or someone dangerous on the other side of the door—is answered, then the Danger Hook dissipates.

**NOTE:** If you raise a question via using a hook or hooks, and then answer the questions raised right away, you'll need to thread in other questions before too long to continue to hold the reader's attention.

One more example of the Danger Hook: this one at the end of chapter one, nine pages into a thriller by Lisa Gardner. At this point of the story, the reader knows we're in the point of view of a woman who has been out to dinner celebrating her wedding anniversary after recently discovering that her wonderful husband has been cheating on her. She lives a very good life, has a beautiful home in an excellent area of Boston, one beloved daughter, and everything that should make her life perfect. Or so she had thought. The reader has been set on edge because the POV character is on edge, which in turn prepares the reader to expect something is about to happen in the story.

At the end of the meal, when they returned home, with her in an acute state of emotional misery but unable to confront her husband, they discover that the front door of their home is ajar. Assuming at first their teenage daughter forgot, again, to lock it, they enter only to be confronted by a masked man, who tasers the husband. He falls, then, the wife is tasered and goes down but is still conscious.

This is a frightening, action-fueled scene, but Gardner does not end it on that note. Instead, Gardner ratchets up the threat, danger, and emotions a step further by building to this point.

> *In my last second of consciousness, I managed to turn my head. I saw two more black forms, one on each side of my daughter's twisting body, as they dragged her down the stairs.*
> *Briefly our gazes met.*
> *I love you, I tried to say.*
> *But the words wouldn't come out.*

*The black-masked figure raised his Taser again. Calmly inserted a fresh cartridge. Took aim. Fired.*
*My fifteen-year old daughter started to scream.*
— Lisa Gardner — *Touch & Go*

In this last example, Gardner uses the shorter length of her sentences to increase the tension, building, building, building, to these last lines and images of a mother unable to do anything, having watched first her husband, a man who'd always been able to do anything, being immobilized, then herself. But the danger doesn't stop there. It's the mother's last conscious thought of not knowing what's happening to her daughter that creates the hook that compels the reader to turn the page and continue reading that next chapter.

**NOTE:** Keep in mind that end of scene and chapter hooks can be longer than a single line.

This next genre, romance, is not one a lot of writers assume is about action or danger, and in some ways they're correct. The focus on these stories is on the romance. However, the Action/Danger Hook can still be present. When we talk about romance we're looking at sub-genres that include historical, paranormal, sweet, erotic, inspirational and contemporary categories. There are a lot of subgenres of romance, so again, be aware of what the reader expects from the type of story you're writing. The first example we're going to look at comes from a historical romance. Remember, historical often means slower paced. This one is set during the roaring twenties. A young, somewhat spoiled, very independent young woman has been sent from the gay life of Paris due to a scandal. She's been banished to Eastern Africa for a year until the furor dies down, if it ever does.

In this particular example at the end of the chapter the protagonist, the woman, has met a man who will be the love interest of the story, but he's not her idea of a lover. There's a conversation that ensues and the hook here at the end of chapter three could have been written as:

ROUGH DRAFT: *"Do you know the men of the club are betting on you?"*
*"Let them bet," I said, "it won't be the first time, hopefully not the last."*

There are hooks here. There are hooks of Foreshadowing and Question(s) Raised, but not the Action/Danger Hook. Let's see how the author wrote this. The first person talking is the eventual love interest, the man:

*"You've already made the betting book at the club," he told me, holding me fast with those remarkable eyes.*
*"Have I indeed? What are the terms?"*
*"Fifty pounds to whoever names the man who beds you first," he stated flatly.*
*I rose and went to the door, turning back just as I reached it. I gave him a slow, purposeful look, taking him in from the battered boots to filthy unkempt hair. "Tell me, who did you put your money on?"*
*He stretched his legs out to cross them at the ankle. He folded his arms behind his head and gave me a slow grin. "Why myself of course."*
—Deanna Rayburn—*A Spear of Summer Grass*

One of the important things to know about this particular example is that it is an emotional and mental type of action and danger, not physical. She's not physically afraid of him. The readers are not physically afraid for her, but this passage at the end of this chapter raises the Action/Danger Hook for these two characters. Something is about to happen between them that has emotional ramifications for both.

## NO ACTION/DANGER HOOK:

Particularly with the Action/Danger Hook, it might be easier to see what exactly is meant by action by comparing sentences that contain movement of people or things on the page but not the type of action that earns the Action/Danger Hook designation. Like this first example:

Mac walked around the corner and picked up a box.

There IS movement of the character through space in the above example but there is no sense of need-to-pay-attention action. Nor is there any danger, so there is no Action/Danger Hook.

How could you add in action or danger? Here are three different examples:

*Mac walked around the corner and picked up a box, stepping through the doorway to descend, unaware that the rivets securing the metal stairs from the third floor loft to the wall had been unbolted.*

*The anthrax virus coated both the inside and outside of the box I sent Mac to collect around the corner.*

*Sliding along the narrow granite ledge, one foot at a time, Mac edged around the last corner and snagged the box.*

Three different scenarios, three possible ways to use an Action/Danger Hook. The first example made it clear that Mac could easily fall three stories. The second rewrite, with the word *anthrax*, and the common knowledge of how deadly this bacteria is, creates danger. And the third example, with the words *narrow, ledge, edged* and *one foot at a time*—show implied danger.

**NOTE:** Each word choice you make when crafting your hooks can enhance—or weaken—your intention.

Here's another No Action or Danger Hook example:

*The paper cut kept aching long after Steve had sliced his finger.*

Yes, for some people, this could be a dangerous situation, but only if you suffer from hemophilia, are a drama queen, or, as a reader, you are aware that a rare poison was on the paper and thus this character is going to die because of that paper cut.

Remember you are asking: would this sentence by itself, or as a result of what's been made clear to the reader up to this point (poison on the paper, for example) lead the average reader to feel the character is in a dangerous situation? If not, then the Action/Danger Hook is not applicable.

Let's examine one more example. This is from a writer who writes Up Market Fiction, stories taken from the headlines, but not in a CSI suspense or mystery approach, rather from a more literary approach. This means the author will want to reel back on an Action/Danger Hook because her readers are not reading for that element. They are reading to understand what makes one human being do something that others cannot easily fathom.

*The night before I got married I woke up, screaming, from my sleep.*
*— Jodi Picoult — Songs of the Humpback Whale*

What's important to look at in this example is that if this had been an opening line to a novel, such as the earlier Walter Mosley mystery passage, a reader could imply danger, knowing nothing else.

However, in this story there had been a prologue. Many writers assume they have to create a strong hook for the opening to the first chapter, but somehow a prologue is a different situation. From a reader's perspective, it isn't.

**NOTE:** Prologues, in a reader's mind, are the first introduction to the story, so they must be strong and clear as to what kind of story the reader is about to encounter, and should contain the same number of hooks you would use in an opening chapter.

The Picoult example is the opening line of the first chapter. The story started with a prologue in the POV of a pre-teen girl, the only child in a family falling apart, very appropriate for a literary novel. The sentence we're examining, which opens the first chapter, is mitigated in intensity, or in other words, the tension is lessened because we know the woman who is screaming will go on to get married and live a number of semi-happy years. The sense of danger has been removed by what's been written already.

**NOTE:** Study what you want to write in order to learn first-hand what types of hooks, how many, and where they need to be placed to continue to engage the reader and draw them deeper into your story.

## ASSIGNMENTS:

1)  Visit a bookstore (online or in person) or a library. Pull out books in a genre you normally don't read (for example, if you normally read literary novels, try science fiction; if you read mysteries, try romances). Don't look at the cover or back cover blurb if possible, because these contain their own versions of hooks. Read the first sentence only. This is where your understanding of the use of hooks really matters. Continue to pull books until you find one that compels you to keep reading. If you find a book in

which you read far enough to turn the page to find out more, look at this book closely, because this author understands how to use hooks. If you can engage a reader that normally doesn't read in that genre, you're doing something well.

**HINT:** The average number of books examined runs between 16-25 books before most writers find a book that works for them. Some writer/readers have gone up to 40-50 books. Since these are not the books or stories you normally gravitate to, it's the writing alone that will keep you reading.

Make sure you're not using books on your bookshelves at home. Why? Because you've already pre-selected these books — either you like the author, had the book recommended, someone else thought you might like this book — whatever the reason, it'll skew your results.

Also, make sure you're using books in a genre you normally don't read. Why? Because if you love what you're browsing through — romance, westerns, general fiction, YA (young adult), etc. — you are once again predisposed to find something you like.

The intention of this exercise is to show you what it's like for a cold reader — one who doesn't have cover art or a blurb — to convince them to keep reading when they don't know you as an author.

2) Now find 8-12 books similar to what you are writing. By that I mean your book would be shelved in the same area in a bookstore; make sure some of these books are by debut authors or authors you have never read. Why? Because their hooks must be stronger to entice you into reading more.

Make sure you haven't read the book yet because you want to be hooked based on that key first line, not by what you know happens on page three. Look at just the opening line. If it's a short line or in dialogue, read until there's a natural stop.

Write the line down so you're not analyzing this line in context with what comes next in the story. Then compare these 8-12 lines and ask yourself is the Action/Danger Hook used? Also, would you keep reading based on just this line?

The intention of this exercise is to train you to see what you might never have looked at closely before. If out of a half-dozen lines in this last set of books you see no Action/Danger Hooks, it's a pretty good guess this is not a common hook in this type of story. However, if you notice that the Action/Danger Hook appears in all the debut authors — which means they had to work harder to compete against published authors who have a following — it means that the hook expectations are changing, and whereas this particular hook was not once as common, it is coming into style now.

**NOTE:** It's always vital to read newer releases as well as your favorite authors when studying the craft of writing. You would not study what was popular on TV or at the movies from ten or fifteen or twenty years ago and expect to break into a competitive marketplace with a script based on those TV shows or movies. The same applies to novels.

### RECAP:

- Write to the largest set of readers who read what you are writing, not the exceptions who might respond differently to your hooks based on where they are personally in their lives.
- To soften the intensity of an Action/Danger Hook, bury it deeper into a longer sentence, or simply imply it.
- Action means more than movement.
- Once the questions created by any hook are answered, then the hook no longer engages the reader as strongly, especially with the Action/Danger Hook.

## HOOK 2: THE OVERPOWERING EMOTION HOOK

This second type of hook is not to be confused with just any emotion. A cry is emotion; a scream is much stronger emotion. A man with a gun is not overpowering emotion; however, the visceral reaction to that gun can create overpowering emotion in the reader. If you don't expect a gun, such as at the opera, or a daycare, or in a genre where the reader doesn't usually expect a gun as a threat, for example a young adult or an inspirational novel or cozy mystery—you can create overpowering emotion by inserting a weapon. But if you're writing a thriller, suspense or police procedural, where a person holding a gun is not as unusual, this situation might create different hooks, such as an Action/Danger Hook, but not an Overpowering Emotion Hook.

The gun can create overpowering emotion in the right situation, but not every situation. This is important to remember and is based on reader expectations.

A man with a shaking hand holding a gun on a stranger is a much more powerful emotion than a hardened criminal holding the same gun on a killer. A midwife holding a gun on the father of the child she just birthed shows more overpowering emotion because of the situation.

**NOTE:** Keep your focus on the word *overpowering* here. Not simply emotion, but *overpowering* emotion.

### EXAMPLES OF OVERPOWERING EMOTION HOOKS:

*People ask whose fault it was. Who caused the accident? Where did the blame lie — on reckless driving, blinding sunlight, a sharp curve in the road? Hidden in their questions*

*is a deeper query. Did Jesse bring it on himself? Was he careless? Perhaps he rode his bike into the middle of the road. Perhaps he insulted God. Maybe that's why he won't be walking me down the aisle, they imply.*
–Meg Gardiner–*Mission Canyon*


The above example is deep into the novel so is longer than what you would expect for an opening line or chapter opening. Once a reader has committed to reading a novel, the hooks do not have to grab them as fast or hard. You can use several sentences to make your hook. By allocating so many words to building the emotion in this example, Gardiner is telling the reader, "pay attention, what's being shared here matters to the story," and creates a stronger Overpowering Emotion Hook than if she simply wrote:

Everyone wondered what happened to cause the accident that paralyzed my former fiancé.

Do you, as a reader, feel any emotion with this telling statement? Do you feel the anguish of the POV character thinking about the man she loves, the man she planned to marry, and the man who no longer wants to marry her? As written, we the reader can understand the emotional tug here, the conflict, the tension. It's built word by word from the image of a young man in a wheelchair to the POV character's internal description of what that wheelchair means to her. Up until the last line of this paragraph, the reader doesn't know that this man is her former fiancé. That's the beat that drives home the emotion.

The first beats key in on what many could focus on — the why of the accident. But Gardiner takes that a step further after starting with the why, a common enough occurrence when we see someone in a wheelchair, especially if it's been made clear this man was a former athlete, a lawyer, a go-getter. To ask what happened is natural and by itself does not create overpowering emotion, or emotion at all. But Gardiner goes deeper and layers from the "why" to "was he at fault" to how that one moment in time changed his life, and hers, forever. And that's where the emotion resides.

Since they are two young people with their whole lives in front of them, the tragedy of the accident is amplified, which shifts the emotion from a shame that something bad happened to a tragic event. That's where the overpowering element comes in.

**NOTE:** With the Overpowering Emotion Hook in particular, you need to keep in mind not all readers will feel emotion in the same way. Aim for the universal middle ground. Could the average reader feel the emotion you're trying to achieve?

Let's look at another example of an Overpowering Emotion Hook.

*The screams had finally ceased.*
*–James Rollins–The Judas Strain*

If Rollins had written: *The sounds had finally ceased*, there would be no overpowering emotion. A Question(s) Raised Hook would apply, but that's all.

As written, the opening sentence contains more than one hook, and the Overpowering Emotional Hook can resonate with a lot of people, especially readers of thrillers and suspense novels, who are looking for that more intense reading experience. Readers of other genres also can identify with certain hooks more than others, so it's important to study published novels in the vein you are writing so you are more aware of what types, as well as how many hooks are expected by the readers of those types of stories.

Here's another Overpowering Emotion Hook, but before we get to the example, let's assume there was a rough draft.

This is an important assumption to make when crafting an opening line hook. Sometimes an opening line appears to a writer and sets off the story. That's wonderful, but too many times writers can agonize over that key first line, sweat it, stop dead in their writing until they craft the ultimate opening sentence when, if they use a place holder and wait until they have finished the initial draft, they might be able to craft a stronger opening based on knowing and grasping the whole story.

So let's build to a stellar opening line showing overpowering emotion.

FIRST DRAFT: *The man had died.*

Death, in any form and to most people, is emotional. So the question here is, based on not knowing anything else about the story except that it's a suspense novel, is this OVERPOWERING emotion? Not really. The man may have been a hundred and ten and lived a good life. The man might have been suffering a terrible disease and death is actually a blessing in ending his pain. The man may be a serial killer that murdered young children.

We don't have enough information that slides this rough draft sentence from an emotional statement of fact in the past tense to a visceral response in our guts that makes us sit up and pay attention.

So let's try again.

SECOND DRAFT: *He was dying.*

Stronger. A better sense of immediacy and urgency. But is it an Overpowering Emotion Hook yet? Not yet. The potential is there, and there are other hooks present, but not that Overpowering Emotion Hook we're going for here.

**NOTE:** Make sure your opening sentence is not too vague—which holds a reader at arm's length, waiting to grasp what is happening—and thus waters down the power of your hook.

Let's see how Frederick Forsyth approached his opening line:

> *The teenage boy was dying alone.*
> —Frederick Forsyth—*The Cobra*

It's the thought of a teenage boy, someone who should have a life yet to live, that shifts this sentence from a statement of fact to one of strong—which can be overpowering—emotion.

**NOTE**: Keep in mind the context of your hook. The reader needs enough info and nuance to make hooks work and make them react the way we want them to.

Remember, the hook at the opening of your story is meant to keep us reading to find out more. If it does, then it's doing its job as a strong hook. If the average reader has to keep reading just a few more sentences to find out what's happening with this teenage boy, not because he's a teenager but because he's dying, then the Overpowering Emotion Hook—the death of a young person—is present.

Here's another Overpowering Emotion Hook that's implied. It's from a suspense/thriller novel, which helps to set up the reader to make some assumptions. If the reader is not familiar with the genre, or the author, the implied emotional power of this short sentence might not be as strong.

> *He is coming for me.*
> —Tess Gerritsen—*The Keepsake*

If the reader reads this in a vacuum, this could mean a plethora of possible scenarios—a youngster waiting to be picked up from school, the principal knocking on a classroom door, a lover picking up someone at the airport; nothing inherently emotional at all.

However, because this is a suspense/thriller, the average reader of those books is going to layer in the threat factor and will thus feel the emotion more. These readers don't need to have it spelled out in the first line that whoever "he" is means danger. Enough danger is implied that one feels just enough fear, the heightened sense of something bad coming directly at a person, something that can be more than scary—until we know otherwise—and the emotion is present and enough to make a reader keep reading until their fears are assuaged or enough is known to decrease the threat level enough to turn away.

**NOTE:** The reader needs the context of the situation, AND the context of genre to experience the strongest hooks.

If we did not know what type of story this is, i.e. where it would be shelved in a bookstore, this line could be less emotionally overpowering because the reader would not necessarily be making assumptions about what's happening. Likewise, if you were a male, especially a male who does not feel vulnerable because of age or health issues, you might feel less overpowering emotion than the average woman, who, simply because she's female, has been made aware that there are dangers in situations a man doesn't think twice about.

This next example comes from a paranormal young adult novel, five books into the series.

Young adult novels often can start with the Overpowering Emotion Hook because the core reading audience for these novels are teens who often expect emotion, and lots of it, in their stories. The emotion can vary—angst, depression, sorrow, fear, etc. —but because these years can often be fraught with heightened emotion, the stories reflect that experience.

Before we jump to the actual example let's assume the author played around with her opening. In this case, the opening line we're looking at is the opening line of the preface.

**NOTE:** Keep in mind that the preface or prologue's first sentence is the first line read by a reader so it must be as powerful as the first chapter's opening line to engage the reader.

ROUGH DRAFT: *As a vampire, I can become aroused at the death throes of a human.*

This example does have hooks — Question(s) Raised, Surprising Dialogue (internal), Foreshadowing, Unique Character — but not the Overpowering Emotion Hook.

This approach is more an intellectual one, a thought more than an emotion, so it doesn't lean into being overpowering; there's no sense of urgency or immediacy.

Let's see how the author approached this sentence:

*Before someone dies, their blood races through their veins, filled with everything that makes them human — adrenaline, fear, the desire to live.*
— L.J. Smith — *The Vampire Diaries, Vol. 5 The Asylum*

By expanding on the rough draft approach, the author keys a reader into the Overpowering Emotion Hook message — three different emotions, all strong, all heightened.

Now if the author continued along this line the story might easily slide into melodrama. Melodrama literally means too much drama. Too over the top; bringing a sense of the theatrical as opposed to reality.

So if you plan to start with an Overpowering Emotion opening line hook, and it's as strong as the L.J. Smith hook we just looked at, remember to balance it. Look at her opening sentence, which follows the Overpowering Emotion Hook of her preface sentence:

*The train whistle pierced the silence of the carriage, startling me out of my reverie.*
— L.J. Smith — *The Vampire Diaries, Vol. 5 The Asylum*

This line has only one hook — the Question(s) Raised Hook. Yes, it includes the emotional word — startling — but that's not *overpowering* emotion so the Overpowering Emotion Hook does not apply. But because of all the emotion of the preface sentence, which is read first, this second sentence gives the reader a chance to catch their breath and thus avoids sliding into melodrama.

The Overpowering Emotion Hook raises specific questions related to the degree of emotion being shown. A scream is stronger than a cry in getting a person's attention, unless that cry has been built up to in such a way that the reader knows this is overpowering, such as a soundless cry wrung from a loved one as they are seeing someone depart to war, or they hear the sound of their mute child's voice for the first time, or when seeing the face of someone they thought had forsaken them.

There are lots of ways to play with the hook depending on the story you are writing.

## NO OVERPOWERING EMOTION HOOKS:

*Aurora sat in the sailboat and cried.*

There is emotion in the above example but not overpowering emotion. The sentence raises a question, which in many genres and sub-genres can be enough of what the reader wants. But not in all genres, and not if you, as a writer, are trying to achieve the Overpowering Emotion Hook.

**NOTE:** There should be emotion on every page of your manuscript, but when you look at using this particular hook you need to think, is this overpowering emotion?

Always keep in mind: use overpowering, over the top, or extreme emotion when looking to build this hook into your work. The emotion must be in context to your story and not tacked on as an afterthought. The emotion can be implied though, given the situation, as you'll see in the next example.

Let's look at a situation, one that could be overpowering, if written in a different way.

ROUGH DRAFT: *She had accepted that she had cancer and had made her peace with it and her family.*

In this example, because the sentence ends with the emotion of acceptance and peace, the residual emotion the reader experiences is not overpowering. It's emotional, but not overpowering. Think in terms of the shock you experience when you first hear a loved one, a dear friend, or someone whom you admire shares the news of having this disease. That type of situation creates the visceral, deep in your gut, emotional response that creates the Overpowering Emotion Hook. If you wrote:

ROUGH DRAFT: *I had cancer.*

This, for some readers could be overpowering on its own, because they are bringing their first-hand experience, memories, or personal associations to the words. But not all readers will have the overpowering reaction. Not if cancer hasn't touched them directly. To make the sentence include the Overpowering Emotion Hook, it could be written something like these next three examples:

*We learned our daughter had cancer on her third birthday.*

*Cancer claws through a body, destroying flesh, destroying families, destroying hope.*

*He never said the word, tap dancing around it as the Grim Reaper danced around an open grave, but I knew, I knew what cancer meant — and looked away.*

These three very different examples indicate much stronger emotion, the kind of emotion that can make a reader pause and pay attention. If you are aiming for the Overpowering Emotional Hook, write and rewrite until there's no doubt in your mind that what you have is emotional and more importantly, overpowering.

**NOTE:** Keep in mind that hooks are often used together. Just because we are focusing on one specific hook at a time, and not mentioning the other hooks, does not mean they are not present in the examples used.

## ASSIGNMENTS:

1) Look closely at a book you've read in the past that you felt showed overpowering emotion — especially in the opening sentence, end of the first page, ending and opening of chapters — the key places you'll find hooks. See if the author threaded in Overpowering Emotion Hooks in these locations and how they did so. Did they build to a strong beat as in the Gardiner example we studied? Or was the emotion layered through the

scenes or chapter? Did the hooks, used at the key places mentioned, tend to be other types of hooks?

The intention of this exercise is to show you how to learn from the authors you read and admire. The more you study each type of hook, the easier it will be to learn how to apply that hook to your own work if it's applicable.

2) Take this sentence: *My father died last year.* A statement of fact with the potential of overpowering emotion. Play with it. Rewrite. Use different word choices, a different approach to the fact, until you can build in an Overpowering Emotion Hook. The intention of this assignment is to show you that, with practice, you can learn to filter whatever type of hook you want, even if you don't have the hook in your first or second draft.

### RECAP:

- The key word in using the Overpowering Emotion Hook is *overpowering*, not simply emotion.
- The overpowering emotion in the Overpowering Emotion Hook can be shown, or implied, given the situation and the characters involved.
- If using an implied Overpowering Emotion Hook, be aware that not all readers might feel as impacted emotionally by what's happening as you do. This can decrease the effectiveness of this hook. Also, be aware of the fact that you can add additional hooks if warranted for what you are writing.

## HOOK 3: A SUPRISING SITUATION HOOK

This next hook requires you to ask yourself, is this situation a surprise to the character? Is it a surprise to the reader? You can have a surprising situation without it being unexpected— i.e., the skin from the rotted corpse slid off (sorry - yuck factor). This would probably be a surprise both to the people handling the corpse, the people watching, and to the average reader. But if the corpse was pulled out of the water by law enforcement professionals who might regularly handle this type of situation, and the body had been submerged for seventeen days, then the situation might not be unexpected. Skin does slough off in that situation. And if this is in a dark mystery, a police procedural mystery, or a suspense novel, the core readers of those genres that regularly focus on the nitty-gritty details of death and violence expect the yuck factor more, lessening the degree of surprise for those readers.

Surprise can be a lot like humor as a hook. It's translated by the experiences of the reader. If in your own work you overuse the same types of surprise situations, the reader will stop being as strongly hooked as they get deeper into the book as they were by a Surprising Situation Hook in the opening lines. Or, if a reader of a particular genre has seen a lot of opening lines that start with someone being killed, or a loved one walking out and slamming the door behind them, or a character walking in on their significant other in bed with another, then these types of situations, while surprising to the character, may not be as surprising to the reader. When that happens, you decrease the effectiveness of the hook.

**NOTE:** Always read a number of the types of stories you want to publish to see what fresh hooks are used and how to turn the expected situation upside down, which then makes it a Surprising Situation Hook.

## EXAMPLES OF SURPRISING SITUATION HOOKS:

*Death was not taking a holiday. New York may have been decked out in its glitter and glamour, madly festooned in December of 2059, but Santa Claus was dead. And a couple of elves weren't looking so good.*
–J.D. Robb–*Memory in Death*

This example is used to illustrate several different points. The first is the Surprising Situation Hook is not present in the first sentence. That's okay, because several other hooks are, and that short sentence leads to the second one quickly, which does contain the Surprising Situation Hook. Two in fact—the year of the event and the fact that Santa Claus is dead—not someone you usually associate with death.

For readers of this particular series, they know the story world is set in the future, so for those readers, the date is not surprising. For new-to-the-series readers, that information does count as a Surprising Situation Hook. Robb is writing to two different reader expectations and making sure each is engaged by having two Surprising Situation Hooks, not just one.

**NOTE:** If you are writing a series where you are juggling the needs of the new as well as the returning reader, be aware you have to engage, or hook, both groups.

So the previous example used hooks in the first sentence. That compels a reader to read at least to the second one, which has different hooks for both new readers, and fans of the series, followed by the end of the paragraph, which contains other hooks.

This is how the best authors approach hooks. They don't stop with one hook in the opening sentence and assume their work is done. They thread in hooks on top of hooks, to keep that reader moving deeper into the story.

What if Robb had stopped with an opening like this:

ROUGH DRAFT: *Death was not taking a holiday. We reached the brownstone off Hancock Street a little after nine where a half-dozen onlookers were already gawking.*

In some types of stories this can work, because the reader will be hooked by the situation. They know from the get-go that this is a type of crime story and the story question — what happened and to whom — has been raised. That can be enough of a hook in stories needing less tension. But there is not necessarily a surprising situation, especially if your reader is used to reading crime dramas.

The rough draft version relies heavily on the Question(s) Raised Hook and Foreshadowing Hook that what is happening in this scene might play out strongly through the rest of the story. But Robb uses so many hooks, and different ones, that if one or two don't work as well for certain readers, they still stand a strong chance of being engaged because of these additional hooks.

Here's another example from an urban fantasy novel, the first in a series.

*First demon you summon, it's kind of scary.*
*— Mary Buckham — Invisible Magic*

Bam! Right from the beginning, the reader knows there will be non-human creatures populating this story, most likely danger (since the word *demon* does not conjure up a warm and fuzzy image) and a surprising situation (unless you or your friends summon demons on a regular basis, in which case this hook would not work). The situation may or may not be surprising to the main character, which we learn is the case by the end of the paragraph, but the first sentence does exactly what it needs to do as an opening; offer enough hooks to keep the reader reading. Keeping the sentence short compels the reader to read at least the next sentence, or to the end of the paragraph. This is where you'll discover another hook the Question(s) Raised Hook (a hook we'll examine in more detail later in this book).

> *First demon you summon, it's kind of scary.*
> *After a few hundred, it becomes just another job.*
> *Unfortunately, I hadn't reached that point.*
> — Mary Buckham — *Invisible Magic*

Short sentences increase the tension and thus the pacing as the target reader for this kind of novel — wanting a complex world of danger and complicated characters, a protagonist with flaws but a willingness to do what needs to be done to protect others, and a hint of an attitude — plus, the story's opening sentence and paragraph hooks keep leading the reader deeper into the story.

Let's look at another example, but let's build up to the final result.

FIRST DRAFT: *My grandmother was killed by the English. That happened the same day I was forced into an arranged marriage.*

There are questions raised by these two hypothetical lines, but the reader is held at a distance because we have no idea who is the POV character, not even if they are male or female. Or the time period. Or why we should care. All of these types of questions keep the reader at arm's length, waiting to find out what's going on. The longer that happens, the easier it is to set a book down.

SECOND DRAFT: *Sir William Scott the Younger of Buccleuch was forced into an arranged marriage the same day his relative died.*

Now we know the *who* of the story, but there are still no strong hooks. Nothing that compels us to keep reading, whether it's one more sentence, to the end of the paragraph, or to turn the page. This is where many newer writers, and those who have become complacent with their writing, will stop. These writers know their stories, so they expect a reader will continue reading to discover the shocking discovery on page eight, or an unexpected revelation a third of the way through the book. Bottom line, a reader will not keep reading if they are not engaged right from the beginning and throughout your novel.

Let's return to our example and see how the author created a Surprising Situation Hook.

> *On the day that his grannie was killed by the English, Sir William Scott the Younger of Buccleuch was at Melrose Abbey, marrying his aunt.*
> –Dorothy Dunnett–*The Disorderly Knights*

Now the reader immediately knows this is most likely a historical, one of the characters is of the aristocracy and, with the use of the Surprising Situation Hook of this man marrying his aunt, must read at least a little further to find out what's up.

Yes, there will be some readers of historicals who can say "it wasn't that uncommon for relatives to marry in days past, particularly individuals with lands and titles." Those readers might not be as hooked as your average reader. Even though the fact a man is marrying his aunt is the fodder for sensational newspapers at grocery store checkout stands. The Surprising Situation Hook isn't meant to carry the reader through the full-length of the novel, but just a little deeper into the story where, the smart writer will re-engage them again and again.

In case you have the impression that to have a good hook you have to write about death or sadness, it's refreshing to realize hooks are in all types of stories. Your challenge as a writer is to discover the types of hooks that work most effectively for what you are writing and who your readers are. How? Read. Study. Read. Study. Read. Study.

Let's look at another example. This one is from a sensual, erotic Regency romance. Assume the author had to work her way up to using the Surprising Situation Hook.

FIRST DRAFT: *I paid him but I didn't want to have sex.*

This is the Question(s) Raised Hook—what's going on—and for some might also be surprising, but it's so confusing that the hook, the engagement encouraging the reader to keep reading to discover questions you are raising, is decreased as the reader focuses on trying to figure out what exactly is happening. We have no idea whether this is a historical or contemporary story, no flavor of a time or place, no sense that this internalization is out of place given the context. Since most readers who pick up the novel realize from the cover that this is a historical, contemporary or otherworldly, there might be a stronger sense of surprise, but not as strong as it could be.

**NOTE:** If it takes reading a sentence multiple times to understand what is happening, then it's probably not working hard enough.

Look at how Sharon Page approaches this opening line, and not only creates a Surprising Situation Hook, but combines it with the Question(s) Raised Hook that will intrigue the reader enough to keep reading, even just a little more.

*How am I going to explain to a man I've paid that I do not want him to make love to me?*
–Sharon Page–*The Club*

Now the reader has enough clarity to understand more of the situation, which is not what one usually associates with a Regency era romance. That's what creates the Surprising Situation Hook. Plus, the language sounds more appropriate for the time period and contrasts nicely with the situation.

**NOTE:** In the Surprising Situation Hook, the contrast between what the reader expects and what is revealed is a very powerful approach, as long as that contrast is true to your storyline.

This next example comes from a memoir. The strongest memoirs incorporate craft techniques found in the strongest novels, including the use of hooks and intentionally guiding a reader through a story. But let's assume the author had to rework her first line until it was as memorable as possible, and contained the Surprising Situation Hook.

FIRST DRAFT: *I didn't expect to see mom that night.*

Pretty bland, even if it does contain a small Question(s) Raised Hook. We learn so little about the POV character, or the secondary character, that we're left wondering "why should we care?" This is not how you want to start a memoir. Memoirs, by their very nature, are about someone else—as if going to a function and meeting a new person and all they talk about is themselves. So finding a way to make someone else's life matter to yours makes a huge difference in whether the average reader will keep reading.

SECOND DRAFT: *I was focused on my clothes when I looked out the window and saw my mother.*

Again, the strongest Question(s) Raised Hook is, "so what?" Why should a cold reader care? So let's see how Jeanette Walls opens her memoir, one that stayed on the NYT bestseller lists for more than six years.

> *I was sitting in a taxi, wondering if I had overdressed for the evening, when I looked out the window and saw Mom rooting through a Dumpster.*
> –Jeannette Walls–*The Glass Castle*

Using contrast between the everyday world that the average reader recognizes—being in a taxi riding along, worrying about something most of us may have worried about—and who the POV character recognizes in a situation (most do not expect to see one's parent)—is what creates the Surprising Situation Hook in this opening line. Plus, Walls' approach to threading in the hook helps build to the surprise. She starts with the normal and builds to the punch line—*rooting through a Dumpster*. If she had buried this key image in the middle of this long sentence, or started with it then watered it down by shifting the focus back to the everyday normal activity, the line would not be as powerful.

Like this:

ROUGH DRAFT: *I looked out the window and saw Mom rooting through a Dumpster as I was sitting in a taxi, wondering if I had overdressed for the evening.*

Or this:

ROUGH DRAFT: *I was sitting in a taxi as I looked out the window and saw Mom misbehaving as usual as I wondered if I had overdressed for the evening.*

**NOTE:** Be aware of the placement of your hooks, particularly if you are relying on one or two only; buried in the middle of a sentence or paragraph. This makes it easier for the average reader to skip over them.

Here's another Surprising Situation Hook from author Marjorie M. Liu. We'll be looking at the opening line and then on to the second and third lines of the opening paragraph to see how she keeps upping the Surprising Situation Hook ante as well as mixing the types of hooks she's using to keep bringing the reader deeper and deeper into the story.

> *There were no zombies at the party. I would have been happy to find some. If nothing else, the small talk would have been less insulting.*
> — Marjorie M. Liu — *Armor of Roses*

First, let's identify which hooks Liu uses here:

*There were no zombies at the party.* [Surprising Situation, Question(s) Raised, Action/Danger, Foreshadowing w/Warning, the Totally Unexpected, the Unique Character hooks]. That's a six-hook opening line. *I would have been happy to find some.* [A different Surprising Situation Hook than the first one, Question(s) Raised Hook, the Surprising or Shocking Dialogue Hook (internal) and the Unique Character Hook.] *If nothing else, the small talk would have been less insulting.* [Surprising Situation and Question(s) Raised hooks].

Now let's expand the explanation for the hooks chosen above to drill down and see why particular hooks apply:

*There were no zombies at the party.* [Surprising Situation Hook, not to the POV character, but to the reader]. How many times have you thought this at a party you've attended? Next is Question(s) Raised Hook, i.e. why did this POV character expect zombies? Is this normal? Who is this person? Then the Action/Danger Hook, since death is usually associated with zombies, danger is assumed here until the reader knows otherwise. If the second line had made it clear the POV character is at a Halloween party, then the Action/ Danger Hook stops applying because the reader's been reassured that all is safe. Next comes the Unique Character Hook, both the POV character, who is expecting zombies, and the zombies themselves. An Unexpected Character Hook assumes the character is not one you personally rub shoulders with on a daily basis, or are familiar with. If, in real life, you are a zombie fighter, this Unique Character Hook would not apply. Another hook present is the Foreshadowing w/Warning Hook; that zombies are mentioned alerts the reader to the fact that not only zombies but also danger might be right around the corner, so the Foreshadowing with Warning Hook applies; and Totally Unexpected Hook; I don't know about you, but this is not what I expected as an opening comment, even though the story is in an anthology of paranormal romance and UF [urban fantasy] stories.

If you read a lot in a particular genre, and have seen the same or similar type of openings, then this Totally Unexpected Hook might not work as strongly for you. Otherwise, this is a six-hook opening line.

Continuing on, we have:

*I would have been happy to find some.* [A different Surprising Situation Hook than the first one — because most of us would not be disappointed at not finding undead creatures at a party. It created the Question(s) Raised Hook: why would the POV character want zombies at a party? Next, adding in the Unique Character Hook; based not on the zombies this time but on the POV character who would look forward to being at a party with zombies. Then a Surprising or Shocking Dialogue Hook; its internal dialogue, but the average reader would not necessarily be thinking along these lines.] *If nothing else, the small talk would have been less insulting.* [Surprising Situation based on internal dialogue from a person who appears comfortable with zombies and clearly prefers them over whoever is at this party; and last the Question(s) Raised Hook;

why are zombies not insulting? Why is the POV character thinking this way?]

Did you note the way Liu power-packed her opening line? In case one or even several hooks did not resonate with a particular reader, there are enough other hooks to keep the average reader moving down the page. Then she adds more hooks in her second and third sentences. Why? Because the goal is to keep the reader intrigued, and thus reading far enough to turn the page. If you can keep that reader moving through the first page, they will most likely purchase your book. If they read past the third page, they will read to the end of the chapter where you will re-engage them into the next chapter.

Page by page, the reader has to find out what's going to happen next, because you keep the hooks and the story questions propelling a reader along.

**NOTE:** If you read predominately in one genre, such as romance, mystery or fantasy, some hooks which are overused in your genre may not be as strong as other hooks. Keep this in mind so that your three or four-hook opening does not come across as only a one or two-hook opening.

Here's another example of a Surprising Situation Hook opening line, one in a different genre — an Amateur Sleuth mystery series. This sub-genre of the mystery genre employs a protagonist not trained as a law enforcement official, but who becomes involved in a murder investigation because they may have some unique insights based on their past or current employment, their knowledge of the people or locale, or their proximity to a crime. They need to find a killer so they, someone they care about, or an innocent person they know won't be unjustly arrested and tried. The amateur sleuth novel at heart is based on the belief that anyone can serve the course of justice if they try hard enough.

Many amateur sleuth novels fall on the slower to mid-levels of pacing needs; this means a lighter read with much less tension on the page than a suspense or thriller novel, which in turn means fewer hooks in places such as opening lines, end of the first page, openings and endings of chapters.

It also means the type of hooks being used can be less about danger and strong emotion and more about raising intriguing story questions — not the kinds of questions that will keep you up late at night as much as keep you curious to know more.

In this next example, let's assume the author, Charlaine Harris, used a placeholder of a first line before returning to it to revise and increase the number of hooks, or, for the sake of a learning experience, decrease the number of hooks.

FIRST DRAFT: (using too many hooks for an amateur sleuth novel): *I watched, not even able to scream, as a man slammed from the sky headfirst in front of me with a hard thud followed by the stench of blood and entrails scattered over the yard.*

This draft contains the following seven hooks: Action/Danger; since most of us do not deal with people dying violently and unexpectedly in front of us; Overpowering Emotion; violent death combined with the inability to scream implies strong to overpowering emotion; a Surprising Situation, since this is not an event the average reader encounters or hears about on a fairly regular basis, it'd qualify as a surprise to the reader as well as a surprise to the character watching; introducing a Unique Character; how many people do you know who have had a person fall from the sky and die in front of them? If it's in the single digits, it makes this character unique; Foreshadowing w/Warning; the assumption here is that this episode will play out in an important way deeper into the story; the Totally Unexpected, we know this by her response; and the Question(s) Raised Hook.

Seven hooks creates a very strong degree of tension on the page, and is not what most readers of amateur sleuths are anticipating for a novel more on the light-reading-before-bedtime end of the reading spectrum.

So let's pretend the author started with these seven hooks and reeled them back.

SECOND DRAFT (Using one hook): *A man fell into my yard.*

Good news, there are fewer hooks in this opening line, but now the trend has slid into the opposite direction—too few hooks to engage the reader combining with a strong sense of vagueness. Did you have to read the sentence twice to understand it? If so it's too vague. There is a Question(s) Raised Hook, but the sentence is weak in that it's not clear at all what's going on or why a reader should care. Did a person fall from a roof or a ladder? Is the man okay? What happened?

The tension has been decreased by this one-hook opening, but so have the reasons for the reader to keep reading. If we know and love the author, we probably would continue reading, but unless you have fierce reader loyalty based on hundreds of thousands of total strangers believing that this lackluster opening is an aberration, this sentence needs some more work.

Let's see how Harris approached this line.

> *My bodyguard was mowing the yard wearing her pink bikini when the man fell from the sky.*
> —Charlaine Harris—*Dead Over Heels*

Now let's pull this apart to understand how hard it's working:

*My bodyguard* [This makes the POV character unique because, while many of us know about personal bodyguards, we don't know why this particular character has one which makes her intriguing—is she a celebrity, a political figure, a criminal? Until the average reader knows more, the POV character is unique.]—*was mowing the yard* [Now we have a visual of what's happening and it seems pretty ordinary and middle-class. No hook here, but that's okay because the lawn mowing image is being created to contrast dramatically with the situation and the bodyguard doing work we normally don't associate them doing.]—*wearing her pink bikini*  [And here we get a Surprising Situation Hook to the reader as our first association with a bodyguard would be 1: male and 2: not in a pink bikini plus it promises a touch of light humor to the story. ] *when the man fell from the sky.* [And everything leads to this punch line. The normal everyday activity—mowing the lawn—the bodyguard in a bikini, —something more unusual—leading to the phrase that contains the strongest Surprising Situation Hook. To some readers, there may be a sense of danger, but the other elements of the sentence help mitigate the Action/Danger Hook because the focus is on the contrast between the everyday and what comes out of the blue (pun intended).]

What Harris did so well in this powerful first sentence is maximize the Surprising Situation Hook while keeping the feel light and humorous. She never lost sight of the fact that her target readers want to be engaged, but not in anything too dark, too gruesome, too violent. She created a five-hook opening line while being very aware of which five hooks work the best for her reading audience.

## NON-SURPRISING SITUATION HOOKS:

*Frank Abbott was seventy-three years old when he died of a heart attack.*

Because of the age reference here, and the type of death that's not uncommon, there is no surprise, especially if used as an opening line hook. If you changed the age or type of death, you could create a Surprising Situation Hook. Like this:

*Frank Abbott was six months old when he died of a heart attack.*

OR

*Frank Abbott was seventy-three years old when he died of childbirth.*

This only works if applicable to your story. The revised examples are used here to show you how combining two disparate images can work to create the Surprising Situation Hook.

Here's another example of a Non-Surprising Situation Hook as initially written.

ROUGH DRAFT: It had rained on Tuesday and Wednesday, and Thursday was looking damp around the edges.

For some readers who live in a climate where rain rarely happens, this might be more intriguing, but not to the average reader. So how could we add in the Surprising Situation Hook?

ROUGH DRAFT: *It had rained volcanic ash on Tuesday and Wednesday, and Thursday was looking to be more of the same.*

OR

ROUGH DRAFT: *Three thousand feet below the surface of the ocean, it rained on Tuesday and Wednesday, and Thursday was looking damp around the edges.*

Adding the unexpected with the expected, and either leading with or ending on your Surprising Situation Hook, can make it more effective.

Let's examine one more Non-Surprising Situation Hook and how we could change it up.

ROUGH DRAFT: *I don't like spiders.*

This last sentence raises a question or possibly foreshadows something that could be happening in the story soon, but since a lot of people don't care for spiders, or snakes, or tarantulas, this comment is not a surprising situation. If you had written:

*I don't like cute, fluffy kittens.*

That is more surprising because so many people do like cats, especially cute, fluffy kittens. Unless you personally don't like kittens or cats, in which case this hook would not surprise you at all.

Let's look closer at the examples of overused Surprising Situation Hooks that we raised at the beginning of this section.

ROUGH DRAFT: *Joe was killed.*

This is a very familiar theme to readers of mysteries, suspense, and thrillers, which means that often the opening hook tries to capitalize on this shock value. But if a reader expects this, then it's no longer surprising. So how could you change it up?

*Joe died this morning, when he was scheduled to have been killed tomorrow.*
OR
*There are a thousand and nine ways to watch someone being killed.*
OR
*The first time I watched someone being killed, I was seven.*

Can you see how, with a little tweaking, you can add intrigue and interest and a hint of I-didn't-see-that-coming? This does impact the story, so it cannot simply be randomly applied because you'd like to use the Surprising Situation Hook.

This next example has been an overused situation in many women's fiction or literary fiction stories as an opening line:

ROUGH DRAFT: *A loved one walking out and slamming the door behind them.*

Yes, this is a Question(s) Raised Hook and foreshadows events that might play out in the story, but it is not necessarily surprising. So let's play around with this and see how we could make it surprising.

*As Fenix walked out the door in a huff of pique and slammed it behind him, I hoped he remembered we were on a space station.*

*I cheered when Martinique walked out the door and slammed it behind her because it was the first time she had walked in decades.*

*My true love, my soul mate, my beloved walked out the front door and slammed it behind her only minutes before my husband walked in the back door.*

A Surprising Situation Hook intrigues a reader just a hint more, or sometimes a lot more, than a simple question being raised type of hook.

Here's another situation that's overused in a lot of romance novels. It's used because it clearly sets up a character who has been burned by love and thus must overcome those wounds in order to love again. The concept is good; the execution, though, can become stale.

ROUGH DRAFT:
*Sue walked in on her fiancée/boyfriend/spouse in bed with another woman.*

Yes, the characters themselves are most likely surprised, but for the average reader of romance novels, this is not surprising. Some readers can overlook this overused cliché because they love the author's work or particularly like this as a story approach. After all, because of this situation or back story, it appears a lot of the angst and emotional pain and bad stuff has already happened before the story opens. It happens off the page, which means the story will focus more on how a character overcomes a bad event to find happiness. That's what some core romance readers want.

Remember, though, if you, as a reader, have read this type of opening, an editor or agent will have read it ten times as often, and most likely passed on the submission, especially if it came from an unknown writer.

What if you wrote:

*Sue walked in on her fiancé in bed with another woman's dog.*

OR

*Brad marched into his fiancée's bedroom dressed in stiletto heels and a red-sequined Bob Mackie knock-off ball gown.*

**NOTE:** Taking a clichéd opening line or situation and altering one element can easily create a much stronger hook.

Something else to look for in your own work is whether you've said too much in a sentence, which can decrease the value of the hook. This is especially true in that opening line hook or the ending of a chapter hook location.

For example:

*The cop patted down the suspect only to discover she was a he.*

This is a surprising situation, especially to the cop. But what if you added two words that reassure the readers that this might not be all that unusual.

*The Las Vegas cop patted down the suspect only to discover she was a he.*

See the key difference? Use the words—Bourbon Street, the Freemont area in Seattle, Trinidad, Colorado—any location where a cop might not be surprised in this situation and you change the impact of the Surprising Situation Hook.

**NOTE:** If the reader is already predisposed to expect the surprise, then the surprise doesn't act as a strong hook.

Don't be afraid to play around with your opening sentence in particular, or one of your end of chapter hooks, to see if you can include a Surprising Situation Hook. It's an intriguing hook and often creates more hooks at the same time.

## ASSIGNMENTS:

1) If you did the assignment in the opening of this book, where you looked at books in a genre you don't normally read until you found one that hooked you, examine that sentence to see if it contains the Surprising Situation Hook. Or look in your TBR (to be read) book stash to see if you can identify at least one Surprising Situation Hook. When you find one or more, pull the key sentence or even the paragraph, if the Surprising Situation Hook is built up to or is at the end of a chapter or scene. Examine it closely to see why it surprised you. Was it the use of contrast

between what you expected to read and what you did read? Was it clear that the surprise was based on knowing enough but not too much about what was happening? Was the hook an opening sentence or ending one? The intention of this exercise is to show you what it's like for you as a reader to be surprised enough to convince you to keep reading. The more you study what works on you, the easier it is to replicate the process for other readers.

2) Now write four or five statement of fact openings. By that I mean sentences that raise no surprise, just like several examples we studied in this section of the book. Hopefully these bland sentences will contain no other hooks either. Once you've selected your sentences, look at just the opening line. And yes, be surprised if this is harder than expected, because I will guarantee you that these rough sentences will most likely contain the Question(s) Raised Hook at the bare minimum. If the opening line is a short line or in dialogue, you can add a second line. Write the line down and then see if you can create five or six ways to make it surprising. Have fun with the process, as you won't have to use any of these results, so there's no right or wrong in what you're creating. The intention of this exercise is to train you to write what you might never have noticed. You might also discover that using this hook actually sparks off potential story ideas you hadn't considered before, or adds twists that add depth to your current story.

**RECAP:**

• A surprising situation can be surprising to the POV character, the reader, or both.

- Write to the largest set of readers who read what you are writing, and only then worry about engaging a larger audience.
- To build on the Surprising Situation Hook, lead or end the sentence or paragraph with it.
- Consider using contrast to create a Surprising Situation Hook.
- Remember that the Surprising Situation Hook works better in some genres than others. If in doubt, read the genre you are writing in and note if this is a hook you see some of the time, most of the time, or rarely.
- If you compel a reader to continue to turn the page when they had intended to stop, you know your hook is working.
- Be careful of saying too much in a sentence, which can decrease the value of the Surprising Situation Hook.

## HOOK 4: THE TOTALLY UNEXPECTED HOOK

If you have a Surprising Situation Hook, you often have the Totally Unexpected Hook, too—but not always. Ask yourself, do you, as a reader, expect this to happen or to have happened? Does the character expect this to happen or to have happened?

Think of the Totally Unexpected Hook as taking a surprising situation to the next level. Your grandmother dancing with your father at a wedding is not uncommon so no hook. Your estranged grandmother dancing with her son-in law, your father, whom she hasn't spoken to in twenty years, is a surprising situation. Your grandmother heading to her job as an exotic dancer after the wedding is totally unexpected.

### EXAMPLES OF TOTALLY UNEXPECTED HOOKS:

*The flying saucer landed on our front yard and a little green man got out of it.*
–John Scalzi–*Zoe's Tale*

Yes, this contains a Surprising Situation Hook but also the Totally Unexpected Hook. Seeing the line all by itself, without knowing it's in a Sci-Fi/fantasy novel, makes the line even more powerful. Within the context of cover art, back cover blurb and where it's shelved in a big box store—under Sci-Fi—the hook may be diluted because the average reader expects a unique world. Yet, it's still an over the top opening sentence, which earns it the right to be called totally unexpected and thus earn the Totally Unexpected Hook quality.

What if Scalzi had written:

FIRST DRAFT: *On the planet Wibwar, during the fourth lunar pass, a flying saucer landed on our front yard and a little green man got out of it.*

Because of the additional verbiage that clearly paints the story as being in an alien world, the shock value of the sentence is decreased, so the hook is decreased. It's the in-your-face punch that makes this example a strong Totally Unexpected Hook that would compel the average reader to keep reading, at least through the first paragraph, where more hooks would be imbedded.

Deeper into the story, when the reader now understands where the story is taking place and has a stronger feel for the story world, this hook would not be as effective.

**NOTE:** Remember that the questions created by your use of hooks can quickly be answered, or shown to be something that is no longer unexpected or surprising given the situation, and that's fine. As long as you raise another hook or reason to keep the reader moving forward in your story, you're good.

Let's look at a different opening hook that involves a Totally Unexpected Hook. But let's assume the author had to work toward this hook.

FIRST DRAFT: *Her life did not change much after leaving the Sultan's harem.*

There is a Question(s) Raised Hook (we'll go into more details about this hook later in this book) and one other involving a Unique Character Hook, but otherwise the opening line is pretty blasé. The sentence does not compel us to continue reading in an active way. We might simply because we have the book in front of us, but otherwise we wouldn't exert much effort as a reader to read more.

**NOTE:** A hint to verify if your opening line hook is as strong as possible is if you separate it from your document and show it to a reader who reads the type of story you are writing. If that person knows nothing about the story and their immediate response is they want to read more, you have a good hook.

The other issue with our hypothetical opening line is that it gives no flavor to what kind of story the reader should expect. No sense of contemporary, historical, fantasy or anything else. Like a heavy stone, the line simply sits there. So let's see how Dorothy Dunnet approaches this opening line to craft a sentence with both a historical flavor and the Totally Unexpected Hook.

> *Not to every young girl is it given to enter the harem of the Sultan of Turkey and return to her homeland a virgin.*
> –Dorothy Dunnett–*The Ringed Castle*

They say sex sells, but the previous opening line is a great example of where the absence of sex can intrigue, given the situation, and also comes as a Totally Unexpected Hook given the association with the word *harem*.

Let's look at another example, this one from a general fiction novel set in the 1940s. That information does not come to light in this opening line, but the premise of the story, which is a hook in itself (even though a different kind of hook), takes what the average reader expects to read and turns it upside down, which can create the Totally Unexpected Hook.

Assuming Lisa Grunwald did not write an initial opening sentence with Totally Unexpected, Surprising Situation, Question(s) Raised and a few more hooks, as her first draft; let's create a progression of lines to see how she might have reached a strong combination for her story.

FIRST DRAFT: *Henry House was used as a teaching tool in a home economics class, which then set the tone of his life.*

This is a good summation of the theme hook—a what-if story based on a true life practice of using orphan babies in some colleges in the late 1940s to give women the chance to experience what it means to care for a young child. The situation is surprising, especially in this day and age of doll babies serving this same role in many of today's high school family and consumer sciences courses. But as a sentence that compels the reader to keep reading, it lacks strong hooks. Let's try again:

SECOND DRAFT: *As an orphan, Henry was unaware that he was a live science experiment, much like frogs in biology or dogs in science classes.*

This is more intriguing because it raises more questions for the reader, which means more hooks are present—a Question(s) Raised, a Surprising Situation, a Unique Character, Foreshadowing and, for some readers, a sense of Danger because the thought of a baby as a project sets off alarm signals.

But this particular rough draft, while having a number of hooks, starts the novel off on the wrong tone, the wrong feel to the story Grunwald crafted. She did not want to imply to the reader that the story is about the initial situation, but more about what happens to this young man as he grows older, given the context of his beginnings. Let's see how she approaches this opening.

*By the time Henry House was four months old, a copy of his picture was being carried in the pocketbooks of seven different women, each of whom called him her son.*
–Lisa Grunwald–*The Irresistible Henry House*

If you knew nothing else about this story, and based on this line alone, would you expect the first part of the sentence to lead to the last part? It's that sensation of "whoa, what's happening" response that earns the Totally Unexpected Hook and intrigues the reader to keep reading, to find out what's going on with this individual.

Let's look at another example, this one in a suspense novel.

> *The last thing Richard Hilzoy thought before the bullet entered his brain was, things are really looking up.*
> –Barry Eisler–*Fault Line*

Again, the juxtaposition between what the reader expects and what the author delivers helps to create the Totally Unexpected Hook. What if Eisler had reversed his sentence construction?

> *Things are really looking up. That was the last thing Richard Hilzoy thought before the bullet entered his brain.*

In the revised version, we have a Surprising Situation Hook and, to some, a hint of the Totally Unexpected Hook, but to others the Totally Unexpected Hook is watered down because we've been focused on the positive thought, then told this man is thinking and finally the surprise. Is it unexpected? Possibly, but he could be in an armed conflict, or escaping a prison, or a hundred other what-if scenarios. The sequence of revelation as Eisler wrote the sentence is what helps ratchet up the Totally Unexpected Hook. As a reader, our attention is in this sequence; bullet-bam-positive thought. That's not the usual progression, and thus twists a surprise into the unexpected.

**NOTE:** All hooks are subjective, eliciting stronger results in some readers than others, which is why relying on one-hook opening sentences in particular can decrease your chances of engaging the greatest number of readers for your work.

Let's examine another example from what's often called a Dude Lit (or Dick Lit) novel, with Dude Lit being the male equivalent of Chick Lit novels. In Dude Lit stories, the focus is on a male protagonist who finds himself at a crossroads, or in a slump, and how the protagonist takes action and makes decisions to deal with it.

In this particular story by author Nick Hornby, the initial POV character is the female love interest to a man obsessed with the life of an obscure musician who fell off the radar after a short career. There's a strong sense of irony and self-deprecating humor, which act as hooks for some readers, but because eliciting these two responses in the average reader is difficult, these hooks are even more subjective than the more common ones we're looking at in depth.

Let's assume Hornby had to write several drafts before he nailed his key opening sentence.

FIRST DRAFT: *We had travelled roughly three thousand, eight-hundred and some odd miles to see what had to have been the most obtuse infamous spot in existence.*

This doesn't grab the reader's attention the way a good hook sentence would, plus it leaves the reader waiting to find out what is being examined. That can be a Question(s) Raised Hook, and in some types of stories, can work as a hook, but let's see how Hornby injected a stronger hook by using the Totally Unexpected Hook.

*They had flown from England to Minneapolis to look at a toilet.*
–Nick Hornby–*Juliet, Naked*

The sentence is short, which creates stronger energy than the rough draft version, but includes  the Question(s) Raised Hook, the Surprising Situation Hook, and ends on the Totally Unexpected Hook. This is what you're aspiring to accomplish—not write a whole paragraph to get as many hooks as possible crammed into it, or write something that doesn't reflect your story told in your way. What you are trying to do is intrigue your reader, give them a reason to keep reading, and make it easy for them to move along to that next sentence, that next page, that next scene or chapter.

The other thing Hornby did well was to use concrete, specific images to help the reader quickly catch the over-the-top-irony he intended, which can be part of the Totally Unexpected Hook. A reader might struggle with seeing what three thousand, eight hundred and some odd miles means, but can easily visualize the distance between England and Minneapolis. This is not spoon-feeding the reader as much as avoiding keeping him in the dark as to your intention, especially in that key first sentence.

**NOTE:** Specific word choices make it easier for your reader to understand your Totally Unexpected Hook.

Our next example comes from a YA novel, the third book in a trilogy. What this means is that the author had to write to engage the new reader with her opening line hook, but also speak to her existing readers who knew the protagonist and her trials in love and life, until the point where this story opened. The protagonist is a young woman, recently graduated from high school in California, whose boyfriend left her to go surfing in New Zealand and she's striking out on her own—in New York City.

Assuming that Rachel Cohn worked up to her opening line, let's see how she might have approached it.

FIRST DRAFT: *The move from California to New York was rough, especially since I ended up moving in with my cupcake-baking older brother.*

The cupcake-baking brother is unusual, which thus earns the Surprising Situation Hook, since it's not a skill one often associates with older brothers, but all in all the sentence is over-wordy, slowing the pacing, and not engaging the reader. A lot like a joke that's poorly stated and, while it might gain a smile, doesn't earn a laugh.

SECOND DRAFT: *I was sitting in a small coffee shop in New York City when I had an amazing epiphany that stood to change my life.*

Now we have a Question(s) Raised Hook, but definitely no Totally Unexpected Hook. Let's see how Cohen crafted her sentence that intrigues just enough to want to read more to find out what's happening.

*A cappuccino cost me my life.*
–Rachel Cohn–*Cupcake*

This sentence is short, which creates tension and increases the sense of pacing, Shocking Dialogue Hook (internal)—a hook we'll examine in more depth later in this book—a Surprising Situation, and the Totally Unexpected Hooks. Part of that unexpected is that this is a novel for teens. Drama or melodrama is often associated with teenagers, but this short sentence doesn't slide into overpowering emotion. It's a statement of fact that grabs the reader and encourages them to read until the next line or next paragraph to find out what this line means.

This last example occurs at the end of the first scene in Chapter Three. In this young adult novel by Alyson Noël, the reader has already been introduced to the protagonist, a young girl named Evermore who has recently lost her parents and younger sister in a terrible car crash. Evermore is the only survivor and not only deals with survivor's guilt but has come away from the accident being able to read other people's auras, hear their thoughts, and know their secrets by touching them.

Uprooted and moved to a new school, Evermore has dealt with all the upheaval in her life by isolating herself with only two friends, kids seen as losers by everyone else, and has kept to herself as much as possible. But now a hot young guy has recently arrived at the school and to the shock of everyone, including Evermore, he seems to take a specific interest and attraction to her.

At the end of this particular scene, we're aware that Evermore realizes that she can't read the new guy's aura, hasn't heard his thoughts, and that getting to know him might not be a total impossibility. But she's not one hundred percent sure yet and is mulling over what it might be like to feel normal once again as she weighs the pros and cons of living with her aunt. Her last thoughts end on this line:

*And I definitely don't let on that I talk to my dead little sister almost every day.*
— Alyson Noël — *Evermore*


The reader already knows a lot of unexpected information about this girl that sets her apart — orphaned, traumatized, able to read auras, hears others' thoughts, is a touch telepath — it seems hard to create one more Totally Unexpected Hook. But the author waited until three chapters into the story to spring this Totally Unexpected Hook at a key location, the end of a scene, where it'd be easy to set the story down if you were reading it late at night.

**NOTE**: Most contemporary readers do most of their reading last thing of the day or in bed. This means they are pre-disposed to setting your book down. Hooks can help you make sure they read a little more, or are intrigued enough to get back to your story as soon as possible.

The author understands the power of using a strong hook to re-engage the reader as the novel progresses, intriguing the reader and compelling them to read just a little longer to find out how this specific information will play out. That's the power of strong hooks.

## NO TOTALLY UNEXPECTED HOOKS:

*The topless dancer met her pimp outside the back stage door at a little after nine.*

This last sentence is simply a bland statement of fact, nothing more. There's nothing here that makes a cold reader want to find out anything else. The sentence contains only facts, and facts alone do not intrigue.

**NOTE**:  An intriguing sentence contains imagery, emotion, magic and the unanticipated. In short, all of the five hooks we've looked at so far in this book do the same.

Let's see what we could do to make drab into compelling by using a totally unexpected element.

*The Topless dancer with only one leg met her pimp outside the back stage door at a little after nine.*

Because the average reader does not visualize a dancer as one-legged, this sentence intrigues a reader just enough to read the next sentence or to find out even a hint more about who this person is and what is happening in the situation. Jarring a reader's expectations is what creates a Totally Unexpected Hook.

**NOTE:** Look at your specific word choices to ratchet the expected up to the unexpected.

> *The Topless dancer met her pimp outside the back door of St. Paul's church a little after she exited the nine o'clock service.*

And here we now have a situation that's at odds with our expectation of the character. If you think about the sentence for a few moments you can easily realize that there's no reason why a topless dancer wouldn't attend a religious service. However, it might not be the first thing a reader thinks when they create an image in their mind of a topless dancer, and that's all you need as an author to create the Totally Unexpected Hook.

Play with your word choices and where you place the emphasis in your sentence; add or subtract until you hit the note, the intention, you as the author want while intriguing your core readers. You won't catch all readers—though the best sentences with hooks can reach the greatest number of readers—so focus initially on the main readers of your genre.

Let's look at another Non-Totally Unexpected Hook sentence.

> *The Friday alarm announcing the end of the shift was ten minutes late.*

This example raises a question, so earns the Question(s) Raised Hook, but until the reader knows more, it's hard to tell if this situation happens often, or if this was the first time. It's reduced to a statement of fact and leaves the cold reader waiting to find more to truly be hooked.

So, how might you change it up to create a Totally Unexpected Hook?

*The Friday alarm announcing the end of the shift was ten minutes late, and then the world ended for Hortense Piddlewacker.*

The reader doesn't know if the world literally ended, but it does intrigue and, with that name, takes this from a Surprising Situation (which it is) to the Totally Unexpected as an opening line. Plus it has the Question(s) Raised Hook and might create a Danger Hook, depending on the genre, and reader expectations. For example, in a YA or women's fiction novel, the phrase *the world ended* would be taken as a metaphor not a literal statement of fact. In a mystery, suspense, RS (romantic suspense) or thriller, the same phrase could easily be taken as the character dying.

**NOTE:** Always keep in mind what your audience expects when weighing the value of a hook; in some genres, a mere hint of a bad thing happening can be assumed to be true, because that's what is expected to happen in those types of stories.

Let's try a different approach to this Non-Totally Unexpected Hook.

*Sunday at midnight, the Friday alarm shrilled, announcing the end of the shift, which should no longer have mattered, but changed everything.*

This example raises stronger story questions and still qualifies as being a Surprise and Totally Unexpected. This version, though, would weigh in more strongly to readers of some genres as unexpected—suspense, mysteries, thrillers, general fiction—than others like woman's fiction, young adult or Sci-Fi, because the readers expect that such a line might contain a lot more meaning behind it. If we go to a horror movie, we expect to be scared; that's the underlying premise of that type of story.

**NOTE**: Never forget that reader expectations play into the power of your hooks. How do you know what those expectations are? Since you should be reading what you are writing, ask yourself what you expect, and what types of hooks intrigue you the most?

## ASSIGNMENTS

1) Take one of the following statements and rewrite until you can create five unexpected openings of that particular sentence. Change the words up, add or subtract words or phrases, do anything you need to ratchet the sentence up to create the Totally Unexpected Hook.

*Mandy always loved brown and white puppies.*

*The school had been abandoned for at least ten years.*

*Mr. Hopkins expected his students to groan when he announced the pop Physics test.*

The intention of this assignment is to practice creating a Totally Unexpected Hook. The more practice you have, the easier it will be to create such hooks in your own work.

2) Look at your own writing, particularly your opening sentence or end of chapter sentences. Play with these particular sentences to see if you can take what you have currently written and add in the Totally Unexpected Hook. You don't need to use the Totally Unexpected Hook in your final draft, especially if it's inappropriate to what you are writing, but learning that words are malleable, that they can be played with to achieve whatever you intend them to achieve, helps

you understand how to create them when you want one. This means that, should you want to use the Totally Unexpected Hook in the future, you have a better idea of how to achieve one.

## RECAP

- Remember that the Totally Unexpected Hook is often seen with the Surprising Situation Hook, creating a double hook.
- Build on a Surprising Situation Hook to reach the Totally Unexpected Hook level.
- The Totally Unexpected Hook can imply one thing about the story before the true reality is revealed. Use this to your advantage, but be careful not to over use.
- Even if the Totally Unexpected Hook is not used in your opening sentences, it can still be effective deeper into your novel, where it can re-engage the reader as your plot develops and twists.

## HOOK 5: QUESTION(S) RAISED HOOK

This is the easiest hook of all for most people to create and identify. It doesn't matter how many questions are raised, you only get one hook point— but if you can get the reader to ask who, how, what, where, why or what happens next—you have this hook.

This hook does not mean a story question that leads the reader several chapters into your novel, or throughout the whole story, though at times it can. It can only raise a question or questions that are answered deeper into the page or that particular scene or chapter.

As long as you, as a reader, have a question, then you as a writer have this hook.

In studying the Question(s) Raised Hook it's important to know that as long as a question, or questions are raised in the reader's mind then the Question(s) Raised Hook is working. That's what makes it so fun, so universal, and seen in all genres.

The Question(s) Raised Hook is all about both direct questions such as Bob said, "Did he do it?" or indirect questions such as—the sun rose thirteen minutes earlier than it should have done. Both create the Question(s) Raised Hook.

When you look at the number of hooks you're creating, it doesn't matter how many, or what kinds of questions are being raised when calculating the number of hooks you have in a given sentence or paragraph, you'll only earn one hook for the Question(s) Raised Hook.

Let's look at a simple sentence to make this clearer.

*Pauline had no idea what Bridget saw in that loser Jason.*

This sentence contains the Question(s) Raised Hook as well as the Foreshadowing Hook but not much else — a gentle, two-hook opening. For genres or types of stories without a lot of tension this is a very appropriate opening — some category romances, children's books, women's fiction and cozy mysteries can fall under this distinction.

The questions raised by this example might include — who is Pauline? Who is Bridget? Who is Jason? Why is he a loser? What's happening? How is this going to play out in the story?

The last question is what earns the Foreshadowing Hook in particular. The assumption is that these three individuals and the situation will be driving the story, at least initially. But as you can see there are at least six questions raised as a result of this sentence, but you as the writer do not have a six-hook opening line, you only have a two-hook sentence.

If a question, any question, is raised as a result of your sentence then you earn one hook point, and only one point, for the Question(s) Raised Hook.

This concept can baffle some writers so I want to repeat to make it clear. No matter how many who, what, when, where or why questions are created you still get only one Question(s) Raised Hook.

The Question(s) Raised Hook raises questions, which is what fiction is all about, but it doesn't always create strong tension or a lot of questions. However, the Question(s) Raised Hook still gives Your reader a reason to keep reading.

Let's look at one more example to make sure this concept is clear:

*Jenn Cartwright was three years old when she entered first grade.*

This sentence has the Unique Character Hook, the Question(s) Raised Hook and the Foreshadowing Hook for a three-hook sentence regardless if you're mentally asking – who is Jenn Cartwright? Why should we care? What kind of school puts a child so young into the first grade? What can she do that she's already in first grade? Etc.

You might be thinking—isn't that unusual to be three and entering the first grade? This type of question created about a specific character is what earned the Unique Character Hook. The questions about whether the story will be about Jenn or the situation earned the Foreshadowing Hook. Because those two hooks were present the Question(s) Raised Hook is present, too.

**NOTE:** Fiction is about questions the reader expects to be answered. How these questions are answered is why we read.

### EXAMPLES OF QUESTION(S) RAISED HOOKS

This first example we'll explore is from a literary fiction novel with a focus on understanding the unexplainable. Let's assume the author, Jeffrey Eugenides, had to work at crafting a powerful opening sentence that has more hooks than simply the Question(s) Raised Hook, but the questions it does raise very clearly indicate what type of novel this is, which the hypothetical rough drafts don't reveal as well.

FIRST DRAFT: *Mary tried to kill herself, being the last remaining sister of five siblings.*

A question has been created. That's why this hook is so common, as it's difficult not to raise some kind of question, but the reader receives no sense of how the story will unfold, or why we should care. Let's try again.

SECOND DRAFT: *Mary Lisbon tried to commit suicide but was unsuccessful the first time, even though her sisters had succeeded.*

Here there are still Question(s) Raised, a Surprising Situation and the Totally Unexpected Hooks, but still no idea if this will be a mystery, western, thriller, or women's fiction. Nor is the Question(s) Raised Hook strong enough to compel the reader to keep reading, because it's written as a bland statement of fact. So let's see how Eugenides created a debut novel that grabbed readers' attention right from the beginning sentence.

> *On the morning the last Lisbon daughter took her turn at suicide — it was Mary this time, and sleeping pills, like Therese—the two paramedics arrived at the house knowing exactly where the knife drawer was, and the gas oven, and the beam in the basement from which it was possible to tie a rope.*
> –Jeffrey Eugenides–*The Virgin Suicides*

The first sentence is almost a paragraph in length, but its length alone, and the lyrical quality of the phrasing makes it clear that this novel is not just about whether Mary died or not, but is already setting up the reader to want to know why this situation happened. It's not a how question but a why question, which is a hallmark of many literary fiction stories. The pacing is intentionally slowed by the length of the sentence, leading the reader to expect to slow down, ponder, consider the ramifications of the story as opposed to race to the end to find out one primary story question—who done it, will they get together, will good triumph over evil, etc.

Let's look at another example, this one from suspense/thriller writer Lee Child. Since he writes a series with a recurring protagonist, Jack Reacher, he has to hook the returning reader as well as the new-to-the-series reader right from the first line.

**NOTE:** Do not be afraid to work and rework your sentences to increase or decrease the number of hooks included in them.

Assuming Child had no idea how he was going to raise questions with his first sentence in his tenth novel featuring protagonist Jack Reacher, let's look at what he might have written.

ROUGH DRAFT: *He saw a man's life change.*

This is a statement of fact that does create the Question(s) Raised Hook—what did he see—but it's a weak question because we have no idea who "he" is or why we should care. There's little flavor, and no idea if this is the story protagonist or some secondary character.

How did Child dig a little deeper and create an intriguing opening line with a strong enough story question to make the average reader want to keep reading to find out what's happening, to whom and why?

> *Jack Reacher ordered espresso, double, no peel, no cube, foam cup, no china, and before it arrived at his table, he saw a man's life change forever.*
> –Lee Child–*The Hard Way*

In this example, Child leads the reader from the mundane, everyday world of ordering coffee, to his hook, which creates multiple questions and not simply one. He's using the power of contrast to ratchet up the questions, which is an effective tool. What if he'd written the sentence like this:

ROUGH DRAFT: *Jack Reacher saw a man's life change forever after he ordered an espresso, double, no peel, no cube, foam cup, no china, and before it arrived at his table.*

In this weaker version, the Question(s) Raised Hook is buried in the sentence and the length of the sentence decreases the tension; the opposite of what a suspense/thriller writer wants. Plus, the Question(s) Raised Hook is also diminished because the rewrite reassures the reader that all is fine with the man whose life is changed. After all, Jack Reacher could and did take a mundane action after his observation. If something suspicious or bad was about to happen, would Jack Reacher be ordering an espresso? If you answer no to this last question, then the assumption is that all is well until the reader discovers otherwise.

**NOTE:** Make sure you do *not* answer your hook question within the same sentence that you raised it; otherwise the hook will not pull the reader deeper into the story.

This next example comes from a lighter romantic suspense novel by Jayne Ann Krentz. By "lighter" we mean not as intense or graphically specific about death, dying and bad things happening on the page. Her core readers want the focus on a couple meeting and falling in love with the external plot line, the suspense being the reason these couples come together, but it is not meant to overwhelm or become more prominent than the romance. What this means is that in a traditional suspense or thriller, with more focus on the external plot line—discovering and stopping a dangerous threat—the opening line might easily include five or more hooks. That key sentence is meant to grab the reader harder and make them whip through the pages with bated breath. However, in a lighter suspense, the number of hooks is decreased so that the tension is not as strong.

Let's assume Krentz forgot her core audience expectations and decided to write for an audience that wanted more thrills and chills right from the first sentence. She might have written something like this:

FIRST DRAFT: *The dead son marched through the halls of the hospital, looking neither right nor left, focused only on paying back his dying father.*

SECOND DRAFT: *"I thought you were dead," the old man wheezed, each breath bringing him closer to his last one.*
*"No, dad. Not before I get my revenge. On you."*

The above two examples keep a very strong focus on a mystery/suspense element. There's a sense that something bad is about to happen, and the second draft not only employs a Question(s) Raised Hook but also creates a Surprising Situation Hook, the Totally Unexpected Hook (the father discovering his son he believed dead is alive), Surprising or Shocking Dialogue Hook, Foreshadowing with Warning Hook and a Unique Character Hook for a six hook opening.

Let's compare to Krentz's final opening sentence below:

*There was nothing like the drama of a deathbed scene to expose the skeletons in a family's closet.*
—Jayne Ann Krentz— *Copper Beach*

By toning down the tension, the reader of this novel knows there will be a mystery element, but that it won't be the kind of suspense/thriller that will keep them awake at night due to the number of hooks threaded through the story. The threat does not feel imminent and the darkness is a little removed from the reader, which works very well for the reader who wants a romance story without nitty-gritty, dark reality.

Here's another example, this opening sentence from a mystery writer known for her psychological tone.

*He found the body on the forty-third day of his walk.*

–Elizabeth George–*Careless in Red*

In comparison to the earlier Child example, here George intentionally keeps the "who" of the story in question, based on this series regarding Thomas Lynley, a Scotland Yard Detective Inspector. This is intentional because the previous novel in the series left a grieving Lynley walking away from his position as a Detective Inspector of Scotland Yard after the murder of his pregnant wife, Helen.

George writes a psychological mystery with the pacing sensibilities often found in English mysteries, where the stories are as much about the in-depth characterization as about the whodunit of murder. By starting her novel with the ambiguous "he," she engages the series readers into finding out how Inspector Lynley is involved and, for the new reader, finding out who the "he" is and what happened.

This is not a fast-paced crime novel, and it's not meant to be, which George deftly shows right from her first sentence. There are several hooks in this sentence, but the one to focus on is the Question(s) Raised Hook.

**NOTE**: If you're writing for a series, you need to keep both of your audiences in mind as you craft a powerful opening sentence. Do not assume your only readers are those who have already discovered you. Be sure and engage and hook the new reader, too.

Here's a different example that comes from a novel that combines a mystery with an insider's knowledge of contemporary Hollywood. Remember, we are simply looking at whether the sentence, as an opening sentence, raises one or more questions for the average reader.

Let's assume Jules Asner, as a debut author, struggled with how to balance the chick lit feel of the novel with the mystery elements.

FIRST DRAFT: *My no-good boyfriend deserved all sorts of bad things to happen to him.*

Here the chick lit feel is present, but with no sense of a mystery, and the only Question(s) Raised might be — what had he done to her or him — but is that a strong enough question to read further, especially for a mystery reader? Probably not. It's ho-hum, especially for a book from a brand new writer with the Hollywood inside connections this author brought to the table. Those qualifications used to intrigue a reader to try this new author — intimate knowledge of a specialized world — might cause a reader (including an editor or agent) to pick up the manuscript or novel, but if the reader isn't hooked on that first sentence and first page, the likelihood of the story being purchased or read is slim to none.

SECOND DRAFT: *It's a fact that most female suicides don't shoot themselves in the head.*

Here we still have a Question(s) Raised Hook — why should this matter — but little else. As a reader, we can assume there might be a mystery involved, but the hooks are not strong enough to compel reading further. So let's look at how Asner approached her first sentence, one that raises a question and says Hollywood, mystery and more.

> *On the day she died, the body of Marilyn Monroe went missing for ten hours.*
> –Jules Asner–*Whacked*

And in this official version of the story opening, we know there's going to be a mystery involved (the day she died), the name Marilyn Monroe conjures up Hollywood, and an intriguing story question — why did her body go missing for ten hours? Not over-the-top unexpected, though for some readers it could be, but more a conundrum that warrants further exploration.

**NOTE:** Your opening sentence must hook, or as close to it as possible, and also engage the reader into the type of story you're about to reveal. Be true to the story.

Here's an example from a literary novel of a Question(s) Raised Hook. This is at the end of the first scene in the second chapter of the story.  Remember, hooks need to be raised throughout your story, and not simply in your first sentence, first page.

This passage is seven pages into a book about the slowing of the earth's rotation and the impact of this event as seen through the eyes of an eleven-year-old girl and told though this child's adult POV. The child is listening to her mother's response to hearing the news about the dramatic change happening to the world, and how the mother shared that information with the family.

> *"Something God-awful is happening."*
> — Karen Thompson Walker — *The Age of Miracles*

This particular quote also contains a Surprising or Shocking Dialogue Hook but that hook, the shock value, is not as strong a hook as the Question(s) Raised Hook for the readers, at this point in the story. In hindsight, from the adult protagonist's POV, we're being shown the exact moment when she hears that her world will never be the same. The author chose to use this key reveal as a direct Question(s) Raised Hook, as opposed to having the mother stating what is exactly happening. This question, this hook here, keeps the reader turning the page to find out more details, to discover what God-awful thing was happening.

**NOTE:** Whether you use an implied question or a direct question, as in the previous example, this Question(s) Raised Hook can be powerful and should not be ignored.

Now let's look at another example where the Raising Question(s) Hook is being employed effectively. This comes from a historical family drama. Let's assume that the author wrote a placeholder opening line.

INITIAL DRAFT 1: *Enoch Root walked around the corner.*

Unfortunately, even that sentence will raise questions — who is this person? What's he doing? What's happening?

See? I told you it's hard not to earn the Question(s) Raised Hook.
Let me try again.

INITIAL DRAFT 2: *His name was Enoch.*

This is about as bland an opening as you can write, but because it's short, it's also natural for a reader to continue reading to at least the next sentence. So let's try and keep no hooks going.

INITIAL DRAFT 3: *His name was Enoch. He was walking down the street on a pleasant spring day.*

Not much going on so far is there? If you read these opening two sentences would you be willing to continue reading? Would you buy the book based on these two sentences?

If you answer no to either question, it's a natural response. Yes, being writers we might try to give the story the benefit of the doubt, but if you had 30-50 opening pages to read in a day, and you would only be choosing one or two to continue reading, would this be enough for you? Probably not, especially if you are used to a lot more hooks in the opening of a story. So let's examine how the author kept the tension low via the number of hooks in his opening line, but still has hooks engaging the reader.

> *Enoch rounds the corner just as the executioner raises the noose above the woman's head.*
> — Neal Stephenson — *Quicksilver*

Now we have the Question(s) Raised Hook — what's happening? Who's Enoch? Who's the woman? — as well as the Action/Danger Hook — the words executioner, noose and the proximity of the noose to the woman's head implies a physical threat to the woman — and the Foreshadowing Hook with Warning — that somehow this situation will play out in the story or that the woman might shortly die.

So, a three-hook opening sentence. Since this is a historical novel, and one that is a little on the darker side, let's see how the author moves from a three-hook opening with a sense of darkness and danger (at least to the woman) to make sure that, by the end of the first paragraph the reader will know if this is the type of historical novel they wish to read.

FIRST PARAGRAPH:

> *Enoch rounds the corner just as the executioner raises the noose above the woman's head. The crowd on the Common stop praying and sobbing for just as long as Jack Ketch stands there, elbows locked, for all the world like a carpenter heaving a ridge-beam into place. The rope clutches a disk of blue New England sky. The Puritans gaze at it, and, to all appearances, think. Enoch the Red reins in his borrowed horse as it nears the edge of the crowd, and sees the executioner's purpose is not to let them inspect his knotwork, but to give them all a*

*narrow – and to a Puritan, tantalizing – glimpse of the portal*
*through which they all must pass one day.*
— Neal Stephenson — *Quicksilver*

Let's break this opening down in more depth so you can
see how using the Question(s) Raised Hook alone, or with
only one or two other hooks, can be built upon with more
hooks to give the reader a clearer idea of the type of story
being offered to them.

*Enoch rounds the corner just as the executioner raises the noose*
*above the woman's head.* [Question(s) Raised, Foreshadowing
with Warning, and Action/Danger hooks.] *The crowd on the*
*Common stop* [Historical detail helping set the scene.] *praying*
*and sobbing* [Overpowering Emotion Hook] *for just as long as*
*Jack Ketch stands there, elbows locked, for all the world like a*
*carpenter heaving a ridge-beam into place.*[More historical detail
and Question(s) Raised Hook — who is this man? Is he a
carpenter? Why is he standing as he is?] *The rope clutches a disk*
*of blue New England sky.* [Setting.] *The Puritans gaze at it,*
[Historical detail that gives time period and a general location
since Puritans tended to live in the New England area of early
America.] *and, to all appearances, think.* [Different Question(s)
Raised Hook here than up to this point.] *Enoch the Red reins in*
*his borrowed horse as it nears the edge of the crowd, and sees the*
*executioner's purpose is not to let them inspect his knotwork, but to*
*give them all a narrow – and to a Puritan, tantalizing – glimpse of*
*the portal through which they all must pass one day.* [This ends on
a Question(s) Raised Hook but different than the ones raised
already, Foreshadowing with Warning Hook, clearer
Action/Danger Hook, and a Surprising Situation Hook. Not
that the woman is going to be hung, but that the spectators
appear to be relish what they are seeing.]

Now let's look at a Question(s) Raised Hook from an
amateur sleuth novel. The tension level the readers often

expect in these types of mysteries is a little more than a cozy mystery but not as strong as a police procedural or a mystery with a stronger suspense slant.

> *The man died fast and hard and in true Texas style,*
> *stepping into a shotgun blast that lifted his feet off the ground*
> *and slammed him backward through the door he'd just opened,*
> *into the powdery dust of the street.*
> —Susan Witting Albert—*Indigo Dying*

Pulling this sentence apart, we can see how and where the author slowed the tension and decreased the potential hooks she used to make it a more appropriate opening for this series set in Texas with a protagonist who runs an herb and tea shop.

*The man died fast and hard* [This is being told to the reader, which creates distance from the actual gruesome death scene.] *and in true Texas style.* [This editorial comment makes this death more an anecdote, creating more distance and a hint of humor, which always decreases tension.] *stepping into a shotgun blast* [Used in another opening, or starting with this phrase here, could have changed this to a much more gruesome situation and a tenser sentence.] *that lifted his feet off the ground and slammed him backward through the door he'd just opened,* [This shifts the focus off the shotgun blast and thus waters down the situation.] *into the powdery dust of the street.* [Ends the death on a mundane note, which again shifts the focus to the setting, not the killing.]

The very length of the sentence decreases tension, but the author intentionally kept the focus off of the Danger, Overpowering Emotion, and Totally Unexpected Hooks and kept the focus tight and less tense by using only the Surprising Situation and Question(s) Raised Hooks.

## NO QUESTION(S) RAISED HOOKS:

As mentioned before, the Question(s) Raised Hook is the most common type of hook you'll find as you analyze others' and even your own work, but that doesn't mean that it's easy to create for all writers.

We have to train ourselves to:
1) Think in terms of hooks.
2) Be aware of the most powerful hooks at our disposal and…
3) Recreate those hooks in our own work where they can do the most to keep a reader engaged and turning the pages.

Here are a few samples of No Question(s) Raised Hooks.

*"I'll meet you to do homework at four, then," I said to my BFF, Kenya.*

This is simply a statement and gives the reader no reason to discover more, based on this sentence alone. Let's see how we might jazz this up a smidge to include at least a Question(s) Raised Hook.

**NOTE:** Many times a Question(s) Raised Hook creates some of the other hooks we've examined because the question(s) can imply Danger, a Surprising Situation or the Totally Unexpected.

REWRITTEN:

*"I'll meet you to do homework at four, then," I said to my BFF, Kenya, "before we make the bomb."*

*"I'll meet you to do homework with you at four, then," I said to my BFF, Kenya, who was also my grandmother.*

*"I'll meet you to do homework at four, then," I said to my BFF, Kenya, which was the last time I ever talked to her.*

Small, incremental, intentional, changes can pay off in making a sentence change from okay to intriguing.

Here's another No Question(s) Raised Hook sentence.

Professor Hornaby enjoyed his daily coffee break, only he always drank tea, simply because he preferred it more.

Some readers may think—I wonder why he called it a coffee break if he preferred tea—but is that enough of a question to keep reading?  Maybe if this was your favorite author or the genre was one you enjoyed, IT WOULD BE enough to give the author a little leeway, but otherwise, probably not. So let's see how we can thread in a stronger question or questions.

On the day the Event happened, Professor Hornaby enjoyed his daily coffee break, only he always drank tea, simply because he preferred it more.

Threading in the key phrase, *On the day the Event happened,* and capitalizing the word *Event* to indicate this was a big thing, creates the Question(s) Raised Hook—what event and what happened as a result? Also, by leading with the Question(s) Raised Hook, then shifting the focus to the more mundane activity, we decrease the tension of the hook while still retaining the questions created.

## HOOK 6: UNIQUE CHARACTER HOOK

All writers believe, and should believe, that their protagonist characters are unique. After all, we spend a lot of time and attention understanding our characters inside and out, what makes them tick, what their fears are, their back story (what has happened to them before the current story begins), their familial relationships, their jobs, likes and dislikes, and the list goes on.

When using the Unique Character Hook, your POV (point of view) character, or the character being introduced (even if they are not the protagonist) must be someone the average reader would not know or meet in their typical day, or expect to see in that particular place or situation.

Well-known types of characters might be cops, mothers, lawyers, cowboys—someone you might personally not cross paths with daily, but have met or know enough about to *not* be surprised with seeing them in a story.

Thus a waitress in the character role of a waitress is not a Unique Character Hook, but a waitress appearing in a beauty pageant could be unique. A mother is not unique (don't tell my mom—she'd kill me), but a mother who's undergoing a sex change operation is unique. A law enforcement officer is not unique, especially in many types of mysteries, suspense and thriller stories, but they are a hint more unique in a children's, young adult, or women's fiction novel, depending on how they are used and introduced. Using a law enforcement officer as the love interest or former spouse in a romance novel makes them less unique because this type of character is often seen.

Keep this in mind as you analyze whether you have a Unique Character Hook (the protagonist or a secondary character) and how and when you want to introduce that unique character to the reader.

If you, as the author, know that within several pages or chapters of your story your reader will discover that the person you portrayed in the opening sentence is a very different or unique person, then that's not a Unique Character Hook opening line. It might be a Unique Character Hook depending on how you introduce a character deeper into the story, at one of the key hook locations — opening or an end of scene or chapter in particular. But it's not a Unique Character Hook if the introduction of that character is buried in the middle of a scene or chapter.

Keep in mind that creating the Unique Character Hook does not mean that your character needs to be quirky or so off-the-wall unusual to stand out. The same character that is very comfortable in one environment can stand out as very unique in another. For example, a nun in a church is not unique; a nun refereeing a mud wrestling competition is unique. A pharmacist in a dispensary is not unique but a pharmacist who sings opera while measuring ingredients is. So be true to your story while being open to the possibility of showing an aspect of a character that can catch the reader's attention a little more.

**NOTE:** Unique Character is all about revealing something the reader doesn't expect about the character, given the type of person that the character is, the job the character does, or the genre being read.

### EXAMPLES OF UNIQUE CHARACTER HOOKS:

*On November the twenty-first, the day of her forty-seventh birthday, and three weeks and two days before she was murdered, Rhoda Gradwyn went to Harley Street to keep a first appointment with her plastic surgeon, and there in a consulting room designed, so it appeared, to inspire confidence*

*and allay apprehension, made the decision which would*
*inexorably lead to her death.*
–P.D. James–*The Private Patient*

This line comes from an older mystery with a slower pacing sensibility than many current ones, which is not a negative reflection on a classic mystery, but a reminder that you, as a writer, must be aware of changes in a reader's expectations—especially if you're studying older novels. What this opening does very well is to introduce the reader step-by-step to a character most of us have never met—a murder victim.

Since what the reader sees here is a normal activity, visiting a doctor's office, even if it's not the kind of doctor every person has personally visited, the average reader is familiar enough with who plastic surgeons are that it's not unexpected to have the character meeting with one. The character is not unique because of her age or what she's doing, but because she will become a murder victim. There's a foreshadowing of future events that builds multiple hooks into this sentence. These are the hooks present:

- Unique Character,
- Foreshadowing with Warning,
- Danger,
- Surprising Situation,
- Evocative.

So while the pace is languid, there are five hooks present, and a clear introduction to a mystery novel.

What if James rushed her opening line?

FIRST DRAFT: *Rhoda Gradwyn was forty-seven when she died.*

Pretty bland, more a plain statement of fact than a sentence that intrigues us with a Unique Character Hook, even if we add in a hint more information.

SECOND DRAFT: *Rhoda Gradwyn was forty-seven when she was murdered.*

Here at least we have a Unique Character Hook (most readers do not personally know a murder victim even if we know of them) but no strong author's voice for the Evocative Hook, no Foreshadowing with Warning Hook, possibly a Question(s) Raised Hook, thus shifting from a five-hook opening to a two-hook opening.

In a literary mystery a two-hook opening can work, the same with some cozy or some amateur sleuth mysteries, where the protagonist is not in law enforcement but brings their knowledge of a community or people to help solve the mystery. Examples of an amateur sleuth could be a baker, a glass blower, a bookstore owner, etc., but even in these types of stories you'd want to follow up with more hooks on that first page. Why? Because a two-hook opening alone will not encourage a reader to keep reading and turn that page unless they already know and love your work.

Let's look at another example, this one from a thriller novel. But before we get to the opening sentence as written by Nelson Demille, let's assume he worked up to including a Unique Character Hook.

FIRST DRAFT: *John Corey was a gruff, wisecracking NYPD homicide cop who'd had a hard life.*

Technically, the majority of readers may not have firsthand or personal knowledge of a NYPD detective. But as a result of TV and movies, this type of character might seem more familiar than, let's say, an Amity, Maine detective or Nacogdoches, Texas detective. These last two characters would actually stand out as more unique because they are from less well-known communities. So let's see how Demille introduces his recurring character in a way that the average reader senses a Unique Character Hook within the opening line.

> *You'd think that anyone who'd been shot three times and almost became an organ donor would try to avoid dangerous situations in the future.*
> –Nelson Demille–*The Lion's Game*

We weren't given a name, a law enforcement affiliation, a marital status or even the sex of the character, but the very fact the character had been shot three times means most readers would consider them intriguing enough to keep reading a little further to find out who this person is. That's how a good hook works.

Let's look at another example, this one from a literary novel.

> *The flight from Newark to Hartford took no more than fifty-eight minutes, but she still managed to get her heart broken three times.*
> –Jean Hanff Korelitz–*Admission*

This particular example was chosen to illustrate several points. Within the next sentence the reader discovers this is not a literal statement but a metaphoric one from a college admissions officer. This opening line sentence still works to pull the reader just a smidge deeper into finding out who this person is and what's happening in their life.

The Unique Character Hook doesn't mean that the POV character in the opening line remains unique throughout the story. It means that for the space of that one sentence this hook can work before another hook, or series of hooks, carry the reader deeper into the novel.

**NOTE:** Hooks are intentional ways to engage the reader's curiosity to continue reading, whether for one more sentence, one more page, or another chapter.

The Unique Character Hook, particularly when used in either the opening sentence or opening paragraph, must promise and entice the reader. Then the book must follow up, if not with that character remaining unique, then with a strong enough story that continues to engage.

**NOTE:** A powerful opening line cannot overcome a weak first page or a weak novel. In fact, the reader may feel cheated by what the author offered but did not follow through on as the story progresses.

The Unique Character Hook, as with most hooks, cannot replace a poorly plotted, clichéd story line. Hooks are not wallpaper that can hide cracks in the walls of your story. Think of a fine appetizer that precedes a mediocre meal. You don't want the reader setting down your book and remembering you for what you didn't deliver rather than what you did.

Understanding and utilizing hooks enhances a solid story and takes your writing to the next level. However, becoming a master of hooks does not mean you can ignore the other elements of storytelling.

Let's look at another opening line, this one from John le Carré, a master of suspense and spy novels. Let's assume that he had to build toward a Unique Character Hook in his opening line.

FIRST DRAFT: *A young boy shadowed the boxing champion down the streets of Hamburg.*

There are hooks in this version — Foreshadowing without Warning, Question(s) Raised, possibly a Surprising Situation. But we're looking specifically for the Unique Character Hook.

Let's see how le Carré created one in his version of the sentence:

> *A Turkish heavyweight boxing champion sauntering down a Hamburg street with his mother on his arm can scarcely be blamed for failing to notice that he is being shadowed by a skinny boy in a black coat.*
> –John le Carré–*A Most Wanted Man*

There's a lot happening in this single sentence that weaves in enough details to create the Unique Character Hook. The man being trailed is not only a heavyweight boxing champion—he's Turkish, in the German city of Hamburg. Most readers, unless they are familiar with the ethnic diversity of this particular city, would not think in terms of a Turkish man in a German city, so it can pique a reader's interest, but le Carré doesn't stop there. He makes sure the man is unique in a second way; that of being a heavyweight boxing champion. The reader now has an image of a large man who is good with his fists. Then le Carré adds in the fact this man is sauntering down the street with his mother on his arm, another image that is not often combined with the words *heavyweight boxing champion*. The author follows up by threading in the clincher: this large fighter is being followed by a skinny boy.

The result is that not only is the Unique Character Hook present, but it's combined with a Surprising Situation, the Totally Unexpected, Foreshadowing with Warning, and Question(s) Raised Hooks. A five-hook opening, which compels the reader to read further into the story.

Let's examine another novel, this one a hard-boiled detective novel published a number of years ago. If you look at a novel written twenty to thirty years ago, or more, you'll often discover slower openings and fewer hooks. Why? Because novels were only competing against television and movies for the attention of the average person at that time.

That same reader today has a lot more entertainment choices—movies at their fingertips with a click of a button, video games, e-mail, Facebook, cable TV with dozens of channels, and the list continues. Which means that in order to engage a reader now, today's writers must work harder to grab a person's attention.

*Grab and hold onto that attention.* We'll dig into how to do this deeper in this book based on hook placement, but for now let's return to another Unique Character Hook in an opening line.

> *When I finally caught up with Abraham Traherne, he was drinking beer with an alcoholic bulldog named Fireball Roberts in a ramshackle joint just outside of Sonoma, California, drinking the heart right out of a fine spring afternoon.*
>
> –James Crumley–The Last Good Kiss

In this example, Crumley took the cliché image of a hard-boiled detective—heavy drinker, a loner, a little on the seedy side—and uses that image with a twist. He makes the bulldog alcoholic. Setting aside the issues of animal cruelty, now the reader is seeing what he expects to see given the subgenre of mystery, but in a very different way—a fresh way. Yes, the main character is drinking, but the focus is more on the unexpected image of the dog, not the man. Then the sentence ends on a very evocative descriptive phrase, which helps showcase a strong author's voice. If Crumley hadn't pushed himself as a writer and stuck with the expected, the opening line might read something like this:

ROUGH DRAFT: *When I finally caught up with Abraham Traherne, he was drinking beer in a ramshackle joint just outside of Sonoma, California.*

No Unique Character Hook here. No Surprising Situation or strong Evocative Hooks either. There might be a hint of a

Foreshadowing without Warning Hook and, when combined with a Question(s) Raised Hook, it creates a weak two-hook opening versus the six hooks Crumley crafted — Unique Character, Foreshadowing without Warning, Surprising Situation, Totally Unexpected, Question(s) Raised and Evocative Hooks.

Before you think that opening lines containing the Unique Character Hook must be long, which can impact and slow pacing, let's look at one from a contemporary urban fantasy novel.

I didn't realize he was a werewolf at first.
–Patricia Briggs–*Moon Called*

The reason this line earns a Unique Character Hook is not because of the mention of a werewolf, because those are fairly common in this genre. It's because the POV character, the one thinking, is aware of what type of creature he or she is facing. That's unusual, until the reader knows otherwise.

In this type of novel, where werewolves, shape-shifters and other preternatural beings abound, the human population might be very familiar with werewolves. But until the reader is clear about that, this short, to the point internalization statement will nudge the reader to keep reading just a little further to find out who this POV character is and why they think they should have realized there was a werewolf in the vicinity.

This opening sentence is also an excellent illustration of the point that a hook does not need to intrigue a reader and draw them through the whole story. Questions raised by hooks can be immediately answered on the same page or the same chapter. The strongest writers, though, continue to use hooks in key locations so the reader always has a reason to keep reading.

Don't assume that in order to create a strong hook, you have to write a whole paragraph to show a character who most readers do not cross paths with in their normal day. Let's look at a line from an upmarket women's fiction novel that creates the Unique Character Hook in one short sentence.

> *In my first memory, I am three years old and I am trying to kill my sister.*
> –Jodi Picoult–*My Sister's Keeper*

Let's examine in more detail why this brief sentence not only shows a unique character, but how the author drills home that point in such a succinct way.

The sentence is paced like a series of stepping stones. The first phrase — In my first memory — sets up the reader to know that the past is influencing the present but by itself offers no hooks. Not yet. The second phrase — I am three years old — might be to some readers a more unique character because not everyone remembers events from that young of an age, but it's the third phrase — and I am trying to kill my sister — that creates the strong punch line and the Unique Character Hook.

The combination, the slow build to an unexpected end of the sentence, offers the reader the following hooks:

- Unique Character,
- Surprising or Shocking Dialogue (internal first person),
- Totally Unexpected,
- Foreshadowing with Warning,
- Danger (if you believe a person who tried to kill her sister from such an early age could be dangerous),
- Surprising Situation,
- Question(s) Raised.

That's a seven-hook opening line that entices the reader to keep reading more to find out who this person is and why this was her memory.

Here's another example, this one from a steampunk novel that requires meeting the reading expectations of historical readers who also want a stronger action-adventure pacing. In this opening line the author, Devon Monk, quickly anchors the reader into the world of her story while using contrast to introduce a Unique Character Hook, not only the protagonist but also in a secondary character.

Let's assume that Monk had a hint of what she wanted to do but wasn't sure of the execution, so she created a weak opening line.

FIRST DRAFT: *Cedar didn't like the woman he met in the shop because she seemed really mean.*

That's a no-hook opening and certainly gives no idea of the type of person who is in this novel, or the world of the story. With a name such as Cedar, we're not even sure if the character is a person, as it could be a dog or another pet. So let's see how Monk creates a four-hook opening sentence.

> *Cedar had stared straight into the killing eyes of rabid wolves, hungry bears, and a charging bull elk, but Mrs. Horace Small had them all topped.*
> — Devon Monk — *Dead Iron*

In this final version, the author created the following hooks:

- Unique Character Hook (most of us have not or do not know a person who's faced all those dangerous animals) or the Unique Character Hook of Mrs. Small (who's being compared to dangerous animals),
- Foreshadowing with Warning (that this woman might play out in the story),
- Danger (she sounds pretty dangerous given what he'd rather face),

- Question(s) Raised (what's going to happen as a result of meeting this kind of woman, who are these people, what's happening in this situation?).

This last example comes from a sci-fi series. This information matters because the author must meet the expectation of her existing sci-fi readers, those who are familiar with the series as well as those new to the series. But let's look at a possible initial draft, one without a Unique Character Hook.

FIRST DRAFT: *If anyone had been watching the graveyard they would be shocked to see what happened next.*

There are Foreshadowing and Question(s) Raised hooks present in this sentence, but there's no character revealed at all, so no Unique Character Hook.

SECOND DRAFT: *Mo Ti needed to escape the high Tariq lords and he had.*

Now we have a character present and, to those readers familiar with the series, this opening could work, because it answers a question raised in Book 2 in the series. For some sci-fi readers new to the series the names might imply enough unusualness to create the Unique Character Hook for them. However, readers new to the series might simply feel confused, as if they've been dropped too abruptly into the middle of a story, without enough anchoring. They have a name, but not much more. So the Unique Character Hook would not be working as effectively as it might.

Let's see how the author approached her opening line and intrigued the reader with a Unique Character Hook.

*He still had dirt under his fingernails from his grave.*
*– Kay Kenyon — City Without End*

Now we have an unusual character, one that an urban fantasy reader more than a sci-fi or high fantasy reader might be familiar with as a zombie. Questions are created about who is this person? What happened to him? What's going to happen next? All questions related to the introduction of him contained in an opening line with the implication that he either is dead or was dead.

If you want to read the next sentence, or more, then the Unique Character Hook is working. In the last example this combination of hooks will make a reader keep reading to find out more.

Now let's look at a few examples of no Unique Character Hooks in opening lines and how a writer could change them to create the Unique Character Hook.

## NO UNIQUE CHARACTER HOOKS:

Mr. Williams, a kindly-looking man with a thick burly mustache, walked with a slight limp.

In this example, we have a description of a man and his name. In a few pages, we might discover he's a lion tamer, a widower with six former wives or a serial killer — only at that point would he earn the Unique Character Hook. Unless by then the reader knows the story is unfolding in a circus, in which case we'd expect to see a lion tamer and other unusual occupations, or he is in a Self-Help Group where the other participants have already indicated they have very unusual relationships, or in a maximum security ward of a prison where one might expect to find serial killers.

**NOTE:** For the Unique Character Hook, ask yourself: have you or would your average reader have met this kind of person in their lives or know about them to the point they seem familiar? If so, it's not usually a Unique Character Hook.

The Unique Character Hook is dependent on what the reader already knows about the story, and when and how the character is introduced. So if you are working to create a Unique Character Hook in an opening line, you might think in terms of your story as a whole and how you could position the introduction of your protagonist or a secondary character on the page in such a way that the reader must keep reading to find out more.

Let's see how we might jazz up Mr. Williams a little more, always keeping in mind that you must be true to your story and not mislead your readers simply for the purpose of squeezing in a Unique Character Hook where it's not appropriate.

*Mr. Williams was a kindly looking man with a thick burly mustache, who walked with a slight limp and looked nothing like the mother I used to know.*

Or:

*Mr. Williams was a kindly looking man with a thick burly mustache who walked with a slight limp, which contrasted sharply with his pet tiger.*

Or:

*At a hundred and ten years of age, Mr. Williams was a kindly looking man with a thick burly mustache who walked with a slight limp.*

Each of the last examples added one small additional piece of information to engage readers and make them want to read just a little bit more. If the author is smart, other hooks have been woven into the page.

If writing a series story, such as a mystery, urban fantasy or western with a recurring protagonist, many times a Unique Character Hook, especially early in the story, involves a secondary character — the victim, a preternatural being or an average person in a very unique situation, such as a school teacher who runs a brothel.

**NOTE:** Creating a unique character applies to any character that might fit that profile, but to use it as a Unique Character Hook means the introduction is not buried in the middle of a paragraph or page or chapter. It must be used in a key location in your story.

We'll discuss where those locations are a little deeper into this book.

### ASSIGNMENTS:

Take any of the following character types (or all of them), or use some of your own and see how you can add one small additional detail that can take the character from average or expected to a Unique Character Hook.

- Mother
- Reverend
- Kindergarten Teacher
- Movie Star
- Thirteen-year-old

Look at your own story. Do you have a unique character present, either protagonist(s), antagonist(s) or secondary character(s)? Look at how and where you're currently introducing them. If you have an unusual or unexpected character, can you introduce them at one of the key locations where they can hook a reader more? We'll go into details as to where those locations are deeper into this book, so for now think opening line, end of the first page, opening or ending of a scene or chapter.

If you are working with a critique partner or writer's group, or even with a group of friends, family or readers who are willing to help, describe for them a character—by name, sex, age, job description and where they are living—from your story and ask each participant to write down 3 ways to make this character unexpected. Having people write their ideas down will allow them to feel less intimidated by off-the-wall ideas—those ideas that just might take your story to the next level. Once you've gathered the ideas, you can read as many as you want out loud because that may create even more ideas.

## RECAP:

- Hooks are subjective and are determined by the type of story you are writing and the speed and pacing of your story.
- Hooks are intended to encourage the reader to keep reading, whether that's from the beginning of the page to the middle of the page, from the end of a chapter to the beginning of the next chapter or simply to read deeper into a scene.
- If you use the Unique Character Hook in your opening line or page, that means that what set them apart as totally unique and different becomes the new norm for this character deeper in the book. If they were introduced as a vegetarian vampire in the opening page, describing them as that deeper into the book does not earn a new Unique Character Hook.
- Use the Unique Character Hook, and all hooks, only if they are applicable to your story.
- The Unique Character Hook can be your protagonist or can be another character in your story.

- Part of creating the Unique Character Hook can involve taking a stereotype and tweaking it in a way the reader would not expect.

## HOOK 7: EVOCATIVE HOOK

This hook can confuse and frustrate many writers. It's one of the hardest hooks to write and to identify. Or, if it comes naturally, you'll find yourself struggling with some of the other hooks that resonate with most readers easily, such as the Foreshadowing with or without Warning Hook, the Action/Danger Hook or the Surprising Situation Hook.

Oftentimes the Evocative Hook is based on a specific setting or the world of the story, but not all settings or all story worlds rate as *evocative*. For example: the sounds of a lot of cars driving could be any city in any place and is not specific to cluing a reader into a story, nor is it evocative. The smell of exhaust, human sweat and hot asphalt of Times Square might tell the average reader they are in NYC and this setting is important to the story, but it's still not evocative, it's simply a specific location. Some settings, and there will be examples further along, conjure up an emotional response to a place that's so strong the reader must keep reading simply to know more about that location.

**NOTE:** Evocative setting as an opening hook MUST be relevant to your story.

Literary word painting, or a beautiful scene, can be evocative but does not always pull the reader into the story. Word painting can be intangible but you know it when you read it. Think—no one else could write it this way, or, this really makes me pay attention—which is why this is one of the most subjective of the hooks. It has to have that WOW! factor, which can be very different for different readers. Expect some of the examples used in this section to make you pause, in order to savor and slide deeper into the word painting, while others might create just the opposite response in you.

Think poetry, or approaching a subject in an unexpected and riveting way. Using Evocative Hooks, especially in the opening line or lines, clearly alerts the reader that they might have to invest more, pay attention more deeply, or slow their reading to absorb what they are about to read.

The way words are combined often indicates a strong author's voice—think Jodi Picoult, Dennis Lehane, Pat Conroy, Nevada Barr, Maya Angelou, Ursula K. LeGuin. Many authors, especially newer writers, assume that their voice is unique because they are unique, and there's validity in that. But what we're looking at here, to earn the Evocative Hook, is an approach to telling a story, word choices and combinations, the different/off-beat phrasing—all of which are what entices the reader to read further . . . or set the book down. These elements create strong reactions in readers who will either love the approach or not "get it," but are rarely indifferent to the voice.

One of the ways a writer often discovers the strength of their voice is with experience, but also with feedback. The stronger the voice, the more likely you'll find readers who either love it or hate it. This is because it is so subjective that the voice either resonates with a reader or doesn't.

It's like going to a blockbuster action-adventure movie where, even if you change the characters, you wouldn't expect much change to the events in the movie. Different villains but same outcome, different male protagonist but it doesn't matter if it's Chuck or Arnold or Tom playing the part of the action-adventure hero—you can pretty well guess what's going to happen by the end of the movie. The movie, or novel, is about getting caught up in the story, knowing where it's going, but you're along mostly for the ride.

Compare this to an Indie or a foreign movie where the pacing is different, how the scenes that are shot can be different, and where you really have to pay attention to all the nuances to understand the story. You, as a viewer (reader) have to set aside what you want/expect to happen next and trust the creator. This doesn't mean that at the end you're not scratching your head and saying, "I don't get it" or "that made no sense," but it does mean that you have to trust the author to guide you through their story with no expectations of how it will unfold.

One of the major issues you need to be aware of when reaching for the Evocative Hook is that it often means you won't have any other hooks present. This is an important consideration, especially at the beginning of a novel or story where the reader must be engaged.

You'll also discover that to truly achieve the Evocative Hook you'll often end up with longer sentences, or maybe a whole paragraph to create the hook. Keep in mind that the more narrative on the page, and the longer your sentences, the slower your pacing will be.

Read what you intend to have published. If longer, more compound or complicated sentences are the rule in the opening rather than the exception, then consider using the Evocative Hook. If a faster pace and shorter sentences are more the norm, especially in an opening line, paragraph or chapter, then you might want to save your Evocative Hooks for later in your novel. But again, only if they are appropriate to what you are writing. Throwing an Evocative Hook into a novel willy-nilly can pull the reader right out of the story.

If you go to a fast-food restaurant knowing exactly what kind of meal you ordered and expecting to have that meal served fast, but then end up waiting thirty or forty minutes to receive a Le Cordon Bleu quality meal, with its subsequent price tag, you will not be a happy consumer. Your story must be consistent with your readers' expectations. Don't promise readers one kind of story then switch to a different type of story simply to show off your abilities as a writer.

**NOTE:** For the Evocative Hook, once the reader is beyond the first page or two, the word painting and voice become what's expected. If you plan to use the WOW! factor of the

Evocative Hook, based on author's voice alone, then this hook usually works strongest on your first page.

### EXAMPLES OF EVOCATIVE HOOKS:

This first example comes from a novel often referred to as a satire, but it's often shelved in Sci-Fi/Fantasy and sometimes, General Fiction. This is because as a novel it straddles genres, which is a clear indication the story is not focused on a specific plot but about the characters. It's also a great example of a unique author's voice that will either engage you or leave you scratching your head. Let's assume the author, Terry Pratchett, wrote a really raw initial draft, with no Evocative Hooks anywhere in sight. He might have started something like this:

ROUGH DRAFT: *The King of Uberwald made a huge mistake when he invited vampires to his daughter's christening.*

This initial draft has these Hooks:

- Foreshadowing with or without Warning,
- Question(s) Raised,
- Danger (the presence of vampires usually indicates danger unless otherwise explained),
- Surprising Situation and, for some,
- Totally Unexpected.

This last hook might not be unexpected for those who read Pratchett's work, but would apply to those new to his writing or this series. So even in a rough draft this example has five to six hooks, and, if Pratchett wrote straight sci-fi or fantasy, this would be a decent opening line. But these hooks are not in Pratchett's style or approach—which is part of his unique author's voice that gives the lines the Evocative Hook—so let's see how he starts his novel's opening.

*Through the shredded black clouds a fire moved like a dying star, falling back to earth —*
*    — the earth, that is, of the Discworld —*
*    — but unlike any star had ever done before, it sometimes managed to steer its fall, sometimes rising, sometimes twisting, but inevitably heading down.*
— Terry Pratchett — *Carpe Jugulum*


This opening has three hooks to engage the reader — Foreshadowing without Warning, Question(s) Raised and the Evocative Hook. It's this last one we want to examine closely. Note how Pratchett doesn't rush into a clear description or hint of what the story is about. He weaves a mood, a sense that the story must unfold in its own time and manner, and the reader is encouraged to adjust to that pacing.

Pratchett's work is known to have rabid fans, as well as detractors who simply don't care/like/understand his approach and thus will either set down his work or not pick up another copy. This opening is an excellent example of why. The reader must buy into the way this story is crafted; not to be gobbled wholly but by suspending disbelief long enough to meet and explore this unique world in Pratchett's distinctive way.

**NOTE:** Don't think that the Evocative Hook requires obscurity or a style that's so out there it's impossible to replicate. Think strong author's voice, poetic word painting, an expressive setting that pulls a reader into a specific world, or  word construction that causes the reader to adjust to the author's approach to their story.

Next, let's examine next mystery writer Nevada Barr, who uses the settings of her story as a strong element and complication to the mystery plot line. What this means is that you cannot remove the place and retain the mystery. It's also part of her voice so that readers of her series expect and look forward to the rich lushness of her evocative descriptive style.

> *The Rambler's headlights caught a scrap of paper nailed to a tree, a handwritten sign: REPENT. Darkness swallowed it, and Anna was left with the feeling she was surely on the road to perdition. God knew it was dark enough. Her high beams clawed the grass on the left side of the narrow lane, plowing a furrow so green it looked unnatural: neon green, acid green.*
>
> *At least it's in color, she thought sourly. Everything she knew — or imagined she did — about Mississippi had been gleaned from grainy black-and-white television footage of the civil rights movement in the sixties.*
> –Nevada Barr–*Deep South*

Let's pull apart the above example to see exactly which hooks are present and why Barr's word choices earn the Evocative Hook:

*The Rambler's headlights* [Use of a specific car hints a little at the character but no hook yet] *caught a scrap of paper nailed to a tree, a handwritten sign: REPENT.* [Foreshadowing with Warning Hook that this might matter later in the story and is being set up here. If the sign said GARAGE SALE or LOST CAT there would not be the sense of warning which is a strong element of the Foreshadowing with Warning Hook.) *Darkness swallowed it,* [powerful verb that creates an Overpowering Emotion Hook in combination with the word REPENT, the sense that a reader feels already that something is about to happen, and they are a little more aware, a little more on edge, almost expecting something to jump out of the darkness any moment] *and Anna was left with the feeling she was surely on the road to perdition.* [More foreshadowing, especially in a mystery novel but it's not an additional hook here because that's already been used in the same way once in this opening.] *God knew it was dark enough. Her high beams clawed*

[Powerful verb which ratchets up tension] *the grass on the left side of the narrow lane, plowing a furrow so green it looked unnatural: neon green, acid green.* [This is where the Evocative Hook, via description, is driven home. The reader is being shown, step by step, the character's impressions of her location and the author does not stop by saying – the lights lit up greenery – but drives home her imagery and creates a specific voice and way of approaching the story.] *At least it's in color, she thought sourly. Everything she knew – or imagined she did – about Mississippi had been gleaned from grainy black-and-white television footage of the civil rights movement in the sixties.* [This contrast at the end of the second paragraph creates clear conflict, which is not a hook but is important to the story as it foreshadows a fish-out-of-water element.]

The Evocative Hook is earned by the slow descriptive build to this punch line in this last example. The reader sees, and experiences, where the POV character is and within two paragraphs, is dragged into a world of conflict and changing expectations which makes you want to read more to find out what's going to unfold. Unlike Pratchett's work, which is about quirky and unusual characters creating mayhem, Barr's stories are about her protagonist, in a specific location, facing the demands of that location and the mysteries created that can only be understood in context of the setting.

Yes, many mysteries take place in a specific location, but not all settings are crafted in such a way as to pull a reader so deeply into a world intentionally. A world revealed by the way the words are combined on the page. That's one of the elements of the Evocative Hook – the strong author's voice, the word painting, the descriptive details that pull a reader in and/or the unique/different approach to what could be everyday when written by most writers – particularly if the hook is used in the opening line or page.

The next example is another look at the Evocative Hook being used in a general fiction novel by an author with not only a strong author's voice, but who is known for his stories set in the South. Often, when an author is identified with crafting stories of a particular region—William Faulkner, Flannery O'Connor, Garrison Keillor, Willa Cather, John Steinbeck, etc.—you can find evocative writing as these writers use their words intentionally to build the power of a particular environment that shapes the events of their stories. The reader buys into the world of their story as being equally, if not more important than the characters. Many of their stories actually start with place to get that message across to the reader.

So let's see how Pat Conroy does just this with his Evocative Hook in his opening paragraph.

> *It was my father who called the city the Mansion on the River.*
>
> *He was talking about Charleston, South Carolina, and he was a native son, peacock proud of a town so pretty it makes your eyes ache with pleasure just to walk down its spellbinding, narrow streets. Charleston was my father's ministry, his hobby horse, his quiet obsession, and the great love of his life. His bloodstream lit up my own passion for the city that I've never lost nor ever will. I'm Charleston-born, and bred. The city's two rivers, the Ashley and the Cooper, have flooded and shaped all the days of my life on this storied peninsula.*
>
> *I carry the delicate porcelain beauty of Charleston like the hinged shell of some soft-tissued mollusk. My soul is peninsula-shaped and sun-hardened and river-swollen.*
>
> —Pat Conroy—*South of Broad*

Did you feel yourself slowed to a pace in tempo with the words until you could feel yourself in Charleston and experiencing the city as this character experiences it? Or did you want to get on to something happening, enough with all the description? This is the challenge and the gift of the Evocative Hook opening—it can impact pacing and turn off readers as much as turn them on. However, if it is *your* author's voice, as it is Conroy's, then to approach a story otherwise would be impossible.

This next example is considered general fiction. It would not be shelved under historical fiction, though it takes place in the past, it's not women's fiction, though it does include the growth and change of at least one female protagonist, and while many consider it literary, which it is, or a classic, which it also is, it's simply filed under the heading 'Fiction' if you went searching in a brick and mortar bookstore.

Let's assume the author used a placeholder for her opening sentence until she could return to it after completing her novel.

ROUGH DRAFT: *Many said the rough-hewn house on Bluestone Road outside of Cincinnati was haunted.*

This approach does contain hooks—Foreshadowing, Question(s) Raised, Surprising Situation and, for some readers Shocking or Surprising Dialogue—for a three to four-hook opening line. But compare this to how the author eases into her story in such a way that, for the average reader, the concept of unquiet spirits is not clear at all, not until several pages into the story.

*124 was spiteful.*
—Toni Morrison—*Beloved*

If you had *not* read the rough draft version would you have a clue what is happening in this story? Not likely. In fact, you might have ended up re-reading this sentence several times to make sure you read it correctly, because it's so unclear you have no idea what is being discussed.

At most this opening sentence earns the Question(s) Raised Hook on first glance. It's not truly evocative yet, as it's too vague, and vagueness can be confusing vs. compelling. However, as we've learned in other hook modules, when a short sentence is used it's natural for the reader to read at least to the next sentence to find out enough about the story to know whether it's intriguing or irritating.

It's the second sentence in Morrison's work that starts showcasing the Evocative Hook. By the end of the third or fourth sentence the average reader will decide to try at least until the end of the page to find out what's going on [Because questions have been raised] or set the book down as not what they want to read. Why? Because a reader has to work harder to accept the author's approach to story telling when the Evocative Hook is present in the opening sentence and opening page. The reader has to read slower and deeper to understand the story.

Let's see what I mean by looking at the first five sentences in this novel by Morrison.

> *124 was spiteful. Full of a baby's venom. The women in the house knew it and so did the children. For years each put up with the spite in his own way, but by 1873 Sethe and her daughter Denver were its only victims. The grandmother, Baby Suggs, was dead, and the sons, Howard and Buglar, had run away by the time they were thirteen years old — as soon as merely looking in a mirror shattered it (that was the signal for Buglar); as soon as two tiny hand prints appeared in the cake (that was it for Howard). Neither boy waited to see more; another kettleful of chickpeas smoking in a heap on the floor; soda crackers crumbled and strewn in a line next to the door-sill.*
>
> — Toni Morrison — *Beloved*

At this point in the story, the reader who is looking for a more direct, straight forward, easy to consume story might give up because they are confused, unclear what's happening, what's going on. But for the target reader, one who loves word painting, values obscurity not as a deterrent but as a challenge worthy of the read, who wants to stretch himself as a reader and thus is willing to put aside expectations of how a story should unfold and allow the author to ease into the story in their own unique way, this opening paragraph will be a siren call—all because of the Evocative Hook usage.

On the opening page sometimes the Evocative Hook is clear in the opening sentence, but sometimes it takes a few more sentences to really bring home the message that this must be read the way the author thinks and tells a story.

Let's look at a very different opening line Evocative Hook, this one from a women's fiction novel with a focus on a woman's growth and change, a journey into self-discovery and a love story. Let's assume the author had to revisit her opening line to create the Evocative Hook before she got it just right.

FIRST DRAFT: *There had been problems in our marriage for a while, but I was willing to go to a marriage counselor if I could get my husband to come with me.*

A statement of where the protagonist is at in the opening of her story and perhaps the Question(s) Raised Hook but not much else. This made-up version is a great example of how many writers might start a women's fiction novel. The situation is not unusual and the approach is not unusual.

**NOTE:** If you're able to write about the usual in a way that makes the reader stop to think—*Wow! I never thought of this kind of situation in this way*—you're closer to the Evocative Hook.

SECOND DRAFT: *I was still willing to fight for our marriage. We had a comfortable life, a son not yet in his teens, and a lot of reasons to stay together, if we'd work a little harder.*

This version has the same issues. The reader will clearly know this story will be about a woman dealing with a dissolving marriage and all the changes that result. But it still hasn't earned the Evocative Hook, the one that grabs the reader more than the subject matter of the story that entices a person to want to find out what's happening, and how it is going to play out.

Now let's examine how the author, Elizabeth Berg, opens her story.

> *You know before you know, of course. You are bending over the dryer, pulling out the still-warm sheets, and the knowledge walks up your backbone.*
> –Elizabeth Berg–*Open House*

This opening doesn't address the why behind the character's emotional response but it encourages the reader to come along on the journey of story discovering. If you picked up the book from a bookstore — online or a brick-and-mortar store — you'd already know it's women's fiction, might have read the blurb, or the pitch ("*Open House* is a love story about what can blossom between a man and a woman, and within a woman herself"), and you might have a strong idea of what the novel will address. So you wouldn't be worried that a stalker is right around the corner or that the woman is in danger. No, she's doing something that millions of women do daily, but it's the combination of that normal, everyday activity and her realization, her visceral, emotional response that calls out to a reader — because of what Berg focuses the reader on and her descriptive word choices. She takes the ordinary and makes it poetic.

In this next example of an Evocative Hook opening, the author, Hilary Mantel, also explores the aftermath of a woman shocked by the dissolution of her marriage, but it's more a side note to the subject matter of spiritualism and the friendship of two very different women characters. The story is considered "dark" which is another way of saying the author goes deeper and deeper into the hidden and shadowed psyches of her characters because that's what the story is ultimately about—why these women make certain choices, what drives them, what scares them, and how their choices impact their lives and those around them.

Because of this approach, and the use of an Evocative Hook opening, the reader isn't rushed into a clear understanding of the novel's strongest themes—disconnection and connection, the world of living with spirits, isolation, etc., but starts with a slower build, a setting of the darkness, the bleakness of the world. By approaching the story this way, which is a hallmark of an Evocative Hook, the new reader clearly buys into the story's promises right from the opening line.

Let's assume that Mantel created a simple opening sentence without the Evocative Hook.

FIRST DRAFT: *Collette, a recently divorced woman looking for meaning in her life, and Alison, a psychic with a troubling spirit guide, have moved to a suburban wasteland in what was once the English countryside.*

The above draft does have hooks—the Unique Character [The troubling spirit guide is not someone most of us encounter on the average day; for many, the psychic also falls into this category]; Foreshadowing with Warning [Because the guide is described as troubling and the countryside is described as a suburban wasteland); and Question(s) Raised. So it's a three-hook opening. That could work if this was a mystery or women's fiction novel, or if the author assumed all of her readers have read her previous work so will trust her to tell a story in the way they've come to expect from her. But it doesn't carry the Evocative Hook.

Let's try again:

SECOND DRAFT: *Travelling after Christmas along the dark motorways around London reflected her mood — endless, pointless and black.*

Definitely more bleak but it still could have been written by any writer striving for a dark tone to the opening of their novel, plus this sentence does not offer an Evocative Hook opening. Not yet. Note how Mantel approaches this opening line in her own, very specific way to earn the Evocative Hook:

> *Travelling: the dank oily days after Christmas, the motorway, its wastes looping London: the margin's scrub-grass flaring orange in the lights, and the leaves of the poisoned shrubs striped yellow-green like cantaloupe melon.*
> –Hilary Mantel — *Beyond Black*

Let's pull this example apart to see how the word choices, and their order, help build the sense that the story will not be light and easy, not a quick read, but something the reader must either engage in, trusting the author's approach, or set aside as not appealing to them.

*Travelling*: [Right here the author sets up motion, the sense of movement, in a way not often described. This speaks to a unique voice] *the dank oily* [Two strong adjectives that paint a bleak image — one by smell and one by touch, again unusual] *days after Christmas,* [Here the image of the time of year contrasting with the season associated with connection, families, celebration] *the motorway, its wastes looping London* [Instead of simply describing a roadway, the author uses the road as a metaphor for life — the loop, the wasteland, being outside of the well-known large city, being outside of the norm]; *the margin's scrub-grass flaring orange in the lights,* [Keeping to the theme of bleakness and darkness here, the reader sees scrub grass but in a specific way that paints a very unusual image] *and the leaves of the poisoned shrubs* [Not any kind of shrub but poisoned ones. By this point the reader is either compelled to find out more about this emotionally dark world or set the book down because it's too edgy, or because it will require the reader to adjust to the complex approach to storytelling that creates the term evocative] *striped yellow-green like cantaloupe melon.*

**NOTE:** Keep in mind that using the Evocative Hook as an opening must be followed up throughout the novel — it cannot simply be tacked on as an opening line because it promises the reader a very specific type of story told in a very specific way.

The following is an example from a historical novel that, right from the first sentence, lets the reader know the word painting will be unique, as will the author's voice. Before we dig into it, let's assume there was an initial draft that didn't contain the Evocative Hook.

ROUGH DRAFT: *You probably don't know anything about my story.*

This version shows the use of the Question(s) Raised Hook and possibly Surprising or Shocking Dialogue Hook. In a young adult novel, it would not be so shocking because it's a sentiment that can often be associated with the angst of the teen years. In a mystery novel it might earn the Foreshadowing without Warning Hook because the reader expects a murder or bad thing to happen at some point in the story. But this is a historical novel and there's no feel of something bad about to happen, nor is there an Evocative Hook.

SECOND DRAFT: *It's been centuries since I lived, but it's important for you to know the truth about me.*

Now we have a hint that this might be a historical novel and that something has happened, which could intrigue the reader to find out more—so it earns the Question(s) Raised Hook but nothing more.

Now let's see how Anita Diamant creates the Evocative Hook in her first sentence and then follows that with Surprising or Shocking Dialogue (first person POV internal), Unique Character and Question(s) Raised Hooks in the second sentence and third sentence.

> *We have been lost to each other for so long.*
> *My name means nothing to you. My memory is dust.*
> — Anita Diamant— *The Red Tent*

Diamant achieved the Evocative Hook via internal dialogue that is not the usual cadence and style most contemporary readers expect, which means it will either intrigue and make a reader want to read more, or set the book down as not compelling. Remember the Evocative Hook is going to create a strong response in most readers and that response can be either attraction to or repellence from the approach.

**NOTE:** It's important to remember voice and evocative word painting do not need long sentences or paragraphs to create the mood or approach to the story. They often do take more words and if so, can slow the pacing and alert the reader that the story is not a quick, light read, but length is not always an indication of an Evocative Hook.

Here's another example, this time from a psychological suspense novel. Contrast it with the Mantel example earlier where, as a reader, the sense was the story would be very dark and bleak. In this next example the author, Lisa Gardner, wants to draw the reader into the situation, while remaining true to the pacing of traditional suspense novels. Suspense and thriller novels tend to be faster paced, creating the race to the end of the story. Most of the Evocative Hook examples we've looked at intentionally slow the reader down. Gardner is straddling a fine line here in creating an Evocative Hook opening that works for readers who want a story more about the psychology of the human condition, which may or may not appeal to her usual readers who want the fast-paced *will-evil-win-or-not* pacing of a suspense/thriller novel.

Let's look at a possible rough draft.

FIRST DRAFT: *Libby Denbe knows her marriage is falling apart and she wonders if it's because she herself has been broken.*

Here we have the following hook—Question(s) Raised. That's it. One hook for a suspense/thriller story is rarely enough to engage the core readership who has high expectations of conflict, danger, fast-pacing, twists and turns driving to the end of the story when all is revealed. Thus this next rough draft approach alerts readers that the story is more like a women's fiction novel than a suspense story.

SECOND DRAFT: *Pain washed over Libby, the pain of knowing her husband was no longer faithful, the pain of a heart breaking, the pain of trust dissolving.*

This version ratchets up the Overpowering Emotion Hook but it's so melodramatic that the average thriller reader might shudder and put the book down because it's too much emotion, too soon, for what they expect in a thriller or even a romantic suspense novel.

So how did Gardner approach her opening?

*Here is something I learned when I was eleven years old:*
*Pain has a flavor.*
— Lisa Gardner — *Touch & Go*

The Evocative Hook here is based on the juxtaposition of the age of the child and the reference to pain. The way the sentence is written creates emotional distance so it's not immediate—the reader isn't shocked or emotionally appalled by a child being hurt at this moment—but this sentence can intrigue a reader about who this character is, which is the Unique Character Hook, Question(s) Raised about what happened or is currently happening, Surprising or Shocking Dialogue (internal), and Foreshadowing with Warning that pain and this view of the world is going to play out in the story. The Evocative Hook exists because in spite of all the hooks described above that are included in this opening sentence, the focus remains on the promise that this story will be more than about a bad childhood or a dissolving marriage. It will be about digging deep into the human psyche to understand what's unfolding.

As a writer, keep in mind what your core reading audience expects/wants from the type of story they are reading and be true to them as well as to the story that you want/need to write. Gardner has a loyal following of devoted readers who were willing to accept a more evocative opening from her, one that's not as traditional in the genre she writes, because they trust she will deliver the type of story they expect from her in the end.

**NOTE:** If you are a debut writer (unknown to a large audience of readers), you may not be able to approach an editor/agent or readers with an opening that contains hooks that they don't expect, unless you make it quickly clear that you will also offer what the readers do expect.

One last example of an Evocative Hook comes from the sci-fi/fantasy genre. Within any category of stories are nuances that the savvy writer understands so that he/she writes to the core readership—or breaks those expectations intentionally. The following example comes from a fantasy story considered high fantasy (as opposed to coming-of-age fantasy, military fantasy, urban fantasy, etc.). Read not only in the genre, but also any sub-categories of that genre in which you are writing to get a stronger feel for reader expectations.

The fantasy author, Patricia McKillip, is known for her lyrical voice, a trait that endears her to her rabid fans but can confuse other fantasy readers looking for a much clearer, straightforward type of story. The author uses the Evocative Hook right from the first line to promise/alert the reader that this is a novel that they must invest in, and without that investment, that willingness to trust the author; they may be left frustrated. Remember that element common to most Evocative Hooks? Readers will tend to love or hate it, but they will not remain indifferent.

What if McKillip did not have such a strong and unique voice? She might have started this story with something like this:

ROUGH DRAFT: *Fascinated with legends and myths, the young man named Corleu was different from the typical dark-haired Wayfolk.*

This opening makes a promise to the reader—that Corleau will be off on an adventure and must call upon his differences to save those he feels estranged from—and contains the following hooks—Unique Character (most of us have never met a Wayfolk, different or not, but to the average reader of high fantasy the expectation is to find unique characters, so this hook would not be as strong for them); Question(s) Raised Hook and possibly the Foreshadowing without a Warning Hook (there is no sense that a warning is involved here but to the average fantasy reader he or she expects the introduction of a character in conflict with their world, or at odds with it, to foreshadow strong elements of the story unfolding). But there is no word-weaving, no strong author voice or poetic approach here, thus no Evocative Hook.

So let's see how McKillip employs the Evocative Hook in her opening sentence.

He was a child of the horned moon.
 — *Patricia A. McKillip — The Sorceress and the Cygnet*

Right from this line McKillip introduces a Unique Character, but it's the way she starts spinning the poetry, her word choices, her promise to the reader that they will not only find an unusual character but also a world to enter step-by-step in order to experience and enjoy it, that spells an Evocative Hook opening line.

## NO EVOCATIVE HOOKS:

The following examples will contain hooks; what they won't contain is the Evocative Hook. Examine them carefully and you'll start to get a stronger feeling for what is missing in great opening lines *if* the author had meant to use an Evocative Hook. Always keep in mind there's a trade-off for authors — most who use the Evocative Hook will not have a lot of other hooks present in that opening line. So an opening line can still have hooks, and lots of them, just not the Evocative Hook.

*The patrolman's black and white sped past the Space Needle on the way to Ballard.*

This is a statement of fact, if you're familiar with Seattle or associate the iconic Space Needle as being in Seattle, this sentence can get a story off and running as to the location of the story events, but has no Evocative Hook. It has Foreshadowing without Warning, Question(s) Raised and the Action/Danger Hooks because a police car going at high speeds can often imply they are racing to a problem. This line could act very well as an opening line to a mystery, suspense, thriller, or general fiction novel, but nothing about it forces the reader to slow down, enter a specifically woven world and experience it as the author intends.

Let's see what we can do to change a sentence around to make it more evocative.

In seven minutes you can order a caramel macchiato, post a comment on Facebook or kiss a loved one good-bye. You can watch half a YouTube video or brush your teeth. You can drive from the Space Needle to Ballard if you know your way through Seattle traffic and your heart is not hammering in your throat.

Or:

*In seven minutes, you can meet your destiny.*

In the above version notice how we stepped away from the image of a police vehicle, the race toward something and the sense that something is about to happen right now. You, as a reader, had to slow down, adjust to the pacing of the opening and either commit to read more (if there was more) or decide that this is too obtuse a story for your reading expectations.

Let's try another version, this time with more of a poetic approach.

*Rain drops; splash, drip, slide; the night gorged with moisture, the vehicle whistling past unaware; adrenaline-jacked driver, crackling radio voices, the flicker of red, blue, red, blue, faster and faster till the rain and colors blur.*

This example has the Evocative Hook, but unless you're willing to commit to the story without having a clue of what's going on, the Evocative Hook isn't working for you.

Let's examine another no Evocative Hook opening and see how it could be rewritten to earn this elusive Hook.

*The pharmacist was thirteen minutes late for lunch on Tuesday, which was very unusual for him.*

In the above opening sentence there might be the Question(s) Raised Hook but not much else. It'd be appropriate to a slower-paced mystery—amateur sleuth, cozy or any novel where the reader does not want a lot of tension in their story.

Here's how we might create a different slant to include the Evocative Hook:

> *A total stranger eating or not eating lunch, whether a*
> *Tuesday or a Friday, matters little to the masses; full-moon or*
> *not.*

Not the usual approach to a story and the convoluted verbiage means a reader must pause and slow to absorb what might be happening as well as be willing to keep reading, more in large part because they have no idea what's unfolding.

Let's try a more poetic slant that can be an element of the Evocative Hook.

> *Tick tock, the clock yawns, the day unfolds; the gray man*
> *behind the counter is not where he's meant to be, tick, tock.*

Again, no idea what the story is about but there's a specific cadence, a tease to the reader and for those who relish literary novels, or stories that make them ponder and question, an Evocative Hook opening.

## ASSIGNMENTS:

1) One of the easiest ways to learn to spot the Evocative Hook is to examine the opening lines of many novels—it will soon leap out at you once you know what you're seeing. So visit an online bookstore or a brick-and-mortar store and browse through the General Fiction section, or, if the store has set aside a section called Literary Fiction, that's a good place to look for examples. Another option is to look specifically at some of the books by the authors mentioned

in this section to get a feel for them. Look at Jodi Picoult, Christopher Moore, Tom Robbins, Jasper Fforde, Robert Goolrick, Gabriel Garcia Marquez, Cormac McCarthy or Terry Pratchett for starters.

2) Take one of the following sentences and play with it— make it more poetic, approach it from a different direction, stretch your evocative descriptive mental muscles until you've created an Evocative Hook:

- The crows flocked across the empty fields and darkened the skies.
- Madeline Marie Mancuzi ended her relationship by using her keyboard.
- Petter was the farthest planet in the Scolari solar system except for one.
- Although the two travelers had heard of the famous valley only now did they gaze upon it.
- Jonny Bodine knew life started and ended with his English teacher's wife.

Read poetry, lots of poetry, not to write but to get a sense of cadence, of approach to a subject. Roger Housden has a delightful series of books that start with *Ten Poems to . . .* that can act as a starting point. Read Rumi, Mary Oliver, or Billy Collins as options, too.

## RECAP:

- Keep in mind that using the Evocative Hook often means you do not have other hooks present so you are trusting your reader to be engaged with a single hook, especially in your opening line.
- Evocative Hooks are the most subjective of the hooks and readers will either be compelled to keep reading or

set your book down because it's not what engages them or not how they want a story approached.

- The Evocative Hook can be created by the author's strong voice, unique slant on a situation, word painting, powerful descriptive details or storytelling approach.
- If you use the Evocative Hook in the opening sentence, then be true to that style/approach throughout your story.

## HOOK 8: FORESHADOWING WITH OR WITHOUT WARNING HOOK

Ask yourself: does the phrase, sentence or paragraph in question hint that whatever is happening is going to play out more in the story? If it does, it probably includes the Foreshadowing with or without Warning Hook, especially if that's all you know about the story. If you, the author, know that fifty pages from now this hint will matter, but the reader doesn't understand that until they get deeper into the story, then it's not foreshadowing.

This Hook is often associated with a stronger sense of warning as opposed to a simple revelation. A warning ratchets the hook up a bit, especially in certain genres, so these two concepts tend to go hand in glove, but it's not a requirement.

**NOTE:** A Foreshadowing Hook, without the warning element included, can still be foreshadowing, but tends to not be as strong a hook as when used in a Foreshadowing with Warning combination.

For example, the first male introduced in many romances is assumed to be the hero, so this can be a form of foreshadowing. The warning is implied to the reader that this man matters, but is not clearly stated. In many suspense and thrillers the opening foreshadows and warns the reader that whatever is happening in Mumbai or Jakarta or a back room in Dubuque, Iowa, is going to play out over the course of the story. Readers who do not normally read either romances or suspense/thrillers might miss these nuances that are specific to the genres, so your Foreshadowing with or without Warning Hook can be weakened.

Thus, "There's your mean neighbor Mrs. Pemberly," can be a Foreshadowing Hook because the reader expects there's a reason you, the author, are directing their attention to this woman. This type of foreshadowing can work as a hook in novels where you don't want a strong sense of tension or fast pace.

"Watch out where you're going or the boogieman will get you!" is both foreshadowing *and* warning and ratchets up the tension.

If your target readers are used to danger, action or threats being associated with Foreshadowing with Warning Hooks, then they may find themselves less engaged by a Foreshadowing reference that does *not* contain Warning. In other words, if your readers primarily read thrillers they would expect a Foreshadowing with Warning Hook to indicate upcoming danger and not a crisis of the heart.

The Foreshadowing with or without Warning Hook automatically creates specific types of questions for readers.

Questions such as:

How is this action or information going to play out in the story?

What's going to happen next?

I wonder what if…?

**EXAMPLES:**

If I wrote:

*Brandon walked in the door.*

This is a flat statement of fact. No questions are raised on the first read. If we study this or any sentence long enough we might find a question, but the average reader isn't reading that way. We're looking at the norm, not the exceptions here.

Now see what happens with only a few more words added.

> *Brandon walked in the door, carrying, very gingerly, a*
> *small package tied with string.*

Now we have a Foreshadowing without Warning Hook. There's no sense that something bad is about to happen, which ratchets up the tension, and thus the pacing, but we do have a sense that something will unfold in the story as a result of what's in *that* package.

That's how the Foreshadowing with or without Warning Hook works. It uses our innate curiosity to create questions in our minds, which in turn compels us to read, even a little bit more, to find out what's happening or about to happen.

Let's add the warning element to the foreshadowing and see if more questions are raised in your mind.

> *Brandon walked in the door, carrying, very gingerly, a*
> *small package tied with string and labeled: Spiders.*

Now for some readers, and yes, I'm one of them, the word spiders is enough to really ratchet up the warning element, but let's see what happens when we are more specific in crafting this sentence.

> *Brandon walked in the door, carrying, very gingerly, a*
> *small package tied with string and labeled: Brown Recluse*
> *Spiders.*

For those familiar with this type of spider they know it's potentially very dangerous. If the phrase: *Beware Poisonous Spiders* was used instead of a specific spider type, the reader would get the same reaction—an increase of the warning element, which increases the tension of the sentence, and also increases the reason a reader MUST read to find out what's happening.

**NOTE**: Depending on YOUR story, and the degree of tension you want or need in your story, you can use the Foreshadowing Hook with or without the warning element.

## EXAMPLES OF FORESHADOWING WITH OR WITHOUT WARNING HOOKS:

These next examples all fall at the opening of a novel, as opposed to the end of a page, scene or chapter. We're focusing on these key sentences because the reader will know little about the story, unless the back cover or book description blurb gives away too much, so it's easier in some ways to create the Foreshadowing with or without Warning Hook and harder in others.

Foreshadowing happens when the reader feels that what he or she is reading will matter later in the story so they are compelled to pay attention. It raises a specific question along the lines of: I wonder what this means or how this will play out?

Here's an example from a young adult novel, part of a series, by the author Pittacus Lore. Before we look at his work let's examine how he might have approached his opening line:

ROUGH DRAFT: *My name is Marina.*

It's pretty blah and doesn't engage us as a reader. It's simply a statement of fact. So let's see how Lore threads in a Foreshadowing Hook, without the element of Warning, and Question(s) Raised Hooks.

*My name is Marina, as of the sea, but I wasn't called that until much later.*
—Pittacus Lore—*The Power of Six*

Can you see how a specific question — what happens later — is raised, which creates the Foreshadowing without Warning Hook, while a different question is raised: who is this person? This creates a two-hook opening, which can work in a young adult novel, especially if followed up with more hooks on the opening page.

When looking at the Foreshadowing with or without Warning Hook you need to make sure the sentence raises a question, or questions, which specifically makes the reader wonder if what is happening is going to unfold deeper into the story. That type of question is what will compel the reader to keep reading, even if it's just a few more sentences or paragraphs.

**NOTE:** All hooks create questions in the reader's mind. The Foreshadowing with or without Warning Hook creates a *specific* type of question.

Another example of a Foreshadowing Hook, without the Warning, comes from a Gothic Romance novel written by Deanna Rayburn. Because the author uses a tag line before the story starts, the reader clearly knows the date and location of the opening of the story — Edinburgh, 1858. With that in mind, here's the two-hook opening:

> *"I am afraid we must settle the problem of what to do with Theodora," my brother-in-law said with a weary sigh.*
> — Deanna Rayburn — *The Dead Travel Fast*

Approaching the challenge of understanding Hooks from a different direction, let's look at why the above example only contains two Hooks by examining why the other hooks don't apply:

- Action or Danger? No, this is simply a conversation that raises a question.
- Overpowering Emotion? There is a sigh, which indicates emotion, but it's not overpowering, so no, this hook does not apply.
- A Surprising Situation? Possibly, and for some readers it's enough of a possibility to count this hook. However, for most readers this is not yet surprising because we don't know enough about the story — is Theodora a habitual runaway, a burden to an overly large family, a child needing punishment? The reader doesn't really know yet, so this hook is not realized fully.
- An Evocative Hook? Do you as a reader receive a strong sense of this author's voice? Are you being pulled into the story because of that voice or because of the unique approach to telling the story? Or the way the words are strung together make you stop and really pay attention? If you can't say yes, then the Evocative Hook is not here.
- Unique Character Hook? There is a character introduced but all we know about her is her name, which, if this were a contemporary, might make her stand out more because this is not a common name now, but because this is a historical story, she's not unique. Yet.
- Foreshadowing with or without Warning? Yes, the average reader could assume this discussion might lead to what happens next in the story. The warning element is absent because there's no sense of a threat or that something bad might happen, so only the foreshadowing element remains.
- Surprising or Shocking Dialogue? Not really. Given this time period, the fact that a male is saying this about a female is not unusual, even if we know nothing else about Theodora. The dialogue raises a question, which

creates the Question(s) Raised Hook, but is not shocking.

- Totally Unexpected? Again, the reader is not given enough information to know if Theodora has been a continual problem, if the problem is unexpected, or if the situation is normal or unusual for the characters. If in doubt, there is no hook.
- Question(s) Raised Hook? Yes, not only is the character raising a question in his dialogue, but that in turn raises a question or questions in the reader's mind. Who is Theodora? What has she done? What's going to happen to her?

So this is a two-hook opening, which reassures the reader this will most likely not be overly tense and fast-paced (as evidenced by the number of hooks present on the first page) which is appropriate for this particular genre.

Let's look at another opening line from a very different genre — the suspense/thriller novel.

Since these types of stories are meant to be very fast-paced (the name thriller comes from the emotional thrill ride type of story the reader expects) the opening line is often shorter, as short sentences increase tension and thus pacing. Opening lines in thriller or fast-paced suspense novels will often contain a sense of danger and foreshadowing, and it's not uncommon to find five- to seven-hook opening sentences, followed by more hooks on the page.

Within all genres there are nuances that must be taken into account. For example, in a psychological thriller the pacing can be much slower than other thrillers.

**NOTE:** Nuances based on reader expectations matter across a genre as well as in comparing genres. Psychological or historical thrillers can be paced more like a cozy or amateur sleuth mystery than the high-octane page-turner most readers associate with the term "thriller".

Let's look at how a master of the high-octane thriller starts the thirteenth book in his series. Assuming he created an initial draft and then revisited it to write what appears in the final novel, we'll start with the draft.

FIRST DRAFT: *The Israeli intelligence agency were the ones who came up with the list of twelve indicators that law enforcement personnel, and those trained to look specifically for the signals, have come to depend on to predict the erratic, but tell-tale behaviors often manifested by potential suicide bombers.*

In this imaginary opening there actually is Foreshadowing with Warning, but the sentence is very long, which slows the pacing and isn't indicative of a high-octane anything. Plus the sentence is convoluted, focusing the reader on a lot of information so that it's hard to tell what this specific novel might be about. It'd be an okay opening for a nonfiction work, or a recap giving the story premise for this particular novel, but not so great for a thriller.

**NOTE:** The more phrases in a sentence that shift the attention of a reader off the primary intention, the easier it is to dilute hooks, *especially* in an opening sentence.

So let's see how the author, Lee Child, approaches his opening line and how many hooks it contains.

Suicide bombers are easy to spot.
—Lee Child–*Gone Tomorrow*

Six words that contain the following hooks:

- Foreshadowing with Warning (the fact someone is thinking this way implies there's a need to know how to spot a suicide bomber),

- Danger (mention a bomb and most times it implies potential danger),
- Surprising Situation (the average person does not know how to spot a suicide bomber),
- Unique Character (both the person thinking along these lines and if there is a suicide bomber present—they would qualify as unique, unless they are in a place, like certain countries in the Middle East, that many readers associate with suicide bombings),
- Surprising or Shocking Dialogue (internal dialogue that if spoken out loud would probably shock most listeners),
- Totally Unexpected (while readers of thrillers might expect bombs and thus bombers in some thriller novels, jumping right into this focus can take the element of surprise and ratchet it up to the unexpected level),
- Question(s) Raised (who, how, why or what's happening next).

Six words for a powerful six-hook opening sentence. The author understands the expectations of his core reading audience and throws them immediately into a sense of danger that is about to happen now. This story will not be a gentle stroll but a sprint to find out what's going to occur next.

The next example comes from a novel described as a cross between memoir and fiction. The author narrates the story based on true events as if she were the protagonist, when the real character was the author's grandmother. This approach means the author, Jeanette Walls, uses a number of fictional devices, including strong hooks in key locations, to create a cross-genre novel.

Let's assume Walls built to her strong Foreshadowing with Warning Hook opening line.

FIRST DRAFT: *It was a hot August day, much like they could be in that corner of West Texas.*

No hooks in this opening, and, if it was simply a memoir, it might work for those readers who read to learn about another time, another person's firsthand experiences, a specific location. But this author wanted to reach a larger audience, fiction as well as memoir readers.

SECOND DRAFT: *I was headed toward the cows to bring them into the milking shed on that hot August day.*

This version might foreshadow for some readers that something is about to happen next simply because the sentence is opening the story. But it's not a strong Foreshadowing without Warning Hook that compels the reader to keep reading to answer the specific question of what's happening next. So let's see how Walls opens her true-life novel.

*Those old cows knew trouble was coming before we did.*
*–Jeannette Walls–Half Broke Horses*

Now we have an opening with the following hooks:

- Foreshadowing with Warning (because of the inclusion of the word "trouble" the foreshadowing has been ramped up from simply something about to happen to a warning that something bad is going to happen),
- Danger (implied with trouble is coming),
- Surprising Situation (unless you were raised on a farm or ranch and expect cows to foretell possible events, in which case this may not contain as much surprise),
- Question(s) Raised (what's going to happen, what's going on, etc.).

For some readers, there might also be a sense of Shocking Dialogue, as this internal thought is not how they expect a memoir-type novel to open. So we have a four to five-hook opening sentence.

Is it enough to want to read the whole story? For many yes. But it definitely makes most readers read more of that first page. Of course she added more on that page to compel them to continue.

**NOTE:** Compelling any reader to keep reading makes a huge difference in whether a manuscript is reviewed by an editor or agent and whether a book is purchased by a reader.

Let's look at an example of an opening sentence in a YA novel with the Foreshadowing Hook without the element of warning.

*I don't know how it happened or what sort of backroom deal went down, but apparently I'm living in a small Texas town with two culturally clueless imposters for legal guardians, when I just know my real parents are out there somewhere.*
—Shauna Cross—*Derby Girl*

Both the length of the sentence, and the lack of a warning element, lets the reader know that while there maybe some angst in the story, and a wry look at life from the POV character since this is first person—there is no sense of danger or high tension.

**NOTE:** Longer sentences tend to decrease tension. Short ones increase tension.

If the author had written an earlier draft like this:

ROUGH DRAFT: *I'm sure I must have been adopted.*

The reader still guesses that this feeling of not belonging might be a theme or story issue to be developed, so it still rates the Foreshadowing Hook (but no Warning).

If the author wrote:

ROUGH DRAFT: *I'm living in a small Texas town with my parents.*

Now we have totally lost the sense of Foreshadowing Hook with or without Warning. The story might play out in Texas, but all stories must happen somewhere so the sense that this story MUST occur here, or the location plays a larger role in the story, is absent.

Let's see, based on the current opening sentence we've been looking at, how we might have added the warning element for a different type of YA:

ROUGH DRAFT: *I don't know how it happened or why, but I'm living in a small Texas town where I just discovered the people who raised me have been arrested for kidnapping me as a child.*

See how versatile the Foreshadowing with or without Warning Hook can be?

**NOTE:** By changing the focus and word choices you as the writer use, you can change the tension of a hook.

The next example comes from true-life events, written by a journalist in the style of a novel. This approach allows readers to absorb information that, if presented in a nonfiction manner, might be harder to face — ethical choices made daily in hospitals around the world, the humanity of doctors who must make those decisions, and the very-real ramifications on everyone involved: patients, family, medical staff and more.

The author, Lisa Belkin, could have chosen a drier, more academic approach to her subject matter in an early draft.

FIRST DRAFT: *There are a number of highly trained and highly paid individuals who meet daily to discuss the pros and cons of a patient's care in most hospitals.*

Unless you need or want to know this type of information because you are in the middle of, or might be facing, such a situation yourself, would this compel you to keep reading? Or does it read more like a textbook on the subject matter of medical ethics in hospitals?

**NOTE:** In nonfiction or memoir, the subject matter itself acts as a hook. The reader picks up and reads a particular book because of that subject and not usually because the author pulls them into a subject that otherwise might not be of interest to them.

So how did Belkin craft a compelling opening sentence for her nonfiction book that, when released, and even now, reads more like a suspense or thriller novel?

> *It was standing room only in room 3485 the day the Committee voted to let Patrick die.*
> –Lisa Belkin–*First, Do No Harm: The Dramatic Story of Real Doctors and Patients Making Impossible Choices at a Big-City Hospital*

Pow! Not only is the Foreshadowing with Warning Hook present, but also Danger (to Patrick), Overpowering Emotion (the very thought that a group of people can make this kind of decision can create a strong emotional response for many readers), Surprising Situation (not how the average reader expects to start a nonfiction book), a Unique Character (how many of us have met or realize we know of someone whose life was voted to end?), Totally Unexpected (that a committee would have the power to save or end a life), and Question(s)

Raised Hooks. So a seven-hook opening in a nonfiction novel that's still required reading for many medical ethics classes.

This next example comes from the prologue to a historical fiction novel. Prologues act as the opening of the book for readers and, as such, the opening sentences need to engage the reader as strongly as a first chapter opening. We're looking specifically at how the author, Bernard Cornwell, foreshadows upcoming events. Pay attention to how he establishes the sense of a time period that is not contemporary. This approach acts as another kind of hook— the kind where if a reader has a specific interest in a specific subject, such as a historical time period, a location, a sport, etc., they will be hooked because of the topic.

Let's assume Cornwell wasn't a master of his craft and wrote a very rough opening line.

FIRST DRAFT: *The cold snow bit through Nicholas Hook's thread-bare clothing as he sat by the roadside of his village and blew on his hands to warm them.*

Any idea of a time period in this example? Or of foreshadowing? That something was about to happen that would either catapult the story forward or play out over the course of the story? Not yet. It's a zero-hook opening that, for a reader unfamiliar with the author's work, or not intrigued by the time frame of the story, or any other of a dozen reasons that let the average reader ignore a so-so written first page, would make it easy enough to set the book down.

Now let's see what happens if Cornwell starts his story with his second and third sentences.

*It was a cold day. And there had been hard frost overnight and the midday sun had failed to melt the white from the grass.*
–Bernard Cornwell–*Agincourt*

Nice narrative description that pulls a reader into the setting of the opening of this story but still doesn't foreshadow anything. Nor are there any hooks present.

**NOTE:** Many newer writers bury a great opening sentence deeper into the first page. The more experienced writers look for that as they return to evaluate the strength of their opening sentence.

Let's examine how Cornwell approached his opening sentence with the intention of hooking a reader:

> *On a winter's day in 1413, just before Christmas, Nicholas Hook decided to commit murder.*
> –Bernard Cornwell–*Agincourt*

Now we have:

- Foreshadowing with Warning (that this decision will jumpstart the story),
- Question(s) Raised (will Nicholas kill someone? Who? Why?),
- Danger (until we know otherwise someone's life is in danger),
- Unique Character (most of us do not make this kind of a decision), as well as word choices that clearly indicates the time period of the story (a hook for a historical reader).

So a strong four-hook opening which works for a historical novel. Five hooks if you include the more subjective hook of a specific time frame for historical readers, but not all historical readers. Some may love a particular time period—U.S. Civil War, Viking invasions of Britain, pre-Shogun era Japan etc.—which is why this hook is not one of the four we examine in detail in this book or the five hooks described in *Writing Active Hooks: Book 1.*

Before we leave Cornwell's opening, let's examine how he builds on his first line to lead the reader to continue until the end of the first paragraph where the author re-engages the reader with another Foreshadowing without Warning Hook.

> *On a winter's day in 1413, just before Christmas, Nicholas Hook decided to commit murder.*
>
> *It was a cold day. And there had been hard frost overnight and the midday sun had failed to melt the white from the grass. There was no wind so the whole world was pale, frozen and still when Hook saw Tom Perrill in the sunken lane that led from the high woods to the mill pastures.*
>
> –Bernard Cornwell–*Agincourt*

At the end of this paragraph, with the introduction of a new character—Tom Perrill—two more hooks are employed: Question(s) Raised (is this Perrill the person Hook will kill? Who is he and why does he matter?), Foreshadowing with a hint of Warning based on the reader now knowing the POV character has made a very specific decision (that this Tom Perrill may or may not be involved in the decision to commit murder).

Now it's easy for the reader to continue to read, even for a few more paragraphs, to find out what's happening and, by the end of the page, the author will show that the POV character will take an action that sets off the events of the story. Hooks draw the reader deeper and deeper into the story. Cornwell uses the Foreshadowing with Warning Hook in his opening sentence, then, by the end of his first paragraph, uses a Foreshadows without Warning Hook with new information to the reader.

**NOTE:** When using the Foreshadowing with or without Warning Hook what is revealed must be new to the reader and not simply a restatement of what's already known.

The next example combines three different genres — young adult, mystery and history — so the author is attempting to include hooks for all three core reading audiences. Because the protagonist, the one the reader meets first, is a young girl and not an experienced detective, the pacing does not need to be extremely tense, but the opening hook still needs to engage readers — three different types of them.

Let's assume the author, Y.S. Lee, worked at her opening prologue line.

FIRST DRAFT: *Mary Quinn had already had a hard and brutal life.*

There's potential in this opening but, as written, the reader is asked to wait to find out more before they are engaged to keep reading. No Foreshadowing with or without Warning Hook either.

SECOND DRAFT: *It wasn't easy being a pickpocket on the streets of London in 1853.*

Here we have a Unique Character Hook, which is combined with Question(s) Raised and Danger Hooks, and makes for a stronger opening. But since we're looking specifically for the Foreshadowing with or without Warning Hook, let's see how the author grabs the reader's attention in her approach to her opening line.

> *August 1853*
> *The Central Criminal Court at the Old Bailey, London*
> *She should have been listening to the judge.*

–Y.S. Lee–ᴀ Spy In The House

The first two lines are tag lines—used often in historical novels to set the time and place—so by the first full sentence the reader knows where the character is and what's at stake, given the location of the event. A Criminal Court hearing gives that element of Warning that's so much a part of the Foreshadowing with Warning Hook, even before the reader reaches the character's internal dialogue. At that point the Surprising or Shocking Dialogue Hook is applied, added to Danger (Criminal Court implies the risks are high) and Question(s) Raised Hooks.

The author managed to create a four-hook opening with a very short sentence. Without the tag lines, the sentence might not have as much power, but the author wisely used a technique that the mystery reader, and especially a historical mystery reader, would not find out of place to set up and power up her opening sentence.

When considering the use of the Foreshadowing with or without Warning Hook, be careful to avoid using author intrusion to foreshadow an event. This approach was once more common and used frequently in mysteries and suspense to raise a story question. But it's not used as often in a lot of writing now because it pulls the reader out of the point of view of a character in order to hint at what might be happening next. It's as if the voice of an announcer pops onto the scene to clue the reader into what is coming up later in the story. Cue up the dramatic music!

The following example comes from a cozy mystery series. This particular novel was published in 1950, which means it was written in the late 1940s. At that time, the technique was used relatively often, but notice how the use of author intrusion here shifts the POV away from the character that had been on scene, a young woman named Stacy, and slows the pacing with a large chunk of narrative. This is a Foreshadowing with Warning Hook used at the end of chapter two in the story.

This means the reader has been in the POV of the main protagonist up to this point, but is suddenly and abruptly pulled back by the use of author intrusion:

> *But everything which happened at Warne House on that Friday night was going to matter. Every single smallest thing, every detail; the exact moment at which everyone came and went; what they did, said, wore; whether they spoke to anyone; whether they wrote or received a letter; whether they telephoned — it was all to matter, down to the last shade of expression, down to the last turn of the head and tone of the voice. But Stacy wasn't to know that. Perhaps none of them knew it yet, though even that was to be in doubt.*
> — Patricia Wentworth — *The Brading Collection*

Next is an example that includes author intrusion, again in an older novel. Read recent releases, published in the last five years, of the types of novels or stories you want to write to see if author intrusion is acceptable or not. Be sure to look at debut authors in particular because they do not have the following that established, well-known authors have, and so are held to a different expectation in some ways. Once you have published a million, or several million books, like the next two authors have, you can get away with using author intrusion because of your strong readership.

**NOTE:** Author intrusion is usually accepted in an opening line versus later in a story, simply because the reader isn't yet deep into a specific character's POV, therefore the distance from the events does not seem as strong. The deeper into a story, the more a writer risks pulling a reader out of POV by using author intrusion.

Let's see how Dean Koontz uses the Foreshadowing with Warning Hook in the opening line of his horror/mystery novel. Before we jump to his actual line, let's assume he built in his hooks during the revision process.

FIRST DRAFT: *Laura Shane was a unique person from the day she was born.*

The above example uses author intrusion, which is telling, with a statement of fact. This approach leaves the reader waiting to find out why Laura is unique, which creates the Question(s) Raised Hook, but also holds the reader at arm's length, waiting to be told enough to make a judgment call of their own. The longer this continues, the easier it'll be to set the story down and find another story that's more compelling.

SECOND DRAFT: *A horrible, awful, no good storm happened the night Laura Shane was born.*

Same issue as already discussed. One hook is present—Question(s) Raised, but otherwise no association between the weather and the character or why we should care as a reader.
Now we'll examine how Koontz crafted his opening line:

*A storm struck on the night Laura Shane was born, and there was a strangeness about the weather that people would remember for years.*
–Dean Koontz–*Lightning*

This approach borders on the Evocative for some readers, because Koontz expanded on the weather, which sets up a feeling, a tone for the story. It's not the fact a storm happened, but the "strangeness" and phrase, "people would remember for years" creating the stronger sense of Foreshadowing with Warning. The reader is promised that the circumstances that surrounded the birth of this character will play out in some way in her life, which compels the reader to read even just a little more to find out how and what happened as a result.

This means the Question(s) Raised Hook is present and, for some readers, the Unique Character Hook, too. So now we have a three- to four-hook opening that will draw us into the story, even if we'd never heard of Dean Koontz before.

**NOTE:** Bottom line is, if you hook the reader from that first page and then follow up with a strong story, you're off and running and can use hooks that may not be the norm for what you're writing.

The next example comes from an author who is said to sell one of her novels every three minutes worldwide. That means an enormous fan base, and, as a result, an editor or agent who will ignore author intrusion as an opening line hook because they know the author will deliver on the story. Let's start from a hypothetical early opening line attempt without a Foreshadowing without Warning Hook.

ROUGH DRAFT: *Cooper Sullivan was content with his life.*

This is a plain statement of fact that doesn't give the reader a compelling reason to keep reading. There are no hooks here, no reason we should care about this character or the story. But Nora Roberts did not become the international bestseller that she is by hoping her readers would continue to read simply because they picked up one of her novels and recognized her name. Let's see how she threaded in a Foreshadowing without Warning Hook in this contemporary romantic suspense novel.

*Cooper Sullivan's life, as he'd known it, was over.*
–Nora Roberts–*Black Hills*

Romance novels, except for the romantic suspense subgenre, tend to average fewer hooks than many genres, but that's not to say they shouldn't have any. In the above example Roberts includes:

- Foreshadowing with or without Warning Hook (something is clearly about to happen or has just happened to this individual. In a romance that doesn't necessarily mean a bad thing, but since this is a romantic suspense novel that suspense element assumes bad events are coming),
- Question(s) Raised (what happened or is happening and why),
- Surprising Situation (or it could be, especially to Cooper).

This creates a three-hook opening until the reader realizes that this is not author intrusion but a story created in two parts—the past and then the current. This line adds in the Surprising or Shocking Dialogue (third person internal POV) Hook but that's not clear until the second line. So now we have a four-hook opening paragraph, which tells the reader this love story is going to have more developing than simply the romance.

FIRST AND SECOND LINES:

*Cooper Sullivan's life, as he'd known it, was over. Judge and jury — in the form of his parents — had not been swayed by pleas, reason, temper, threats, but instead had sentenced him and shipped him off, away from everything he knew and cared about to a world without video parlors or Big Macs.*
–Nora Roberts–*Black Hills*

In her second line, because the reader knows this will be a story as much about the romance as the suspense, the reader assumes (correctly) that this is the hero at a younger age. So we have stepped away from author intrusion and the author builds in more hooks in the second sentence—Surprising Situation, Question(s) Raised, Foreshadowing without

Warning (that where this young man now is will play out in meeting the heroine of the story) and Surprising or Shocking Dialogue. Now the new reader is enticed to keep on reading to find out even just a little bit more, and the reader who is a fan of Nora Roberts knows the romance element of the story is about to jumpstart this story.

**NOTE:** Like the other suggestions we're covering in this book, you can find exceptions. The more you read, the more likely that will happen. These are not hard and fast rules, never to be broken. Understand the suggestions, understand your target audience and what they expect to read on the page, and understand what your intention is on the page.

## NO FORESHADOWING WITH OR WITHOUT WARNING HOOKS:

*The Spanish trees ringing the colonial style home looked as regal as I'd always expected them to look.*

In this example, the natural response might be *so what?* — especially if used as an opening sentence. There's no sense that this view of trees sets off a story or is going to play out in some way, even deeper on the page. This line might work in a women's fiction novel, a memoir, or any story that does not need a lot of tension right from the opening sentences, but there had better be some hooks, some questions raised in the reader's mind soon, to give the reader a good reason to keep reading or the writer stands to lose a reader before they can engage with the story deeper into the novel.

Here's another example that lacks a Foreshadowing with or without Warning Hook, or any hooks at all.

*I graduated from high school the day after my eighteenth birthday.*

Since the above opening line relates information that is not that unusual, given the situation and age, there's no sense of a warning that something is about to occur set up in this sentence.

Let's play around with the sequence of words, or add some that clearly contain the Foreshadowing with or without Warning Hook.

*The three events happened on the same day: I graduated from high school, I turned eighteen and I met Manny Rodriguez.*

*If I were to ever graduate from high school again, which I won't, I'd make sure it wasn't on a day right after my eighteenth birthday and definitely not on the day my father hanged himself.*

*I didn't expect a lot from my parents, especially my stepmother, but the day after my eighteenth birthday, when I graduated from high school, she hit an all new low.*

Small, incremental changes can build in the Foreshadowing with or without Warning Hook and create a more compelling opening for readers.

**NOTE:** If you use a Foreshadowing with or without Warning Hook, make sure it plays out in some way as your story progresses, even if it's proven to be not what you expected or is resolved quickly. Do not foreshadow then leave the question this hook creates in the reader's mind unanswered.

### ASSIGNMENTS:

1. Study a good number of the type of novels or stories you wish to write to see how common or unusual the

use of the Foreshadowing with or without Warning Hook is, especially in the opening sentence. If you find this particular hook, look at the authors who use it—are they multi-published authors, debut authors, or NYT authors with strong fan bases? If the Foreshadowing with or without Warning Hook is used rarely among the debut authors, sometimes among the multi-published and often by the NYT authors, this will give you an idea whether you want to explore and utilize this hook depending on where you're at in your writing career.

2. Take the following writing prompts and see if you can turn them into Foreshadowing with or without Warning Hooks:

For example:
*Nancy knew Bob.* Could become:

*It had been fifteen years since Nancy had seen Bob and that was still too soon for her.*

*Nancy had been young, dumb and a risk-taker when she'd known Bob, but she'd learned her lesson, the hard way.*

*Nancy had known Bob as well as she'd known any man, before he'd been sent to prison.*

Here are a few more prompts to play with:

- There was a lot of fog driving up to Jerome.
- I had always planned on having three children.
- Mountain climbing was not the sport for me.
- Julie knocked on the door.
- Eduardo deMingus was from an old and highly esteemed family.

## RECAP:

- Keep in mind that the warning element is a strong component of the Foreshadowing with Warning Hook. Without that sense of warning, that the reader is being directed to something important, this hook will not be as strong.

- 

- If you plan to use author intrusion — the telling of a future outcome that the character could not possibly know about in advance — make sure it's an acceptable approach for opening sentence hooks, as well as end of chapter hooks in the type of stories you want to write.

- 

- If you want to use the Foreshadowing with or without Warning Hook, make sure the question(s) you created are addressed and answered deeper in your story.

## HOOK 9: SURPRISING OR SHOCKING DIALOGUE HOOKS

This hook can be created via internal or external dialogue: internal dialogue is a character's thoughts — clearly their thoughts — and not omniscient POV (point of view of the author with omniscient POV being as if from a great distance from the events); external dialogue includes any speaking that another could hear.

Ask yourself if you expected the character to say *that*? Did the character expect to hear *that*? Given the context, is this dialogue expected? If you have a Surprising Situation or the Totally Unexpected Hook(s) present, you usually can have a Surprising or Shocking Dialogue Hook, too.

*"F\*\*k," the nun said*—is shocking.

*"F\*\*k," the Hells Angel biker dude said*—is not.

*"My mother will not allow me to discourse with total strangers,"* said by a spoiled and pampered teen, is not surprising,

*"My mother will not allow me to discourse with total strangers,"* said by a thirty-five-year old, is more surprising.

The average reader might expect a mother to warn her children about being a teen and traveling with a wild crowd so dialogue along those lines would not be surprising or shocking. However, if the mother is a vampire warning her offspring about hanging out with the werewolves, or a cookie-baking, hover-parent-type mom suggesting to her child to try some drugs, unprotected sex, or running nude during a graduation event, that could be seen as a clear Surprising or Shocking Dialogue Hook.

**NOTE:** Always think in terms of the context of the words. Would the average reader expect to hear this type of dialogue coming from this type of character in this specific situation?

When we talk about the Surprising or Shocking Dialogue Hook the focus is on two things: the emotional response in the reader as a result of the dialogue and the fact that we're literally talking about dialogue.

Let's look at the latter initially. Remember, dialogue can mean internal—a character's thoughts—or external—meaning another person could hear what is being said even if the POV character is alone or mumbling. This type of dialogue *could* be heard *if* there was another person around.

Pretty straight forward. Now let's examine what we mean by the emotional response in the reader, the reason this hook intrigues and raises a question or questions in the reader's mind. It must raise enough emotionally tinged questions for the reader to want to find out even a smidge more to have created the emotional response.

Remember that hooks are like breadcrumbs. They are meant to lead the reader in small increments deeper into your story. While some hooks might raise a question that will not be answered until the end of your novel, most will be answered in a few pages, the next scene or chapter, or in a few chapters.

With that in mind let's look at why the Surprising or Shocking Dialogue Hook is not only one of the powerhouse hooks in the 10 Universal Hooks, but can be found across every genre, every type of story. It's that versatile.

Why? Because as humans we tend to be hardwired to find answers to the unexplained. We're not talking about being an explorer willing to go into unknown lands, but every day we can find questions that cause us to seek answers. Why did that car stop so suddenly? What was your boss thinking when she made a co-worker lead in an important project? Who turned on the hall light when you had turned it off not fifteen minutes ago?

Our innate curiosity is wired into our DNA because knowing usually, not always, but usually can protect us. Since we've crawled out of the primordial swamps we have known that survival is good.

So what does this have to do with the Surprising or Shocking Dialogue Hook? Everything—in large part because being surprised or, the stronger emotion, being shocked; is hardwired into creating a response in us. For writers this response means a stronger reason for someone to keep reading.

Pretty nifty!

Let's dig a little deeper into our overall understanding before we start exploring a number of Surprising or Shocking Dialogue Hook examples.

Think of the word 'surprising'. It means unexpected, without warning, astonishing, from out of left field, unpredictable.

Think of a car parked next to you in a parking lot. A brown, white, red or blue car are common enough to not warrant a second glance. Now what if a bright pink, neon orange or zebra striped car pulls in beside your vehicle? The surprise would arrest your attention enough to have you pause, have a reaction, maybe even think about it after you leave the parking lot. It raises questions in your mind and that's exactly what a good hook does.

So what's the difference between surprising and shocking? The degree of emotion changes, increasing in intensity; and that intensity builds tension on and off the page.

Shocking means it can include atrocious, distressing, appalling, horrible or terrible as well as amazing or mind-bending. These are much stronger emotional responses than surprising, yet either or both can be contained in the Surprising or Shocking Dialogue Hook.

## EXAMPLES OF SURPRISING OR SHOCKING DIALOGUE HOOKS:

Let's look at some examples to anchor in the Surprising or Shocking Dialogue Hook. This first example will be from a literary novel that made headlines upon its release, in part because of the death threats received by the author. But before the furor there was his opening line, and before the author's opening line let's assume there was a rough draft.

ROUGH DRAFT: *Gibreel Farishta fell from the sky but he lived.*

This version does have hooks, including the Unique Character, Foreshadowing, Surprising Situation, Question(s) Raised and Totally Unexpected, so a five-hook opening sentence. This is where many writers would pat themselves on the back and not return to revise this sentence.

But the author wanted something stronger, more memorable, more shocking than simply surprising.

So this is what he wrote:

*"To be born again," sang Gibreel Farishta tumbling from the heavens, "first you have to die."*
—Salman Rushdi—*The Satanic Verses*

This version takes the surprise element and ramps it up into shocking. Hooks present here are Foreshadowing, Unique Character [Over the top unique to be saying or even thinking these words given the situation], Surprising Situation, Totally Unexpected [Because of the situation but also because of how the character is acting in the situation], Action/Danger [Which the previous example did not earn because the threat to the person was in the past tense and the reader knows immediately that the POV character lived], Question(s) Raised and the Surprising or Shocking Dialogue Hook.

Now the sentence has a strong seven-hook opening line without feeling like it's commercial fiction. In part that's because of the absurdity of the dialogue, the contrast between event and dialogue, and the incongruity of what's being shown. All of these elements of this sentence clearly alert the reader that the story will not be so much about this character's death as much as the fact that irrational death is a metaphor for what the story is truly about.

The Surprising or Shocking Dialogue Hook does not always need to be over the top to grab a reader's attention.

This next example comes from a romantic comedy novel. The reader doesn't need any other information about who the speaker is or why they are saying this internal dialogue (thought) for the average reader to be surprised or shocked.

Let's assume the author, Kathy Carmichael, had to work up to her killer opening sentence.

ROUGH DRAFT: *I really didn't like birthdays.*

Nothing really surprising in this thought, because not everyone is excited about having a birthday. It's a plain statement of fact, and while it might contain a Question(s) Raised Hook, it's not strong enough to keep most readers reading. So let's see how Carmichael changed up a blah opening line to something that would keep most readers intrigued enough to continue.

*Birthdays are like a box of Tampax.*
–Kathy Carmichael–*Hot Flash*

How often have you heard this combination of internal thoughts? If it's rarely to none, then you have a Surprising or Shocking Dialogue Hook. Other hooks present include a Surprising Situation (for the same reason this is Surprising Dialogue—it's very unusual) and Question(s) Raised Hooks. It's not the Totally Unexpected Hook, because the reader doesn't know if this is the type of thought or verbiage that this character habitually uses. It doesn't show Action/Danger or Unique Character Hooks—though there might be a hint here, depending on what's revealed about this character next, and if the focus of the sentence was more on a warning, the Foreshadowing with Warning Hook might apply, but the emphasis is not so much the birthday as much as how the birthday is regarded.

**NOTE:** Good opening line hooks will keep a reader reading long enough to turn the page. Great opening lines can intrigue a reader to continue even further into your story.

The next two sentences we'll be examining come from the opening line of the first chapter. Sentences that follow a powerful prologue and two quotes — all of which clue the reader into the fact this romantic fantasy will be tense, dark and heart-pounding.

The author might have simply started right into action, which is not unusual in the romantic fantasy genre. Deeper on the first page is a hint of that approach, rewritten here as an initial draft.

ROUGH DRAFT: *I squatted on the edge of the cliff, looking into a deep and deadly abyss.*

Again, this sentence is not without hooks — Action/Danger, Foreshadowing, Surprising Situation and Question(s) Raised but no Surprising or Shocking Dialogue Hook.

So let's see how the author used, repeatedly, the Surprising or Shocking Dialogue Hook (internal) not only in her opening chapter but right from the first words read by the reader.

OPENING QUOTE:

> *I feel it deep within*
> *It's just beneath the skin*
> *I must confess that I feel like*
> *A monster.*
> *— Skillet — Monster*

Here the tension is already building with Foreshadowing with Warning, Action/Danger, Surprising Situation, Question(s) Raised, a Unique Character and the Surprising or Shocking Dialogue (internal) hooks—all from a few lines of a song. This leads into the prologue, again all internal dialogue.

PROLOGUE:

*You wish to know me?*
*Posit yourself as the pinpoint center of one of your kaleidoscopes, and grasp time as one of the colorful fragments erupting from you in a multiple of dimensions that constantly expand outward in an ever-widening, ever-shifting infinite array.*
—Karen Marie Moning — *Shadowfever*

Here the tension is again being built. The immediacy of this internal dialogue is almost a threat. The reader may not know who or what is creating the internal dialogue, but it's very clear that this is not your average individual so in addition to the Surprising or Shocking Dialogue Hook there's also the Surprising Situation, Foreshadowing with Warning, Unique Character [different than the monster already alluded too in the quote] and Question(s) Raised Hooks.

This one-page prologue leads into the next two opening lines which, being short, are read as one.

*Hope strengthens. Fear kills.*
—Karen Marie Moning — *Shadowfever*

Bam! Surprising and Shocking Dialogue (internal) and very powerful, while promising that something dangerous is just around the corner. Since this novel is the fifth book in a series, the opening lines must re-engage and intrigue readers who are already fans of the series while quickly alerting readers new to the series as to the type of story to expect.

If this had been the first book of the series the author might have approached the story more directly, orienting the reader as to the who and the what of events. In fact the opening of her first novel did exactly that, so here, taking a risk that she might lose a reader before they were anchored into the story was not as large a risk as it might have been. In part because she kept both the quotes and the prologue short which reassured the reader that, even if confused about who the initial quote was about or who was thinking about themselves as a still point, etc., that soon at least some of the answers to all the questions raised were going to be answered or clarified.

This next example is from a YA novel that started creating a buzz from its initial release. Before we examine how the author, John Green, handled a subject many readers could find difficult to delve into, that of a seventeen-year-old girl with cancer, let's look at a possible opening line that does include the Surprising or Shocking Dialogue Hook but at the risk of alienating his core readership.

ROUGH DRAFT: *I was seventeen and dying of cancer.*

The above sentence is so short and in-your-face abrupt as to be shocking because of the contrast between the age of the character and having such a horrible disease. It does have a Unique Character Hook [Most readers don't automatically associate cancer with a seventeen-year-old], Foreshadowing with Warning, Surprising or Shocking Dialogue (first person POV internal dialogue, not external), Overpowering Emotion [the potential death of a young person tends to create a strong emotional response in the reader] and Question(s) Raised Hooks, so the rough draft is a five-hook opening. But it does so at a cost. Remember how too many hooks, creating too much tension, can work against an author if readers do not want or expect that type of opening and story.

So let's examine more closely how Green slides a reader into an opening that's not overwhelming with too many hooks and too much tension, but at a slower pace, letting them adjust to the painful subject matter by using fewer hooks in a very intentional and evocative manner.

Keep in mind this is a YA book, so Green focuses on the issues that are common to many teens—parents who don't understand them, having roiling emotions that are hard to explain and feeling isolated and alone. His primary target audiences are teen readers—adult readers are his secondary market. So his approach is to connect with emotions/feelings common to most teens before he leads into the uniqueness of the protagonist.

> *Late in the winter of my seventeenth year, my mother decided I was depressed, presumably because I rarely left the house, spent quite a lot of time in bed, read the same book over and over, ate infrequently, and devoted quite a bit of my abundant free time to thinking about death.*
> —John Green—*The Fault In Our Stars*

No mention about cancer, about the chances of the protagonist dying, about anything except what the average teen might feel or think about in their teen years. The author's promise is that this story is about an individual who's very much like the core reader—creating an empathetic bond—before he slips in how this character is different.

If he started with the Unique Character Hook he might lose the very readers he wanted to reach. Keep in mind that teens are often trying to determine where they fit in as opposed to *how do I understand a character going through something I don't even want to think about.*

Let's examine how mystery author, Steve Hamilton, uses the Surprising or Shocking Dialogue Hook at the end of a chapter. In this example, the protagonist has been asked by a good friend to visit that friend's mother who explains that her other son is missing and she's worried about him. She is Native American and is avoiding asking outright for the protagonist's help so, until this point, she has been explaining the meaning behind her son's name, how it was chosen by the boy's paternal grandmother, and how the mother felt it had and would bring bad luck to her son. This information is not necessary, but allows her time to build up her courage for a request that puts her in a position of supplication.

At the end of this chapter the author could have simply told the reader the following via dialogue:

ROUGH DRAFT: *"I want you to travel to Canada and find my missing adult son."*

Here there's dialogue but it doesn't really surprise or shock as the whole conversation had been leading to this point. So how did the author build in some more compelling hooks, and especially the Surprising or Shocking Dialogue Hook?

> *It took a moment to sink in. When it did, I knew I was committed. There was no way I could sit in that room with that woman and have it turn out any other way.*
> *"I want the two of you to find him," she said. "Prove me wrong. Go find my son with the unlucky name and bring him back home."*
> —Steve Hamilton — *Blood is the Sky*

The reader has been given more reasons to keep reading by the employment of Foreshadowing without Warning, Question(s) Raised, Action/Danger and the Surprising or Shocking Dialogue hooks here, plus the author kept this secondary character consistent with being a worried mother and strong matriarch who found it hard to ask for help, especially from a white man.

This next example is from a YA series, and this is the first book in the series. If the first book in a series keeps a reader wanting to read more, then the series can continue. So wisely using hooks throughout that first novel, and creating a strong and compelling story, helps sell your second or third novel in the series.

Let's look how Stephen Westerfeld approaches the opening to his futuristic world novel that keeps in mind the YA reader. He needs to engage and speak to readers from the 6th grade up in a way that reassures them that this novel is about their world, their experiences, their POV, even if they live in a contemporary environment.

Before we jump to his sentence that uses Surprising or Shocking Dialogue Hook as a powerful opening line, let's assume he had to play around a bit.

ROUGH DRAFT: *Tally Youngblood can hardly wait until her sixteenth birthday when she can become a Pretty.*

Not bad because it does contain the Question(s) Raised Hook and the Surprising Situation Hook, while giving a hint that there might be something different about this world, but a two-hook opening rarely holds a reader's attention for long. In a competitive marketplace, which is the world of contemporary publishing, a two-hook opening in a genre that expects more, makes for a harder sell to a reader new to this author's work.

Here's how author Scott Westerfeld made sure he snagged his YA, and later adult, audiences' attention.

> *The early summer sky was the color of cat vomit.*
> —Scott Westerfeld—*Uglies*

Now we have the Surprising or Shocking Dialogue Hook (internal first person), Question(s) Raised, Surprising Situation and Foreshadowing without Warning for a four-hook opening line. Would you, especially if you are a YA reader, want to continue reading even a few sentences more? If so, this line hooked you and works.

The next example comes from the prologue of an urban fantasy story. We'll go into more explanation about prologues deeper into this book, but don't forget a prologue's opening line must be treated with the same care and intention in engaging the reader as the opening sentence of the first chapter. Let's look at how Marjorie M. Liu does this utilizing several hooks, but most importantly the Surprising or Shocking Dialogue Hook.

> *When I was eight, my mother lost me to zombies in a one-card draw.*
> — Marjorie M. Liu — *The Iron Hunt*

This is a short, punchy sentence that alerts the reader that the story will most likely be fast-paced. As for hooks, Liu used:

- Surprising or Shocking Dialogue (first person POV internal),
- Action/Danger (given the age of the character and the fact zombies are mentioned, most readers would assume danger was involved),
- Surprising Situation (unless you know many mothers who lose their children in this type of situation, it's pretty safe to say it's surprising),
- Totally Unexpected (for the same reasons the Surprising Situation Hook applies),
- Unique Character (three actually, the mother who lost her child in such a manner, the child who has been lost and zombies),
- Foreshadowing with Warning (assumption being made, especially since a prologue is being used in the novel, that what happens here will impact the course of the current story),
- Question(s) Raised.

This then is a seven-hook opening that will compel most readers, even readers who normally don't read in the urban fantasy genre, to read just a little more into the story to find out what happened or what's going to happen next. Readers who love urban fantasy would most likely dive into the story and read through until the end because of such a strong opening line.

The next example comes from a contemporary category romance novel. A category or series romance is a sub-category of the romance market.

Readers of category romance purchase and read these books with clear expectations for the tone and kind of story they will be reading. They also have a specific understanding of the degree of sexual intensity on the page from sweet (no sex) to very, very sexy. So a reader who picks up a Harlequin Blaze romance expects a story that's contemporary, sexy and steamy. This is an important fact to remember as we examine the next opening sentence by author Lori Wilde.

> *A modern-day chastity belt?*
> *–Lori Wilde–Sweet Surrender*

In the above example, the author uses the contrast between what the core reader expects given the subgenre of this category romance — contemporary, sexy and steamy stories — and a reference to a historical relic associated with no-sex and thus no-steam. What Wilde achieves, then, is a Surprising or Shocking Dialogue Hook, a Foreshadowing Hook and a Question(s) Raised Hook. A three-hook opening, which might not be enough hooks in some types of stories, is perfectly acceptable for category romance readers who are not looking for a lot of pacing tension in their stories, but do expect and want a strong focus on the challenges and foibles of finding love.

If Wilde had approached the above opening sentence as if it were meant for an audience expecting five or more hooks to engage and entice them to continue reading, she might have tried something like this:

*ROUGH DRAFT:* Wear this modern-day chastity belt or I'll sell you to the sleaziest pimp on Hooker Row.

Now we have Action/Danger, Foreshadowing with Warning, Question(s) Raised, a Surprising Situation and Surprising or Shocking Dialogue Hooks. It's a very different feel than Wilde's opening line but brings home the point how important it is to not only have hooks, but the right kind and number of hooks for the core reading audience.

**NOTE:** Too many hooks, based on what you are writing, can cause a reader to set down your book just as quickly as too few.

This next example comes from a mystery series featuring Hispanic PI (Police Investigator) Lola Cruz. It's not considered a police procedural mystery, though the occupation of the protagonist means she might have some law enforcement experience, but has the pacing sensibilities and expectations of an amateur sleuth novel—fun, fast, and in this case, with a strong dose of humor—which means the pacing is faster.

Let's see how Ramirez uses the Surprising or Shocking Dialogue Hook to clue the reader into the tone of this second book in her series. But first, we'll assume the author had to struggle to thread in her hooks.

ROUGH DRAFT: *My grandmother was sobbing her heart out at my funeral.*

There are hooks in the above version, but also a degree of confusion. If the reader stops reading because they are confused, the power of your hooks is decreased. Plus there's nothing to give the flavor, the tone of the story. So let's see how Ramirez approached her opening sentence:

*I can't even begin to count the number of times my grandmother told me that she would die a happy woman if only I'd join the Order of Benedictine Sisters of Guadalupe and live a chaste and holy life.*

–Misa Ramirez–*Hasta La Vista, Lola!*

Now this opening contains a Surprising or Shocking Dialogue Hook (first person POV internal) that sets the tone of a fun, tongue-in-cheek character — not a Unique Character, not yet, because we don't know enough about her to determine if we've met, know, or have heard of a person like her — but the Question(s) Raised Hook is also present. So we have a two-hook opening, which indicates it'll be a lighter, less tense read, a sense of the world of the story and enough reasons — particularly if a reader enjoys lighter, fun mysteries — to keep reading.

**NOTE:** Be aware that if your author's voice or your story warrants humor, by all means use this hook, just don't expect to throw humor into a story simply for the sake of humor.

Here's another opening line from the opposite end of the mystery genre — this time a romantic suspense novel — which means a faster pace than the last example, with more focus on the romance aspect, but the romance does not have to be the first element introduced to the reader because it's a larger, stand-alone novel and not a category romance. The core reading audience knows there will be a romance, so the story can be opened on the suspense element, which is shown below.

Before we get to the opening sentence, one that clearly spells out strong danger elements sought by suspense readers, let's look at a possible rough draft.

ROUGH DRAFT: *Carlos Delgado was in a plane waiting for information from his bosses.*

No Surprising or Shocking Dialogue Hook here. No sense that there's danger either, or that the story will be fast-paced, or that it's a suspense novel at all. If there is a hook, it'd be a Question(s) Raised Hook, but not compelling enough to promise an exciting story to those who love and read these types of novels. So let's see how the co-authors who wrote this novel, Sherrilyn Kenyon and Dianna Love, created a much stronger opening sentence.

*If he had to die today, he'd have preferred a warm climate and a bullet between the eyes over this.*
–Sherrilyn Kenyon and Dianna Love–*Whispered Lies*

Now we have:

- Surprising or Shocking Dialogue Hook (third person POV internal),
- Action/Danger,
- Surprising Situation (to the reader, not necessarily the character, but it might be to him also),
- Unique Character (the thought expressed is not necessarily one that most readers have ever considered),
- Foreshadowing with Warning,
- Question(s) Raised.

So we went from a rough one-hook opening to a six-hook opening line, which creates the tension and interest for the suspense reader to keep reading.

The following opening line comes from a historical mystery series set in London in 1888. The reader knows this even before the story opens by the use of a tag line (that's found after the chapter heading but before the first paragraph) which can help orient the reader as to a change of locations or the passage of time if used deeper into a novel.

*"Julia Grey, I would rather see you hanged than watch any sister of mine go haring off after a man who will not have her,"* my brother Bellmont raged.
— Deanna Raybourn — *Silent on the Moor*

The above dialogue might not be shocking in a contemporary novel, but given its Victorian historical context, it's not what the reader or the character might expect to hear between siblings. The dialogue also includes both a Question(s) Raised Hook and a Foreshadowing Hook, one without the Warning element, so a three-hook opening line which is very appropriate to the genre. Too many hooks and the tension would feel too much, fewer hooks and the tension would be decreased.

Here's another example, this time via internal dialogue. This comes from a contemporary literary novel and is the opening line starting with internal dialogue.

*Jail is not as bad as you might imagine.*
— Anna Quindlen — *One True Thing*

If this had been the opening line of a mystery, suspense or thriller novel, the reader might not be as surprised or shocked by this internal dialogue/thought because in those genres there are more often than not characters who deserve to be, or have been, in jail. Not so much in a novel centered on relationships; in a middle class family in a nice community.

**NOTE:** The reader reads in the context of the type of novel they have picked up, so if they do not expect a person to say or think something in the story context, then that can create the Surprising or Shocking Dialogue Hook.

The reader knows nothing about the character sharing this thought, but because of the context promised to the reader by the back cover blurb, the cover art and where this book might be shelved in a bookstore, this counts as a Surprising or Shocking Dialogue Hook. There's also a Question(s) Raised Hook, and a Foreshadowing with Warning Hook (assuming something in the book leads to this insight or results from it and the reference to a jail). It could also qualify as a Unique Character Hook because of the type of story it is, the context being at odds with what the core reading audience of literary or women's fiction stories expect.

Always ask yourself if the average reader of your genre expects the hook or hooks you are using. Too out of the realm of expectation and you might turn off your readers. For example, a character tripping over a dead body in a mystery would be expected, but in a young adult novel or women's fiction, such a hook could turn off the readers. However, if you move the dead body off the page, off scene, the same concept as a hook might be Surprising or Shocking Dialogue, or a Surprising Situation or the Totally Unexpected.

To use this idea of the dead body not being as well received as a hook in a young adult novel, you, as the author, might approach it obliquely such as this:

*If Mr. Hinton hadn't picked today to have a heart attack*
*just when I was calling over the fence at him, then I would be*
*on my way to the mall to meet Tyler Hinchley.*

Yes, there's a dead body, but the focus is more on the interruption to the POV character's plans than the shock and violence of death on the page. In the made up example, some readers will still see this as a Shocking or Surprising Dialogue Hook because of its lack of empathy or awareness that the man was dead. But the core YA readership might not be surprised or shocked if they know people in their world who would have these exact kinds of feelings given the situation.

Let's look at an example that combines an Evocative Hook opening with a Surprising Dialogue Hook. Surprising but not Shocking Dialogue, though some readers might disagree, and that's perfectly acceptable. This is why hooks are very subjective; they are not going to be read the same way by every reader. We're not looking for 100% agreement on the impact of a hook, but we are looking at particular hooks and why they work for most readers given the type of story.

The novel, written by Chris Cleve, is considered a literary novel and one of the hallmarks of these stories is to promise the reader a thought-provoking read. We'll assume Cleve had to work at creating a powerful opening line and one with a Surprising Dialogue Hook.

ROUGH DRAFT: *I am an orphan who is only seeking justice and political asylum in a new country.*

There are hooks in this draft, but not the Surprising Dialogue Hook or the sense that this is a thought-provoking novel. Given the subject matter it could be, but the approach comes across more as a writer with an agenda as opposed to using the power of story, and the development of two very real, empathetic characters, to entice readers to become aware of a subject many would avoid otherwise.

How did Cleve open his story? Like this:

*Most days I wish I was a British pound coin instead of an African girl.*
–Chris Cleave–*Little Bee*

What the author manages to do with this very succinct, very focused opening is to engage the reader with:

- Surprising Dialogue (first person internal POV),
- Evocative Hook,
- Unique Character (most readers would never think of a person with this view of their world),
- Foreshadowing without Warning,
- Totally Unexpected,
- Question(s) Raised.

A six-hook opening that still—because of the Evocative Hook, it's alerting the reader that the story will unfold as it needs to unfold—does not create the type of tension associated with most openings that start with six hooks.

This last example comes from a general fiction novel. We haven't discussed a lot of these types of stories but you'll find this section in a brick-and-mortar bookstore under the heading: Fiction. In other words, it can be a novel that isn't simply one genre or another but rather a crossover of several genres. Literary novels are usually shelved under the Fiction heading, and, in some ways this novel could be considered literary, but one of the two main protagonists, Annie, is on a quest and that becomes apparent on the first page.

Let's focus more on the hooks that Nick Hornby, the author, deftly threads into his opening line, including the Surprising or Shocking Dialogue Hook.

> *They had flown from England to Minneapolis to look at a toilet.*
> —Nick Hornby—*Juliet, Naked*

The Surprising or Shocking Dialogue Hook is clearly present (third person internal dialogue), but we also have:

- Surprising Situation,
- Totally Unexpected,
- Unique Character (not many would make such a journey to view a toilet),
- Foreshadowing (without the sense of a warning that something bad is about to happen),
- Question(s) Raised.

That's a six-hook opening line that makes it almost impossible not to read even a little further to find out what's happening and why.

If Hornby had been a little less aware of the power of this strong opening line, he could have started deeper into his novel with a less intriguing sentence that he wrote.

> *Most people are unaware of Tucker Crowe's music, let alone some of the darker moments of his career, so the story of what may or may not have happened to him in the restroom of the Pits Club is probably worth repeating here.*
> —Nick Hornby—*Juliet, Naked*

This sentence, which opens the second scene of the novel on page three, is not nearly as intriguing or engaging as Hornby's opening sentence with only two hooks present; Question(s) Raised and possibly Foreshadowing without Warning (that what's about to be revealed plays out in some way through the story). But there's a huge difference between a two-hook and six-hook first sentence, especially when the six-hook opening engages you with the protagonist from the first sentence.

## NO SHOCKING OR WITTY DIALOGUE HOOKS:

"Brandon, did you leave the milk container out on the table again?" Mom shouted.

I know I shouldn't have yelled at him like I'd done, but he always knows how to make me mad.

"Brittany, I'd like to introduce you to Sharon."

After reading the powerful examples of internal or external Surprising or Shocking Dialogue Hooks that we've examined in this section, can you see the difference between the openings that strongly engage versus these last three examples? The last three sentences do contain hooks, but very few, and, if given your choice to choose only one book to read, would you choose one from the last three sentences (knowing nothing else about the story) or from one of the earlier examples?

**NOTE:** If submitting to a traditional publisher, keep in mind that an editor sees hundreds of submissions cross their desks in a month, and sometimes in a week. They have to think: Will this story engage the average reader? If the opening in particular doesn't, it's very easy to pass on that novel to grab for the submission that does.

### ASSIGNMENTS:

1. Take any one line of dialogue from your current writing as a starting point. Then play with it until you create 10 examples of Surprising or Shocking Dialogue. Have fun with this—there's no right or wrong approach. You can delete everything once you're done, but the more you do this exercise with a random line of dialogue, internal or external, the easier it'll be to create this hook intentionally.

2. Examine 20-30 books like the one you are writing (online bookstores let you examine the first few pages at no obligation, so you can easily find examples). Look at debut authors as well as established and award-winning authors. The intention is to see if this hook is common or uncommon in what you are writing. Reviewing 20-30 books is a start. The more you review, the better idea you have as to the use of this hook in what you want to write.

3. Remember, hooks are used in more than the opening line. In the books you're examining, or in a brick-and-mortar store, or on your own bookshelves, look for this

hook at the end and beginning of chapters to see how common it is in those locations. You may be surprised.

## RECAP

- The Surprising or Shocking Dialogue Hook can be in the ear of the reader, or the ears of the characters given the situation and type of story, or a combination of both.
- If you choose to use this hook, make sure the dialogue relates to the story. Be wary of using a shocking statement simply to shock. The dialogue must be relevant and lead logically to the next lines of your story.
- Keep in mind the context of your story to look for ways to tweak your dialogue to create this hook. If you've created a character who is acting out of character and revealing this via the Surprising or Shocking Dialogue Hook, make sure your motivation for this is clear to the reader, either before or after the communication.
- You can have the Surprising or Shocking Dialogue Hook in the middle of a page, a scene, or a chapter that can engage your reader, but when we're examining hooks we're looking at specific key placements to make it work most effectively.

## HOOK 10: HUMOR HOOK

In previous recaps about hooks in general I mentioned that all hooks are subjective. Another way of saying that is that if you read and write in only one genre [i.e., mystery, romance, fantasy, westerns, children, young adult] or sub-genre [police procedural mysteries, inspirational romance, high or epic fantasy, steampunk-westerns, etc.] you are probably used to seeing certain types of hooks that resonate with these specific readers.

But not all readers can be lumped into a homogeneous category. If you are writing a mystery with a strong romantic element or a fantasy western with steampunk overlap, you'll be writing for readers who read multiple genres. This is important to know because one hook will not, nor should, fit only one genre. The writer who is able to understand the power of and the versatility of all 10 Universal Hooks is the writer who can engage more readers.

I'm bringing up this point because while all hooks are subjective, and all of us as readers and writers, will respond in different degrees to all hooks, it's a foolish writer who assumes that since they are not writing a light or comedic story that they will never need to use the Humor Hook.

Humor can provide the breathing space all readers need after a particularly emotional or intense scene. This is why buddy movies are so popular. By using a comic relief secondary character — Watson to Sherlock Holmes, Sanchez to Don Quixote, Chewbacca to Hans Solo — the writer can ease the reader out of a very tense scene and allow them to process what just happened. Too much continuous drama — physical, mental or emotional — is exhausting. Humor, in its many forms, can help diffuse and transition a reader from one scene before they are thrust into the next one.

Humor also serves another story function. It can open our emotions so that when a particularly emotional event is *about* to happen, the reader is impacted even stronger. William Shakespeare used this approach many times throughout his plays. Have the audience chortling at the antics of secondary characters or witty repartee and then BAM! Hit them with a tragic event that the viewer did not expect.

One other important issue to keep in mind when thinking and working with the Humor Hook is that humor itself is very subjective. Some readers love dark humor, others prefer slapstick. Humor can be subtle, wry, laugh-out-loud and anywhere in between. When I was growing up my mother used to groan out loud when she knew my siblings and I had been watching the Three Stooges because we'd get so wild and rowdy, but that was the type of humor used by Larry, Curly and Mo.

Not only is humor subjective, it can also depend on where the reader is at in their life, whether the humor resonates or not. You'll have experienced this yourself if someone told you that you'd really enjoy such and such book or story but when you picked it up you just couldn't get into it. Later, you tried again and wondered why you ever stopped the first time.

Certain subjects used in humor can also push some people's hot buttons. Jokes about sex, body parts or situations can just as easily repel readers who don't find those subjects particularly funny or think they are in poor taste.

When using any hooks you must be true to your story. Do not force the Humor Hook on your reader to prove you can use it. Humor in the wrong locations can jar your reader out of a story just as humor in real life situations can be anything but funny.

**NOTE:** Keep in mind too that humor can be used in degrees. Not all humor must be slap-your-knee funny. Some can generate a simple smile or other feel-good response.

Yes, there are a lot of nuances to keep in mind when using the Humor Hook but before you start to worry too much or stop your writing to perfect a specific Humor Hook at a key location, give yourself permission to write your first draft. Then, and only then, reread for hook consideration and placement. You'll have a far stronger idea of where your story might need a quick quip or breathing space, especially at the end of a chapter or the opening of one.

One other point to keep in mind. Using the Humor Hook does not mean you are writing comedy. Humor can mean that moment when, in the midst of drama your character can say or do something simply because if they don't th,ey feel they may break. For example, you have a character who has been lost, afraid, exhausted and all hope is gone when they recall a comment or reference said to them earlier about what to do when at the end of their rope. Maybe sing, or whistle or recite nursery rhymes. Something they would never consider otherwise, but they decide—why not? The next scene opens up with someone finding them singing ninety-nine bottles of beer on the wall and assuming they are drunk. That can be humor.

As a writer it's your goal to write for more than simply yourself. Your goal is to study and understand all 10 Universal hooks, one by one, to see what you might be currently missing in your craft toolbox.

The more hooks you can use, the less often you will fall back on the same story openings or the same chapter endings. We don't see this situation very often in published work, but when it does happen, as a reader you start to pick up on the stale feel of the writing. The more that happens the easier it becomes to set a book down and you become reluctant to pick up the next one.

In studying the Humor Hook it's important to know that as long as there's an emotional response—from light to intense—decreasing the tension—the Humor Hook is most likely working. There are exceptions—a strong sense of relief also reduces the tension but doesn't have to be humorous.

For example, we're reading a novel where the protagonist and a potential romantic interest have been butting heads, reluctant to deal with their attraction. Then the love interest physically disappears. If this character has been missing and presumed hurt or dead the end of a scene might end like this:

WITHOUT HUMOR: *She heard the crunch of a boot against stone and turned around. "Oh, thank heavens! I thought you were dead."*

This scene ends on relief and maybe one hook—the Question(s) Raised Hook—what happened to the person? How could they still be alive?

So this is a one-hook ending. Let's try again by including the Humor Hook. Same situation—reluctant attraction, the grief of thinking the love interest has been killed, the regret for missed opportunities and the friction of their behavior, etc., only this time the scene ending includs a twist of humor.

WITH HUMOR: *She heard the crunch of a boot against stone and turned around, not believing whom she saw, or the rush of relief roaring through her. But no way was she going to admit it given that cocky grin creasing his face. "So what took you so long?" she demanded, turning away and throwing over her shoulder. "Next time if you're going to die, then stay dead."*

Okay, it's rough, and it does take more words, but as a result more hooks have been built in. The Question(s) Raised Hook has been ratcheted up by creating more questions—what happened to the person? How could they still be alive? What's going to happen with the relationship now? Does she mean her words or is she reverting to hiding her true feelings? Plus we have the Surprising or Shocking Dialogue Hook, given this response is not the usual response to finding someone is alive and well after it's believed they were dead and the Humor Hook—because of the wry, tongue-in-cheek statement the protagonist has made. It's not a laugh-out-loud moment, nor will all readers find it funny, but if it is in-character for this protagonist to deny, avoid and hide her emotions, especially her attraction emotions—this would come across as humor.

That's what makes the Humor Hook so fun, so universal, and seen in all genres.

As we start looking at specific examples of the Humor Hook—in the opening sentences and deeper into a story—I'll try to make clear from the context why the hook is present. Sometimes it's because the line is clearly funny. Sometimes it's because of what happened leading up to a line. Sometimes it's because of the character or characters involved, or the context.

Let's look at some examples from a variety of genres where the Humor Hook is being employed effectively. This first example is from a middle grade novel, which means the target reading audience is from about grades 4 through 6. Let's assume that the author wrote a placeholder opening line. She created a character who feels like a fish out of water in a new school environment—a very common premise for this age range. But there's something different about this particular character—she is able to see ghosts—and is having a very hard time dealing with that issue.

The author might have written an initial draft that focused on the most universal issue—the feeling of being different.

ROUGH DRAFT: *I didn't want to be at this new school, or the one before, but my mother gave me no choice.*

Now, if this was a contemporary story about the trials and tribulations of being fourteen and the new kid in a new environment, this opening could work. It does have hooks—the Foreshadowing Hook given the average reader would assume this situation, being in a new school, would play out in a strong way throughout the story, and the Question(s) Raised Hook because the average reader might wonder: Who this character? Why are they in a new school? What's happening?

But there's no sense of the uniqueness of this character that creates a twist to the fish-out-of-water story. Like this:

> *The undead are ruining my life. I blame my mother.*
> —Elizabeth Cody Kimmel — *Supernatural: School Spirit*

Here we have not only more hooks, creating a stronger reason to keep reading, but also a clear idea that this particular story will have an interesting character and situation. Hooks seen here are the Foreshadowing Hook [That the issue of dealing with the undead will play out strongly throughout the story]; Unique Character Hook [Since the average reader doesn't see or deal with the undead on a regular basis, whomever the POV character is they are not the average person.]; Surprising Situation Hook [Given the age-range of the targeted reader they would not expect someone their age dealing with the undead.]; Surprising or Shocking Dialogue (internal) [Again, not what you expect someone to be thinking.] Question(s) Raised [Is this for real? Does this person really deal with the undead? What's happening? Why is it mom's fault? Etc.] and the Humor Hook [Because of the contrast between the expected—it's mom's fault—and the unexpected—involvement with the undead ruining their life—creates a wry twist of perspective that creates that sense of lively fun, as opposed to angst or resentment that the rough draft contained.]

We went from a mild, two-hook opening line in the presumed rough draft version to a much stronger six-hook opening. The fact that it takes two sentences doesn't decrease the effectiveness because the sentences are short and thus read as one longer line. This final version also clearly gives the potential reader an idea that there will be a strong paranormal element to the story so that those readers who do not wish to read in this sub-genre can pass on the book. And that's okay. The humor of the situation will not resonate with them.

But if those very same readers had picked up or purchased the book based on the rough draft opening line they could be very upset that the story was not what they thought it was. We've all seen those reviews or heard those comments—I thought I was going to be reading X but it turned out to be Y. Nothing wrong with the story —just not what the reader expected and therefore a disappointment.

Defining our core readership market is important, as well as determining who our readers are not. This process starts creating not only a stronger fan base for the author but a clearer branding too. The sooner the author can get the message across to their potential readers—that this will be a fun, light read or an emotional roller-coaster of a read with humor as an element, the better chance to create a stronger win-win for everyone.

This next example comes from a cozy women's sleuth mystery. These stories are not meant to have a lot of high tension so the Humor Hook is often employed. Not as laugh-out-loud humor but with a gentler touch. The author chose to open her story with a line that does not contain the Humor Hook, but sets up the mystery of the story. She used the Humor Hook in her second line and as a way to reveal the protagonist.

> *Maybe I'd have had a drink with the guy if I had known the next time I saw him he'd be sprawled out in a dumpster enclosure, with a greasy newspaper tented over his face. Then again, maybe not.*
> —Rosemary Harris — *The Big Dirt Nap: A Dirty Business Mystery*

Let's pull this example apart to see which hooks the author used so effectively and how the Humor Hook continues the set up of the first line while bringing in a different feel specifically by her use of the Humor Hook.

*Maybe I'd have had a drink with the guy if I had known the next time I saw him he'd be sprawled out in a dumpster enclosure, with a greasy newspaper tented over his face.* [Opening sentence contains the Foreshadowing Hook—that this death, and investigating it, will play out over the course of the story. The Question(s) Raised Hook—who is the person thinking this thought? What happened to the man? The Surprising or Shocking Dialogue Hook (internal) as well as the Surprising Situation Hook—because of the contrast between the current situation [dead man in a dumpster] and the reference to previously meeting the deceased [drink with the guy] and a Unique Character [we know nothing more about the protagonist except that 1) she's found a dead body and 2) her response to that body is not the average response one expects given the situation. That's a solid five-hook opening.] *Then again, maybe not.* [Here is the Humor Hook, which reveals more of the POV character's personality while offering a wry, tongue-in-cheek internal observation of the situation. That second part helps create not only the humor but adds a new Surprising or Shocking Dialogue Hook (internal) for a two-hook second line.]

While dropping the reader quickly into the genre—a mystery—but without blood, gore or violence, and using a five-hook opening line followed by a two-hook second line; the author has intentionally revealed to the reader the theme, tenor and a strong hint of the personality of the protagonist via these two lines. She did not jump too fast into the mystery like this:

ROUGH DRAFT: *Maybe I'd have had a drink with the guy if I had known the next time I saw him he'd be sprawled out in a dumpster enclosure, with a greasy newspaper tented over his face. I grabbed my cell phone to report the crime to the 911 operator and buttoned up my jacket because I knew it'd be easily a half an hour or longer before the first responders arrived.*

See the difference? The author's version kept the focus on the protagonist. This rough draft version shifted the focus very quickly to the situation and as a result, revealed a very different type of protagonist. The rough draft version might be more appropriate to a police procedural with its business-as-usual feel from a person experienced with death.

As a reader, if you were seeking a lighter, less intense and more fun read you'd more likely reach for the author's version because it's clear that's what she's offering her readers. If you, as a reader, wanted a story that's all about the crime and pits an experienced investigator against a criminal, you might lean toward the rough draft version.

Remember there is no right or wrong here. It's about being aware of what the readers of a cozy mystery want and expect and the author making that very clear to all readers as soon as possible in her opening. She jumped into the story with a strong enough sentence to indicate that the story is not as much about place or occupation or cast of familiar characters — that will come later — but about this specific protagonist with her specific view of the world. Using the Humor Hook so close upon the first sentence makes that point very clear.

Let's look at another example — this one again an internal thought or dialogue opening. Why? Because, when all is said and done, we care about plot because we care about a specific character. Without wanting to know more about the protagonist of a story the external events — such as a car chase, eating an ice cream cone on the front steps, an unexpected package arriving — don't really matter after a while. It's the impact of those external events on specific characters that make a story matter.

That's why in action-adventure stories, such as a movie where a volcano is exploding in a small town, a tsunami gobbles up a coastal town, an earthquake hits a large metropolitan area, etc, and in the background all these people are swept away in lava or water or are being swallowed by sudden fractures in the earth serve only one story purpose—to show the reader what could happen to the main protagonists. Sad, but true. The viewer might feel for the unknown masses but not as much as for the individuals we're rooting for to survive.

Humor, revealed through internal or external dialogue, can quickly create an empathetic bond with the reader. It doesn't mean we have to like the POV character but humor, even a hint of it, allows the reader to relate to a character. It's the difference between riding on public transportation where everyone averts their gazes or are focused on their phones, and catching a quick smile, from another passenger. Which person do you recall if someone asks you about your fellow passengers, given that situation?

**NOTE:** Using the Humor Hook in an opening sentence or page is a quick way to create reader empathy with your protagonist or the story world via a secondary character but only if the humor element is true to that character or situation.

In young adult novels, which this next one is, it's vital to make sure you let your target reading audience connect quickly with the protagonist. Why? Because, given the age of these readers, most of their real lives revolve around their peers. Their world-view can be myopic in this sense. Again, this doesn't mean the protagonist must be likeable as much as easily identifiable to the reader. Add this need—to identify who the protagonist is, what kind of person they are, and whether you are drawn to that person or not—with the high degree of emotional intensity found in a lot of novels for this age group—again because the readers in this group tend to feel intensely and you can start to understand the nuances necessary to write for this audience.

When I say intense emotion it doesn't mean only negative ones such as fear, anger, bitterness or apathy. It can also mean embarrassment, frustration, isolation, or shame. It's the intensity that can make the difference and help alert the reader as to whether this is a book truly written for and about teens, or a book written by an adult to instruct teens.

The author of this next example, if her intention was to instruct teens, might have written her opening line something like this:

ROUGH DRAFT: *It is hard enough being thirteen and dealing with all the accompanying emotions associated with this age, but accepting that emotions might feel heightened due to the increase of hormonal activity in a young adult's body, might help temper the moments of frustration and embarrassment.*

Sounds a lot like a work of non-fiction, doesn't it? Plus it's preaching, which is a turn-off for many, if not most, of the target audience. So let's see how the author uses the Humor Hook to quickly engage a teen reader while creating a sense of familiarity—*I know this feeling* response in those same readers. The protagonist is a fourteen-year old male in a story that's fast-paced and at times over-the-top breathless.

*"I am a socially awkward mandork."*
— *Sherrilyn Kenyon—Infinity: Chronicles of Nick*

Without knowing anything else about the story the humor shines through while being spot-on for the readers. Kenyon manages to create not only the Humor Hook—both with the character's comment but also with whatever situation created the comment—even without knowing anything more. Because this humor is revealed via dialogue the Surprising or Shocking Dialogue Hook also applies. The third Hook present is the Question(s) Raised Hook—who is talking? What's going on? And since it's a short sentence it makes it easy for the reader to gobble up the next few sentences which adds in a different Humor Hook as well as clarifies and increases the humor of laughing with the protagonist.

*"I am a socially awkward mandork."*
*"Nicholas Ambrosius Gautier! Watch your language!"*
*Nick sighed at his mother's sharp tone as he stood in their tiny kitchen looking down at the bright orange Hawaiian shirt. The color and style were bad enough. The fact it was covered in l-a-r-g-e pink, gray, and white trout (or were they salmon?) was even worse.*

—Sherrilyn Kenyon—*Infinity: Chronicles of Nick*

Now the reader knows what created the initial dialogue, so some of the questions that were raised have already been answered, but so has the sense of relating to this character's situation. In less than a paragraph, Kenyon makes the reader care about her character and his situation as well as relate to the universal experience of knowing that by pleasing/obeying a parent it will definitely make them stand outside the group that defines their world.

This next example also plays up that sense of being different, but with a sense of irony and unexpected humor. It's a literary novel, which, on the whole are not known to be or contain a lot of humor. That's okay because we're not saying that the whole novel is going to be comedic. Even in stories of tragedy, loss or disillusionment, the Humor Hook can reassure the reader that while life might be painful there are still moments of relief. Or, the author might use humor to assume that there is hope, as this next novel does.

The author might have started his story that's been described as a "bizarre novel of obsessively apathetic love (that) is really quite bad," in a way that clearly let the reader know that the tone of the story would be bitter, disillusioned, and generally unhappy. That way the potential reader who did not want to be dragged through the mire might have skipped this novel. Something like the following sentences that come from deeper in the same novel:

*Bill, I've been starving for you.*
*He finds in it a refuge. Sometimes I'm glad he has*
*something in which he is not locked up and incoherent, but it*
*frightens me in him. So remote.*
—W.H. Manville—*Breaking Up*

These lines include the Evocative Hook for its lyrical language and phrasing which forces the reader to adjust to the author's style as opposed to jumping in and gobbling up the story. There might even be a Question(s) Raised Hook for some readers, as long as it's not based on confusion. What's going on is a question that would compel a reader to keep reading, but a—huh? question creates vagueness and makes it easier for readers NOT to be engaged. But clearly there's no hint of the Humor Hook.

So let's see how the author managed to give the sense of humor, by introducing the POV character with a sarcastic internal thought.

*I don't know how other men feel about their wives walking*
*out on them, but I helped mine pack.*
—W.H. Manville—*Breaking Up*

This is a good example of an opening line that some readers might not think was funny. But if a comedian on a stage made this comment most of the audience might give some kind of a smile or chuckle. That's another gauge to see if the Humor Hook is working. With the Manville version he also added in other hooks—Foreshadowing [The assumption being made that the break up of the marriage will play out in some way in the story.]; Question(s) Raised [What happened? What's going to happen next? Etc.]; Surprising or Shocking Dialogue (internal) and the Humor Hook. So this version went from a weak two-hook opening sentence to a stronger four-hook opening line.

A rule of thumb is that when using the 10 Universal Hooks to create the most opportunities for engagement for the average reader, having less than three hooks is the mildest, least intense of openings. Four to five hooks give the reader that many more reasons to keep reading, it keeps the pacing faster but is not over the top tense. Anything from six hooks or more ramps up the pacing, builds in more questions to engage the reader and increases tension on the page.

The next Humor Hook example comes from a non-fiction book—a travelogue. Being aware of the power of hooks to catch and hold a reader's attention throughout a story and incorporating these same types of hooks into non-fiction work in key locations can pay off for the author. In this case not only does the Humor Hook promise the reader a fun and light read, but clearly indicates that this travel book will not be dry and simply fact-filled. It takes an armchair travel guide and places it in a cross-genre position—a non-fiction work with the engagement and ease of reading a work of fiction.

The author might have started his story of searching for his small-town roots with something like this:

ROUGH DRAFT: *I had been away from America for over twenty years, living and writing abroad but it was only after I returned, and was able to see America from the perspective of both an insider and an outsider that I decided to revisit the world of my childhood, a small town in the Midwest.*

This approach sounds more like a memoir, and the final book has large elements of memoir, but that's not what the book is about. The richness of this book, and this author, is in his sense of humor, poking fun at the world he sees and himself, but not in a mocking way. This particular travelogue is described as "With a razor wit and a kind heart, Bryson serves up a colorful tale of boredom, kitsch, and beauty when you least expect it."

So how does he use the Humor Hook to entice his readers to keep reading?

*I come from Des Moines. Somebody had to.*
—Bill Bryson—*The Lost Continent: Travels in Small Town America*

Self-deprecating humor can be very subtle while being very effective, given that some folks, those who belong to the Des Moines Booster Club for example, might not think these two short sentences are funny at all. They might even be seen as blasphemous. But for anyone who has grown up in a town or environment that simply did not fit, and were able to josh about this—not with an anti-Des Moines feel or a complaint— just simply a wry look at what it meant to this one person— and impart that information via a Humor Hook in their introductory paragraph, stands a great chance of finding their ideal reader who can become loyal fans. It's not a bait-and-switch sense of humor as you can see by the end of the first paragraph.

*I come from Des Moines. Somebody had to. When you come from Des Moines you either accept the fact without question and settle down with a local girl named Bobbi and get a job at the Firestone factory and live there forever and ever, or you spend your adolescence moaning at length about what a dump it is and how you can't wait to get out, and then you settle down with a local girl named Bobbi and get a job at the Firestone factory and live there forever and ever.*
—Bill Bryson—*The Lost Continent: Travels in Small Town America*

The Humor Hook continues in the third sentence because what's being revealed is a different topic—a wry description of the town itself. The buying decision is most times made by the first page for the average reader who buys a book from an author new to them. For a fair amount the decision is made by the first paragraph, *if* the author started with hooks and built more in.

Bryson does an outstanding job of using the Humor Hook again and again to help his ideal reader determine if this is the type of non-fiction book they want to read.

This next example of an opening sentence containing humor, or the possibility of humor comes from a literary novel. When we examine the Evocative Hook in this book we'll see it used very often in literary novels, but using only that hook can backfire. The reason this can happen is that using only one type of hook means the author is missing connecting with a broader range of readers.

Focusing too much on only one type of hook narrows your reading audience to only those readers who are drawn to that specific hook. With 10 Universal Hooks to choose from, the more versatile you are as a writer in intentionally using multiple hooks throughout your work, the more reasons you are giving a reader to keep reading.

The author might have started his novel on an Action/Danger Hook, like this:

ROUGH DRAFT: *The explosion that killed my grandmother started like any average Wednesday.*

This version contains not only the Action/Danger Hook, but the Foreshadowing, Surprising Situation, Totally Unexpected and Question(s) Raised Hooks too. That's a little too much tension for most literary novels and can give the reader the impression that they are reading a suspense or mystery and not a complex family drama.

So let's see how the author approached his opening line.

*It was the day my grandmother exploded.*
—Iain Banks—*The Crow Road*

This version contains the Surprising Situation, Foreshadowing, Shocking or Surprising Dialogue (internal), Questions Raised and for a lot of readers a sense of tongue-in-cheek humor that earns the Humor Hook. Not every reader will feel that way, which is why I chose it as an example. This is enough of a shocking, out there image conjured that it passes the comedian on stage test. If you heard a comedian on stage raise this topic in this way, would you sit up and take notice? Would you possibly expect a punch line to follow?

Let's now see how the author follows up this sentence with his next one to clearly alert the reader as to a stronger hint of what kind of story they are diving into.

*It was the day my grandmother exploded. I sat in the crematorium, listening to my Uncle Hamish quietly snoring in harmony to Bach's Mass in B Minor, and I reflected that it always seemed to be death that drew me back to Gallanach.*
— Iain Banks — *The Crow Road*

This is a one-two punch of an opening. The questions raised by the multiple hooks in the first sentence, including the Humor Hook, followed up by a visualization that can keep the humor in place. Not laugh-out-loud humor, but the self-deprecating kind that can have you nodding your head in commiseration.

Let's examine a different type of opening sentence that uses a spoof on a classic as a Humor Hook. Again, not every reader, especially those who are die-hard Jane Austen fans and feel that the following is a cheap shot at an iconic writer and story. But keep in mind, humor comes in a lot of varieties and, for the target audience who enjoys making fun of recognizable works, this example does hit the funny bone.

*It is a truth universally acknowledged that a zombie in possession of brains must be in want of more brains.*

—Seth Grahame-Smith and Jane Austen — *Pride and Prejudice and Zombies*

One sentence, that's all it takes to let the reader know if this take on Pride and Prejudice will suit their sense of the absurd, or is not worth purchasing or reading.

The next example also falls under the inappropriate for some readers and spot on, tongue-in-cheek humor for others. No one book will appeal to all readers equally. By making sure the initial sentence and the first page let a reader know if they are selecting their type of read, you start building your die-hard readership.

This opening comes from a novel described as having dark humor and satire. Right there many readers will be either intrigued or repelled. If the author had shied away from the Humor Hook and tried for other, safer hooks in her opening line she might have written something like this.

ROUGH DRAFT: *I wanted the cheapest manual on knot tying I could find.*

Not much here to give offense or raise a lot of questions, unless the reader is passionate about knots. Even then, they'd probably lean toward a work of non-fiction on the subject vs. fiction.

So how did the author speak to her target audience using the Humor Hook?

*Balloon Tying For Christ was the cheapest balloon manual I could find.*
—Monica Drake — *Clown Girl*

Now we have the Humor Hook along with a Surprising Situation, Surprising or Shocking Dialogue, Foreshadowing and Question(s) Raised Hooks. We went from a zero-hook opening to a five-hook opening. Possibly a six-hook opening sentence if you feel that a person who wants to learn about balloon tying is unique.

The next example comes from a general fiction novel that many consider a romance, or at least one with very strong romantic elements. It is about a man who realizes that he might be missing something by not being in a committed relationship. It's clearly a love story as well as a feel-good read. Even if the male protagonist is not what many think of when they think of as a romantic hero.

The author might have started his novel with something without gentle humor. Like this:

ROUGH DRAFT: *There comes a time in many men's lives when they realize that having a wife might be a nice thing.*

Here we have the Foreshadowing Hook along with the Question(s) Raised Hook but no sense of humor and thus no reactions raised in the reader because of that humor. So let's look at how the author started his novel.

*I may have found a solution to the Wife Problem. As with so many scientific breakthroughs, the answer was obvious in retrospect.*
—Graeme Simsion—*The Rosie Project*

Technically, these are two sentences, but because the first one is so short it's easy to continue reading the second one. At this point in the story the reader doesn't know anything at all about the POV character, unless they read the back cover blurb or heard about the book from a friend. So the humor is coming from the initial internal statement, which, if stated on a stage by a comedian, would earn some smiles along with a few groans. Because the concept of marriage as a challenge is as old as the concept of marriage, it counts for some of the humor. The other element of humor is raised by contrasting the idea of a scientific breakthrough and marriage. So the

Humor Hook is present as well as the Foreshadowing, Surprising Situation, Surprising or Shocking Dialogue (internal) and Question(s) Raised Hooks for a strong five-hook opening.

The next sentence is drawn from a cross-genre novel that is called dystopian, political and literary. Not a combination you see every day and the opening sentence could have started in a number of ways.

ROUGH DRAFT: *The present future was bleak, fraught with danger and not unexpected given the rise of the challenges Luz faced everyday.*

This contains Foreshadowing with Warning and the Question(s) Raised Hooks but clearly not the Humor Hook. So let's see how the debut novelist started her story that earned award upon award.

*Punting the prairie dog into the library was a mistake.*
— Claire Vaye Watkins — *Gold Fame Citrus*

Does it intrigue you? Does the contrast between prairie dogs and a library make you want to know more? Not a large chuckle sense of humor but a dry, what's-happening hint that while the overall theme of the book — being literary, political and dystopian, not the cheeriest of subjects — might be a little something different and worth reading more to find out. If that was your response then the Humor Hook is working. Remember that humor can open senses and intrigue in a way that might compel readers to give this novel a second glance, even if they normally don't read any of the sub-genres it contains.

Let's examine a mystery series that is known for its zany characters, laugh-out-loud humor and fun spin on a mystery that runs hand-in-glove with a strong romantic triangle. The author might have started out with the romance element with a first draft something like this:

ROUGH DRAFT: *Some days are more challenging than others given my love life.*

This might not be too bad an opening if the author wanted to use Foreshadowing (without Warning) and Question(s) Raised Hooks while letting potential readers of the series know this particular story, if not the series, would appeal to both mystery and romance readers. But instead she chose to focus on the main protagonist and use humor to reveal a little, or a lot, of her personality.

*For the better part of my childhood, my professional aspirations were simple—I wanted to be an intergalactic princess.*
—Janet Evanovich—*Seven Up*

This version not only contains the Humor Hook but a Surprising Situation, Surprising or Shocking Dialogue (internal), Question(s) Raised and, for some, the potential of a Unique Character Hook. That last earned not because the protagonist once thought along the lines of career choices including that of an intergalactic princess, but because it's clear she believed she could be that princess.

Humor used to create empathy with a main character is a common way of using the Humor Hook—especially if you are picking up a novel that could be dismal, threatening, scary or bleak. By using the Humor Hook right from the first sentence you are promising the reader not only an engaging character, but a read that can make them smile as part of the mystery, literary tale, suspense, etc.

The next is an example of creating immediate empathy between a reader and a protagonist using humor. Let's assume the author wrote a placeholder as an opening sentence like this:

ROUGH DRAFT: *When Cleveland private eye Milan Jacovich reluctantly attends the fortieth reunion of his St. Clair High School graduating class, he gets a rude surprise: one of his classmates is found shot dead and another quickly becomes the main suspect.*

Sounds more like a summation sentence doesn't it? We're being told about who the main character is via his occupation, the area of the country, a hint of back story and the set up for the mystery. But we're not shown who the protagonist is by his personality. Like this:

> *Three surprises make a high school reunion strongly resemble a visit to hell.*
> — Les Roberts — *King of the Holly Hop* (Milan Jacovich Mysteries #14)

If you as a reader had been looking for a mystery that grabs your attention, makes you relate to the protagonist even in a small way, and know that there's more to the story than simply a mystery, which of the two versions would you select? The author's version clearly uses the Humor Hook as well as Foreshadowing, Question(s) Raised and Surprising or Shocking Dialogue (internal) Hooks.

Up next is an example from an urban fantasy novel. It can be helpful to keep in mind that the Humor Hook can and is used across every genre. In this case, it's employed as a way to connect the reader to the protagonist. Urban fantasy is a sub-genre of the larger fantasy/sci-fi genre and often, but not always, has a female protagonist who can take care of herself physically while taking a sarcastic, wry approach to life. The fact that life often contains werewolves, vampires, demons and the like makes the stories that much more interesting. The author, who introduces her protagonist's personality via the first sentence of the book might have written an early version.

ROUGH DRAFT: *Sabina Kane lived in a world that was sassy, hip and lethal.*

In this version the reader is being told about the main character, not shown. There is an element of Foreshadowing and Question(s) Raised Hooks but the reader is being asked to wait to find out more, instead of becoming engaged with the protagonist as soon as possible. Like this:

> *Digging graves is hell on a manicure, but I was taught good vampires clean up after every meal.*
> —Jaye Wells—*Red-Headed Stepchild*

Right here the potential reader gets a glimpse into this vampire protagonist with a Humor Hook as well as a Foreshadowing, Surprising or Shocking Dialogue (internal), Unique Character [unless you have met or know any vampires], and Question(s) Raised hooks for a strong, and fun, five-hook opening line that makes the average reader, and definitely the target reader of urban fantasy, want to know more.

Now we'll look at using the Humor Hook at places other than the opening line in different types of stories. This first comes from a children's book, one of a series of tongue-in-cheek stories about a most unlikely protagonist—twelve-year-old Artemis Fowl who is a millionaire, a genius-and above all, a criminal mastermind.

Keep in mind that hooks used at the end of scenes or chapters can be built with several sentences as opposed to the single opening lines we've been examining, so the examples are longer and need the context to make the Humor Hook obvious.

But what if the author had written a placeholder ending to his pre-prologue, one without strong hooks, like this:

ROUGH DRAFT: *Artemis becoming involved with the goblin uprising was going to cause him some problems.*

Because of the mention of a goblin uprising, this version does contain hooks that include Foreshadowing with Warning, Surprising Situation, Unique Character [The goblins or, if this is the first book in the series that a reader had read it would also include Artemis as not the typical twelve-year-old expected], Action/Danger and Question(s) Raised Hooks, so it's not a bad ending. However, the author wanted to keep the focus on both the improbable situation as well as Artemis as a character and here's his version:

> *[Leading Up to the Prologue Ending]*
> *Artemis avoided other teenagers and resented being sent to school, preferring to spend his time plotting his next crime.*
> *So, even though his involvement with the goblin uprising during the year was to be traumatic, terrifying, and dangerous, it was probably the best thing that could have happened to him. At least he spent some time outdoors, and got to meet new people.*
> *It's a pity most of them were trying to kill him.*
> — Eoin Colfer — *The Arctic Incident*

Let's look a little more closely at this example to see how the hooks come into play. Keeping in mind that if you use a prologue, or any notes to the reader before the prologue, as in this example, you must treat that text as what a reader first reads, and thus the needs for hooks in this material is as strong as an opening chapter.

*Artemis avoided other teenagers and resented being sent to school, preferring to spend his time plotting his next crime.*

[Surprising or Shocking Dialogue (internal, this passage is from the thoughts of the doctor of Artemis. If that was not clear this hook would not apply.), Foreshadowing, Question(s) Raised and Unique Character Hooks]

*So, even though his involvement with the goblin uprising during this year was to be traumatic, terrifying, and dangerous,* [Action/Danger, Foreshadowing with Warning, Question(s) Raised and Unique Character (goblins) hooks as well as the possibility of Overpowering Emotion Hook. Since it is not the protagonist here actively experiencing the events as they happen but the reader is instead being told about them from another character who is removed from the emotion, the emotion is not as strong as it might be for a truly Overpowering Emotion Hook.] *it was probably the best thing that could have happened to him. At least he spent some time outdoors, and got to meet new people.*

*It's a pity most of them were trying to kill him.* [Humor Hook here because of the contrast between what a reader might expect to follow the benign comment of getting to meet new people and be outdoors more, as well as Foreshadowing with Warning, Action/Danger, Surprising Situation, Totally Unexpected, and Question(s) Raised Hooks to end on a six-hook lead into the prologue.]

The next example is from a PI (private investigator) mystery series with two lawyers turned investigators, set in the Florida Keys. The couple are partners as well as lovers, and their on-again, off-again relationship as well as the fact that one comes across as a laid-back, bend-the-rules surfer boy and the other as high-society, born-with-a-silver-spoon-in-her mouth woman creates much of the humor involved.

The context of this particular scene ends after a snake was released in the hotel bathroom of the female protagonist who has her challenging mother staying with her. Victoria, the protagonist, has just killed the deadly snake. Some writers might have stopped at that point, with a chapter ending like this:

ROUGH DRAFT: *Victoria felt the after-burn of the adrenaline coursing through her system and making her whole body shake. Who could have left the snake in her shower? Intentional or not? And why her?*

This version keeps the focus very much on the external mystery plot line and while there are hooks present, that do raise questions, it's more of a summation, wrap up chapter ending when what the author was going for was a stronger breathing moment using the mother-daughter dynamics. The character speaking first is the mother.

> [End of scene, chapter 28]
> "Are you all right?"
> "I fell pretty hard, but I'm fine." Victoria rubbed her hip; there'd be a bruise within hours.
> "Thank God. I should get some ice—"
> "It's okay, Mom. Don't worry about me."
> "Not for you. For the snake."
> Oh. Her mother thinking more clearly than she was. "For evidence. That's a good idea, Mother."
> "Evidence? What evidence? I've got a craftsman in Miami who can make a killer handbag out of that beauty."
> —Paul Levine—*Deep Blue Alibi*

Instead of drama this ending builds up to the Humor Hook and ends with it as well as with a Surprising Situation, Totally Unexpected, Surprising or Shocking Dialogue and Question(s) Raised Hooks. A five-hook ending that also gives the reader a chance to catch their breath after the high-tension fight between poisonous snake and protagonist.

This next example comes from a steampunk novel. The variety of examples here helps show the versatility in using the Humor Hook to relieve tension, impact pacing, give the reader a breath before plunging your character(s) into greater danger or to create stronger empathy between the reader and character.

At this stage of the story we're reading up to the climax [or black moment as it's called for romance writers] so the tension is increasing but the author wanted to keep the focus not only on the external events in the story—a threat to a Queen Vampire's hive—but also on the protagonist who, while not a traditional vampire killer, is soulless, which makes vampires very wary of her proximity. The series of books with protagonist—Lady Alexia Maccon—is known for her wit as well as her ability to find herself in the middle of funny, tongue-in-cheek situations in a character-driven romp of a series.

In this particular end of chapter the author might have stopped with a sentence leaving all of the focus on the approaching external threat. Like this:

ROUGH DRAFT: *"Now," said Alexia, "I do so hate to do this to you all. But really, our safest bet would be to get out of here."*

Because the reader knows a dangerous mechanical beast called an octomaton is coming after the vampire queen and, if the queen does not leave (or swarm as leaving is called in the story) she will certainly die, which will upset the balance of power in Victorian England. So Alexia's challenge is to make the queen act. The rough draft leaves the question of escape open but gives no flavor of the comedic elements of this story, even here while approaching the do-or-die moment of the story. If Alexia remains to help the vampires, she and her unborn child might die. If she escapes without trying her utmost to get the vampires to swarm, and they die, there can be dangerous and long-reaching impact to Alexia's family and her world.

Let's see how the author approaches the end of chapter 13 of 17 chapters - leading to the climax/black moment.

*"Now," said Alexia, "I do so hate to do this to you all. But really, our safest bet would be to get out of here."*

*The countess shook her head. "You may leave, of course, Lady Maccon, but — "*

*"No, no, both of us, I insist."*

*"Foolish child," said the Duke of Hematol..."How can anyone know so little of vampire edict... Our queen cannot leave this house. It is not a matter of choice — it is a matter of physiology."*

*"She could swarm." Lady Maccon swung her gun once more toward the vampire queen.*

*Lord Ambrose hissed.*

*Lady Maccon said. "Go on, Countess, swarm. There's a good vampire."*

*The duke let out an annoyed sigh. "Save us all from the practicality of soul-suckers. She can't swarm on command, woman. Queens don't just up and swarm when told they have to. Swarming is a biological imperative. You might as well tell someone to spontaneously combust."*

*Alexia looked at Lord Ambrose. "Really? Would that work on him?"*

*At which juncture the most tremendous crash reverberated through the house, and guests at the party below started screaming.*

*The octomaton had arrived.*

*Lady Maccon gestured with her gun in an arbitrary manner. "Now will you swarm?"*

— Gail Carriger — *Heartless*

See how building to the humor element in the very last line keeps the focus squarely on this delightful character, who is not swashbuckling or intense as much as she's over-the-top zany; her and the antics she finds herself in.

This last example can be found at the end of a chapter from an urban fantasy novel. It's about mid-point through the story where traditionally something very unexpected occurs in the plot line that changes the external drive of the story.

The author might have had a dramatic fight scene with her vampire killing protagonist who works hand in glove with humans of the St. Louis police department to fight preternaturals; creatures whom most of those in the area don't even know exist. Something like this:

ROUGH DRAFT: *Anita Blake didn't want to come up against one more psychopathic preternatural killer but that was her job so here she was.*

There is potential in this line but no Humor Hook and no sense of Anita's personality or the tension of the scene. So let's see how the author ends her chapter with a conversation with Dolph and Zerbowski (human law enforcement) who are with Anita as they are approaching an unknown threat.

> *[End of chapter 17 – mid-point of the story.]*
> *"You're our expert. Why don't you sound sure?" Dolph asked.*
> *"If you would have asked me if a vampire could plow through five feet of silver-steel with crosses hung all over the damn place, I'd have said no way." I starred into the black hole. "But there it is."*
> *"Does this mean you're as confused as we are?" Zerbowski asked.*
> *"Yep."*
> *"Then we're in deep shit," he said.*
> *Unfortunately, I agreed.*
> — Laurell K. Hamilton — *Circus of the Damned*

Can you see how the tension builds via dialogue which, when ended on a black sense of humor external line by Zerbowski and followed by the last internal dialogue line by Anita creates a one-two punch of sometimes you have to laugh when you would rather cry type of witty humor. This earns the Humor Hook along with Surprising or Shocking Dialogue (both external and internal), Foreshadowing with Warning, Action/Danger, a Surprising Situation (that the expert is as clueless as the humans), and Question(s) Raised Hooks for a strong six-hook end of chapter.

Would this make you want to turn the page and find out what's about to happen? By combining humor (breathing space) with a focus on the external threat and adding in the fact that all three individuals have no idea what they will be dealing with except to know it's deadly and capable of the unbelievable makes this end of chapter a hook winner.

## ASSIGNMENTS:

1.  Study comedians or comedy shows that grab your attention. The monologues of late night show hosts are a perfect venue to listen to comedic lines. Pay attention to how a subject is presented or not presented. What causes you to be surprised, smile or laugh out loud and want to hear more? What are comedians if not masters of understanding and using hooks?
2.  Reading creates an opportunity to focus closely on what grabs your attention with humor, and therefore how you can also do so with tight, focused and powerful words (when they work).
3.  Even in dark or gently-paced stories you can find humor and thus humor hooks. Look at where they are used: after a major turning point in a story or to help decrease tension? Read intentionally to study humor, and to identify the type of humor that works for you and works for the kind of a story you are reading.
4.  Another tool to study humor is to watch movies or TV shows, and not just the comedic ones. Buddy movies

use a lot of humor to keep the tension in check and to reveal friendship, love or emotion in a subtle but impactful way.

### RECAP:

- If your story is not comedic you can still use the Humor Hook.

- The use of the Humor Hook at the end of scenes or the end of chapters can give your reader some breathing space before you plunge your character back into action, trouble, or danger.

- Because humor can be very subjective, make sure if you are using the Humor Hook that it is appropriate to your genre and core readership.

- Humor can include a continuum of emotional intensity from a slight smile to laugh-out-loud funny.

- Using humor, in any way in your story, tends to bring about a decrease of tension on the page.

- Use the Humor Hook strategically at key hook locations in your story vs. always buried in the midst of a scene.

- The sooner the author can let the reader know the tone and type of story they are offering—a fun, light read vs. an angst, emotionally-volatile story—makes it easier to target your core reading market.

- Using the Humor Hook can be a quick way to create empathy with your protagonist.

- To see if you are using the Humor Hook, especially in the opening sentence or page, ask yourself if a comedian was saying the line or lines out loud on stage would you expect some kind of reaction from the audience? No reaction probably means no Humor Hook.

- The Humor Hook is often revealed via internal or external dialogue, which also serves to give your readers stronger reasons to root for your characters.

- Inappropriate to you humor does not mean it's inappropriate to all readers.

- Inappropriate humor to you as a reader, reading a specific genre where the topic, situation, phrasing, etc., is inappropriate; means you're starting to recognize the nuances of using a Humor Hook.

## SECTION 2: UNDERSTANDING HOOK PLACEMENT

Hooks can be used on every page, but there are several places in your manuscript where you'll want to pay particular attention. Why? Because these key locations are logical places where the reader can set your book down—that's not a good thing, even if it's sometimes necessary. Your intention in using hooks is to give your reader an incentive, a little nudge, to keep reading even just a smidge more to learn the answers you've raised via your hooks. The more this happens, the easier for the reader to seek out your other work or share this experience via word of mouth.

The locations where hooks can make the most difference include:

- Opening sentence of a book (whether it is a prologue or chapter).
- Opening line of the paragraph following the first sentence.
- End of that first paragraph.
- End of the first page (or approximately 225-250 words into your manuscript).
- End of the third page (which is where many editors/agents will read to before either flipping pages to see where the story really starts or looking to your synopsis to see if the rest of the story might hold up to your great opening and, if it does, deciding to invest more time reading).
- End of the third chapter (or whatever arbitrary page number you are using in your submission to editors

and agents package—fifty pages, one hundred pages, etc. Near the end of your submission pages make sure there is a strong hook even if you have to submit fewer pages. Why? So the editor/agent will want to keep reading because you raised a question or reaction in them as a reader).

- Opening a chapter.
- Ending a chapter.
- Opening and ending a scene.
- If writing a series, then near the end of the current book.

## PART 1: OPENING PARAGRAPH AND PAGE

*An opening line should invite the reader to begin the story. It should say: Listen. Come in here. You want to know about this.*

—Stephen King

The reason it's so important to thread hooks throughout your first page—opening sentence, opening paragraph and the end of the page—is because the average reader must be engaged enough on this page to want to turn the page, whether it's on a reading device or a printed page.

The moment a reader moves on to the second page is the moment that most readers decide to purchase a book. Of those readers who didn't buy based on that first paragraph a certain percentage will still buy, but only if you hook them deeper in the first page and convince them to keep reading.

**NOTE:** Understand and use hooks correctly and you have a stronger chance on that first page to land a sale. Get them wrong and lose your sale within the first paragraph.

Without engagement, without pulling a reader deeper and deeper into that first page and on to the next, it's easy for a reader to find another book. The more book options available, the more important it is to engage and compel a reader to keep reading. Give them good reasons to want to discover more about YOUR story, YOUR characters, the situation and the world you've created.

Earlier we looked at the first three sentences of Anita Diamant's novel, *The Red Tent*, as an example of the use of the Evocative Hook in a historical novel. Let's look at how she keeps the unique language that helps create that hook while crafting more hooks deeper into her first paragraph.

First, let's examine a rough draft, assuming the author focused on the information she was trying to impart to the reader before she wrote deeper into the POV of her protagonist and focused on crafting hooks.

ROUGH DRAFT: *You might know my name if you've read your bible, except the names of my brothers are more well-known. My story was shared incorrectly. So wrong that my name became lost. But I had a name. It was Dinah.*

The above reveals what the author wants to share to the reader in her first paragraph but that's about all it does. Unfortunately, in this draft the reader is not only being told the story versus being shown, but also the writing is choppy and contains few hooks, which means there's not a lot of incentive to keep reading. Let's compare the above to Diamant's actual approach to see if you'd be engaged enough to read more. I'll include the first three sentences that set up the next two paragraphs so you can see the flow in context.

*We have been lost to each other for so long.*
*My name means nothing to you. My memory is dust.*
*This is not your fault, or mine. The chain connecting mother to daughter was broken and the word passed to the keeping of men, who had no way of knowing. This is why I became a footnote, my story a brief detour between the well-known history of my father, Jacob, and the celebrated chronicle of Joseph, my brother. On those rare occasions when I was remembered, it was as a victim. Near the beginning of your holy book, there is a passage that seems to say I was raped and continues with the bloody tale of how my honor was avenged.*
— Anita Diamant— *The Red Tent*

At this point Diamant's target readers—those who love historical novels or women's fiction, literary novels, or just beautiful word painting—would be clearly engaged. Other readers might too, which is the secondary target market. Readers who only read the same type of books—westerns or action-adventure or thrillers—might not keep going because they've been given enough of a sense of what the story is about and how it might unfold to know this is not their type of read. And that's okay. There's a book for every reader, which also means not every book is meant to be appreciated by every reader.

**NOTE:** Focus on your core reading audience first, meet their expectations and don't worry about the outliers, until you've nailed the story for your core audience.

Now back to the Diamant story. Let's pull apart the previous first paragraph to see what hooks are included:

*This is not your fault, or mine.* [Evocative Hook plus Surprising or Shocking Dialogue Hook—first person internal.] *The chain connecting mother to daughter was broken and the word passed to the keeping of men, who had no way of knowing.* [Question(s) Raised–why? What happened? Who is this?; Foreshadowing without Warning Hook and possibly a Surprising Situation Hook.] *This is why I became a footnote, my story a brief detour between the well-known history of my father, Jacob, and the celebrated chronicle of Joseph, my brother.* [Unique Character because the reader might recognize that these are historically important names so the POV character relating the story is not your average person, plus the Foreshadowing without Warning Hook.] *On those rare occasions when I was remembered, it was as a victim.* [Surprising Situation and Totally Unexpected as well as new Foreshadowing with Warning Hooks because of the word "victim".] *Near the beginning of your holy book, there is a passage that seems to say I was raped and continues with the bloody tale of how my honor was avenged.*

[Action/Danger, Foreshadowing with Warning, different Question(s) Raised Hooks.]

There are strong reasons that this debut novel of the author hit the major bestseller lists and remained there for years, and one of those reasons was how she skillfully and intentionally kept the reader engaged in a novel about women in a time period relatively unknown, even if the original story idea came from one of the most well-known of books — the Bible.

Let's go deeper into another first paragraph in a mystery this time to show you how the author threads in several more hooks before the reader comes to the end of the paragraph and, in this case, to the end of the page.

OPENING LINE: *I celebrate the dawn of my seventy-fourth birthday hand-cuffed to a lead pipe.*

MID-PAGE: *They dragged the boy in during the night and we struggled to communicate . . . tears of despair carved uneven grooves down his bloody cheeks.*

TWO-THIRDS down the first page: *He didn't live to greet the new day.*

END OF PAGE: *But his soul was free. I envied him that.*
    — Colin Cotterill — *Love Songs From a Shallow Grave*

Now let's look at these key sentences closer to see the hooks they contain. Remember that once you've used a hook, such as the Unique Character Hook in that opening line, the reader now knows the POV character is an older man, given he just turned seventy-four, in this Surprising Situation and Totally Unexpected Hook reveal. Which means the reader accepts those elements as the norm so they cannot be used again to hook us in the same way deeper into the story. However, they can be used to build upon and craft new hooks. So let's see how Cotterill did just that:

OPENING LINE: *I celebrate the dawn of my seventy-fourth birthday hand-cuffed to a lead pipe.* [Unique Character, Foreshadowing with Warning, Surprising Situation, Totally Unexpected, and Question(s) Raised Hooks here.]

MID-PAGE: *They dragged the boy in during the night* [The reader knows by this time the POV character is in a cell so adding in this new secondary character builds in an Overpowering Emotion Hook as well as Action/Danger Hook—given the age of the individual. If the author had said a man was brought in, the reader most likely would not feel as strong an emotion because we've heard of men in cells, not boys.] *and we struggled to communicate . . . tears of despair carved uneven grooves down his bloody cheeks.* [This increases the Overpowering Emotion as this boy is not resigned, he's in despair, which is a stronger emotion than the previous line created. The first emotion the reader experienced above was because of the situation, this emotion here is because of how the boy is responding to his inability to communicate *and* the situation.]

TWO-THIRDS down the page: *He didn't live to greet the new day.* [Surprising Situation Hook. This does not earn the Totally Unexpected Hook because inmates do die in the type of conditions these two are in, but for some readers it still might be unexpected for them. Plus the danger is increased for the old man because the reader is clearly shown that prisoners die here, which ratchets up the Action/Danger Hook for the protagonist.]

END OF PAGE: *But his soul was free. I envied him that.* [Surprising or Shocking Dialogue Hook. It's internal dialogue but still not what most would say, plus a Foreshadowing with Warning Hook that the POV character too could die, and a

Question(s) Raised Hook for the same reason—what will happen to the remaining man?]

Here's another example. This one from an urban fantasy series with this first page opening the first book in the series.

OPENING LINES: *First demon you summon, it's kind of scary. After a few hundred it becomes just another job. Unfortunately I hadn't reached that point.*

MID-PAGE: *I'm part shaman, part witch, not a card-carrying Wiccan, but a blood-born witch, and one of my abilities was to summon others to me, both human and non-human, but only within a limited range.*

TWO-THIRDS down the page: *Embracing magic was not a piece of cake, because it came at a cost. Always.*

END OF PAGE: *So now I was more witch-wanna-be who had to produce an Echo-demon, and fast, to keep my spot on the team.*
　—Mary Buckham—*Invisible Magic*

Let's pull these passages apart to see which hooks were used and woven in throughout the page to keep a reader having to read just a little bit more and, hopefully, turn to the next page.

OPENING LINES: *First demon you summon, it's kind of scary. After a few hundred it becomes just another job. Unfortunately I hadn't reached that point.* [Unique Character—unless you know a lot of people who are able to summon demons, or know a lot of demons. So two different Unique Character Hooks—a person who can summon demons and the possibility of demons, though this is not as strong yet because the reader doesn't yet know if there are going to be real demons; Foreshadowing with Warning—the assumption that this ability, and its result if achieved, will play out over the course of the story; Action/Danger—demons can be associated with danger; Surprising Situation; Totally Unexpected, Surprising or Shocking Dialogue and Question(s) Raised Hooks. So a seven-hook opening sentence combination and paragraph.]

MID-PAGE: *I'm part shaman, part witch, not a card-carrying Wiccan, but a blood-born witch, and one of my abilities was to summon others to me, both human and non-human, but only within a limited range.* [Unique Character—now the reader learns a different aspect of who this character is, which makes her not the average person you meet on a normal day; Foreshadowing with Warning—that this ability, which is new to the reader, will matter in the story; Action/Danger—the ability to summon non-humans can imply danger to either them or her; Surprising Situation—unless you know people who can do this and Question(s) Raised that are different than those already raised. Five hooks here.]

TWO-THIRDS down the page: *Embracing magic was not a piece of cake, because it came at a cost. Always.* [Different Foreshadowing with Warning Hook than has been revealed so far, Surprising or Shocking Dialogue (internal first person) and Question(s) Raised. Three hooks here.]

END OF PAGE: *So now I was more witch-wanna-be who had to produce an Echo-demon, and fast, to keep my spot on the team.* [Unique Character—an Echo-demon; Surprising Situation, Totally Unexpected, Foreshadowing with Warning—if she succeeds there can be a fallout, and if she doesn't, there can be a fallout, Action/Danger—with an Echo-demon, and Question(s) Raised for a six-hook end of page.]

Can you see how the author kept compelling the reader, through her strategic use of hooks, to keep reading throughout the page?

Let's examine the first page of NYT suspense/thriller author Lee Child's novel, *The Enemy*, and how he doesn't stop with hooks in the opening sentence but continues to thread and build on them as the page continues. Keep in mind a thriller is meant to be fast-paced, which means strong hooks to keep the tension high. This book also straddles another issue series authors must deal with—writing to the reader who knows the other books in the series and writing to the reader new to the series. On top of that, this particular novel is a prequel to the very popular Jack Reacher novels—meaning the events in this story happen to a younger Jack Reacher so the author fills in background details for fans who've followed the series for years while introducing the series to new readers.

OPENING LINES: *As serious as a heart attack. Maybe those were Ken Kramer's last words, like a final explosion of panic in his mind as he stopped breathing and dropped into an abyss.*

FIRST PARAGRAPH: *He was where he shouldn't have been, with someone he shouldn't have been with, carrying something he should have kept in a safer place.*

END OF FIRST PARAGRAPH (midpoint of page): *He had no time to put anything right.*

END OF PAGE: *He just dropped dead and took his secrets with him, and the trouble he left behind nearly killed me too.*
    —Lee Child—*The Enemy*

Let's pull out which hooks have been created to keep the reader moving down this page and engaged enough to continue with the story.

OPENING LINES: *As serious as a heart attack.* [This sentence, being so short, makes it easy for the reader to read the next sentence as the true opening of the story.] *Maybe those were Ken Kramer's last words, like a final explosion of panic in his mind as he stopped breathing and dropped into an abyss.* [Action/Danger — the reader only knows that the character died, but not how, which creates a sense of danger as opposed to an assumption of a natural death. Once the reader knows the character died of a heart attack, this hook disengages. Foreshadowing with Warning — that this death is going to kick start further events that will unfold in the story. Question(s) Raised. Overpowering Emotion given key words — explosion, panic, abyss. At this point, the reader's own emotions are ratcheted up to feel what this man felt dying, and it is not portrayed as easy or peaceful.]

FIRST PARAGRAPH: He was where he shouldn't have been, with someone he shouldn't have been with, carrying something he should have kept in a safer place. [More Foreshadowing with Warning that is different than what's already been introduced to the reader as well as different Question(s) Raised Hooks.]

END OF FIRST PARAGRAPH (midpoint of page): He had no time to put anything right. [Different Foreshadowing with Warning than what's been introduced so far and new Question(s) Raised Hooks.]

END OF PAGE: He just dropped dead and took his secrets with him, and the trouble he left behind nearly killed me too. [Surprising Situation — why should this death possibly lead to the POV character's death question; different Foreshadowing with Warning; Danger; Surprising or Shocking Dialogue (first person internal including author intrusion) and new Question(s) Raised Hooks.]

So Child starts with a four-hook opening line, re-engages the reader throughout the page and ends on a five-hook end of page. The author intrusion that the author used at the end of the page is an approach that once was more common in novels, and we still sometimes see it in veteran writers who became used to this approach. Know it can stand out as old school or, and this is more dangerous, can pull the reader out of the story.

The issue is switching POV, from deep POV (in the emotions, mind and skin of the protagonist Jack Reacher) to author intrusion POV (where the reader is given information from the author through the character as if the character knows what's going to happen in the future). In other words, the reader is being told something bad might happen to foreshadow, raise questions, create danger, etc., even if at this point in the story the POV character doesn't know how events will play out.

One last important issue about using author intrusion is that it alerts the reader to the fact the character survives the upcoming events of the story, which does decrease a story's tension. In this particular story, since it's a prequel to the series, fans of the series already know this fact so it can be a moot point.

This approach, using author intrusion, can be a crutch for an author and, for the newer writer, it is important to consider whether another hook approach might be just as effective. When you reach the status of Lee Child, and know when and how to use author intrusion, you can use it more effectively.

Here's a different example, this one from a young adult novel—a sci-fi/fantasy story.

**NOTE:** When writing to two or more target markets (the primary readers of what you write), you need to think of the expectations of all the intended markets when considering pacing, number and types of hooks to use.

*My name is Marina, as of the sea, but I wasn't called that until much later. In the beginning I was known merely as Seven, one of the nine surviving Garde from the planet Lorien, the fate of which was, and still is, left in our hands. Those of us who aren't lost. Those of us still alive.*

—Pittacus Lore—*The Power of Six*


Let's pull apart this example to see how the author worked hooks throughout this paragraph and ended on a strong ending hook in particular.

*My name is Marina, as of the sea, but I wasn't called that until much later.* [First sentence has two hooks: Foreshadowing without Warning, and Question(s) Raised.] *In the beginning I was known merely as Seven, one of the nine surviving Garde from the planet Lorien,* [Here different questions via hooks are created than were already revealed, so the Question(s) Raised Hook applies as well as a Surprising Situation, Totally Unexpected—if you had not read the series or the back cover blurb in particular, a Unique Character, and different Foreshadowing with Warning Hooks—given the fact that this is an alien being—than that raised in the first sentence] *the fate of which was, and still is, left in our hands.* [The length of this middle sentence slows the pacing so the reader can digest the implication of what they're reading and sets up the hooks in the next two sentences.] *Those of us who aren't lost.* [Foreshadowing with Warning Hook and Question(s) Raised; who are the others? How many are there?] *Those of us still alive.* [Here one of the Question(s) Raised in the previous sentence is answered but another Question(s) Raised Hook is created—What happened? Why? How many are left?—as well as the Foreshadowing with Warning and Action/Danger Hook—the fact some of her fellow Garde are dead.]

So the paragraph starts with two hooks, five are filtered through the second, longer sentence, then two, then three. The author never lets up, leading the reader from the opening line through the end of the first paragraph, not overwhelming them but keeping the tension taut.

**NOTE:** Hooks are built upon one another, so rather than repeating what the reader already knows, find a new insight, a twist, a different way to write what you've written to create new hooks.

Another example, from a psychological thriller which, because the focus in these stories is delving deeper into the human mind and the reasons behind a character's actions and choices, is slower paced than most other thrillers. The pacing is closer to a literary novel, so expect to see pacing sensibilities closer to those types of stories.

Before we get to the actual example, let's pretend the author's initial drafts did not contain the hooks finally achieved.

ROUGH DRAFT: *I'm a crazy guy who is not always sure about what's real and what's not real.*

This sentence might contain a Unique Character Hook if the reader doesn't know many crazy individuals, but the fact that this crazy person had issues with reality is simply a statement of fact for many people in the general population who are at least familiar with some types of mental illness. It's also an example of telling not showing. The reader is not in the skin or deep into the mind of this character, but is being told about the character as if outside his or her head.

Let's see how the author added in hooks to his opening, especially in the first line and the last line of the paragraph and created a strong showing at the same time. Be aware that in this genre there can be a lot more internal narrative, which does slow the pacing of the story. That's why this approach is not used commonly in all genres, especially in thrillers.

*I can no longer hear my voices, so I am a little lost. My suspicion is they would know far better how to tell this story. At least they would have opinions and suggestions and definite ideas as to what should go first and what should go last and what should go in the middle. They would inform me when to add detail, when to omit extraneous information, what was important and what was trivial. . . .*

*A memory that seems one instant to be as solid as stone, the next seems as vaporous as a mist above the river. That's one of the major problems with being crazy: you're just naturally uncertain about things.*

— John Katzenbach — *The Madman's Tale.*


Let's pull apart this opening paragraph to see which hooks are used and where those hooks are working the hardest.

*I can no longer hear my voices, so I am a little lost.* [Surprising Situation, Foreshadowing with Warning, Surprising or Shocking Dialogue, Question(s) Raised and the hint of a Unique Character Hooks.] *My suspicion is they would know far better how to tell this story.* [Foreshadowing without Warning and the Unique Character is cemented here because this is now a person who had once relied on the voices in his head to make decisions for him or her and most readers would consider that unusual, new Question(s) Raised — what story and why would they tell it better? — plus Foreshadowing without Warning that whatever is about to be revealed changed this person to one who cannot hear the voices any more.] *At least they would have opinions and suggestions and definite ideas as to what should go first and what should go last and what should go in the middle. They would inform me when to add detail, when to omit extraneous information, what was important and what was trivial. . . . A memory that seems one instant to be as solid as stone, the next seems as vaporous as a mist above the river.* [The length and word choices of these long, languid sentences create the Evocative Hook as well as show characterization, how this POV character thinks, which is not a hook but creates

Question(s) Raised about how this character will react to events as the story unfolds.] *That's one of the major problems with being crazy: you're just naturally uncertain about things.* [This last line confirms what was a strong guess up to this point, that the POV character can be considered crazy, which cements even more the Unique Character Hook already raised. However, it's not new information so it's not a new hook; Question(s) Raised Hook; Surprising or Shocking Dialogue Hook also applies here because of what the person is saying about himself.]

So the author went from a four- to five-hook opening line and kept building until, by the end of this long, almost page-length paragraph, the core reader of psychological thrillers would be definitely engaged, and readers who want to experience the story from a perspective different than their own, would also clearly understand this book will do that.

Here's a different example, one from a historical mystery series. In a series, for consistency, the author must juggle intriguing a new-to-the-series reader while not repeating the same hook approach, or too much information to the returning reader who already knows about the protagonist or series. It's a fine juggling act. The other issue being handled here is quickly orienting the reader to the fact this story is in a specific historical time frame. The reader wants to quickly be grounded into the world of the story, and the sooner that happens, the better.

The returning reader of this series knows it's set in Victorian London and the protagonist, a man named Monk, is a former policeman now working as a private inquiry agent, a term meaning a detective. Let's see how mystery author Anne Perry achieves so much in hooking the reader into this opening page:

> *When she first came into the room, Monk thought it would simply be another case of domestic petty theft, or investigating the character and prospects of some suitor.*
> — Anne Perry — *A Sudden, Fearful Death*

In the above opening sentence the hooks used are Foreshadowing without Warning and the Question(s) Raised. Two hooks, which can work for the slower pacing of this subgenre of mysteries. What the author does so well here is trade off a lot of hooks for easing the reader into the cadence of the times, the acceptance that 'investigating the character and prospects of a suitor' clearly says we are not in a contemporary mystery.

At the end of this opening page, the reader is again re-engaged, and compelled to keep reading, by new hooks that continue the pacing sensibilities set up by the opening. Look at how the language is very time appropriate, while setting up a stronger Foreshadowing with Warning Hook and Question(s) Raised Hooks that are different than those created by the opening sentence.

> *It was not easy to engage an inquiry agent. Most matters about which one would wish such steps taken were of their very nature essentially private.*
> — Anne Perry — *A Sudden, Fearful Death*

**NOTE:** Balance the number and types of hooks throughout your opening page with the readers' expectations of what they are reading.

## PART 2: PROLOGUES

Prologues tend to confuse a lot of writers as being of lesser importance than the first chapter. That's a mistake. Prologues to the reader, and that includes an editor or agent reader, are to be treated as the opening chapter or scene of your story, so the rules of hooks — first sentence, end of first paragraph, end of first page, end of chapter — all apply.

Let's look at an example from a PI (private investigator) type mystery series set in Alaska. This is the fifteenth book in the series, so the author is writing both for readers new to the series and returning readers. A PI mystery can run the gauntlet from light — two sisters in a small town offering their services for friends and family because they both lost their jobs, or an older retired individual with some type of law enforcement background pulled into solving crime as an amateur with experience — to darker stories — the gritty, stark, dark side of catching a killer from someone with a lot of experience — or something in between.

This example falls into the in between story category, with some darker story themes and occasional on scene violence, but most stories are more about an Alaskan native who walked away from her career in the legal system but finds herself, based on her knowledge of the area and the people, called in to solve mysteries.

These are the opening two sentences in the prologue:

> *She'd had to spell the word weary in a spelling bee in grade school. She'd spelled it correctly, but she never really understood what it meant, until now.*
> — Dana Stabenow — *The Deeper Sleep*

Let's pull apart this example to see which hooks are used and how many hooks the author, Stabenow, is employing here:

*She'd had to spell the word weary in a spelling bee in grade school.* [Question(s) Raised Hook—who is she and why is this important to know; and Foreshadowing without Warning Hook.] *She'd spelled it correctly, but she never really understood what it meant, until now.* [Different story Question(s) Raised and for some readers Overpowering Emotion depending on the reader's firsthand experience with extreme weariness.]

The combination of the two sentences creates a four-hook opening but only after the reader gets to the end of the second sentence. If fewer hooks had been used, the reader might expect a light PI story. If two or more additional hooks were used, the tension would be increased and the reader might expect a darker or faster-paced story.

As written, the author eases the reader into wanting to find out just a little more about who this character is and why she's feeling this way. It's a gentle reeling in of the reader, learning a little more about this woman who'd fallen in love with the wrong man, endured an abusive relationship and saw no way out. The reader is engaged enough to keep reading as the prologue is short and can quickly be read just to find out the answers being raised throughout its pages until they reach the end of the prologue where they find the following two lines:

*A quick hand moved the bucket out of the way so that her head dropped through the hole she had chopped in the ice.*
*The soft splash when her face hit the water was the gentlest kiss she ever received.*
—Dana Stabenow—*The Deeper Sleep*

Here stronger and more hooks—Question(s) Raised, Foreshadowing with Warning, a Surprising Situation, the Totally Unexpected, Surprising or Shocking Dialogue, Action/Danger and a Unique Character [a murder victim is unique even to a die-hard mystery reader]—compel the reader to find out why this woman is killed and who did it.

This next example comes from a fantasy novel that is more epic fantasy than the earlier example we reviewed by Patricia McKillip. Before we jump to George R.R. Martin's prologue opening, let's assume he dashed off a less than stellar initial attempt.

FIRST DRAFT: *Three men rode into a dark forest.*

No epic feeling here and no hooks, not even the Question(s) Raised Hook, though some readers might want to know why they rode into this forest. This approach leaves the reader waiting to be told more as opposed to being drawn into the world of this story or hooked enough to continue reading.

SECOND DRAFT: *The youngest of the guards looked around nervously, not liking the feel of the dark woods.*

A better attempt because now there's a sense of Foreshadowing with Warning and clearer Question(s) Raised used as hooks. This is the point where most writers will stop and call the attempt good. But not George R. R. Martin. Not in creating an epic fantasy series with a dark feel and huge world building.

Here's his prologue opening line:

*"We should start back," Gared urged as the woods began to grow dark around them. "The wildings are dead."*
—George R.R. Martin—*A Game of Thrones*

Now we have:

- Surprising or Shocking Dialogue,
- Action/Danger,
- Foreshadowing with Warning (with the death of these beings there might be ramifications),

- Totally Unexpected (the introduction of the creatures called the "wildings" to new-to-the-series readers can be Totally Unexpected, more so than to existing fans who may be familiar with these beings),
- Unique Character (unless you as a reader know of or have met a wilding, these creatures are unique),
- Question(s) Raised.

This creates a six-hook opening, a sense of an unusual world (with wildings) and enough reasons to want to keep reading to learn more.

The next example comes from the end of the same prologue as above—in the same epic fantasy novel. Here we're building on one line to create a stronger ending line. Before we see how George R.R. Martin builds hooks into this powerful ending to his prologue, let's look first at an assumed original draft.

ROUGH DRAFT: *The man was killed by someone he didn't expect to be killed by.*

There are so many problems with the above sentence, it's hard to focus on what we need to focus on—the hooks, or lack thereof. As written, we end up with one hook—Question(s) Raised. That's it. For some readers that might be enough, particularly if they are already fans of the author. However, for the writer who is growing his or her audience of readers, or who is submitting to an editor or agent, a one-hook ending to a prologue in a dark fantasy would not be enough to keep them reading.

Let's look then at how Martin approached this prologue ending.

*Long elegant hands brushed his cheek, then tightened around his throat. They were gloved in the finest moleskin and sticky with blood, yet the touch was icy cold.*

—George R.R. Martin—*A Game of Thrones*

In more detail:

*Long elegant hands brushed his cheek, then tightened around his throat.* [Question(s) Raised, Foreshadowing with Warning, Action/Danger Hooks.] *They were gloved in the finest moleskin* [Surprising Situation and Totally Unexpected because the average reader isn't expecting a killer described like this] *and sticky with blood, yet the touch was icy cold.* [Surprising or Shocking Dialogue Hook (internal.)]

Can you see how in two powerful sentences Martin compels the reader to turn the page to find out who killed the character at the end of this prologue and why?

Here's another example from a paranormal romance novel. Notice how the author, J. R. Ward, treats her prologue's opening page in the same way a smart author treats their first chapter page. She builds in the hooks in the first sentence; mid-page and end of page.

OPENING SENTENCE: *Some two years after the fact, when Jim Heron was no longer in special ops, he would reflect that Isaac Rothe, Mathias the Fucker, and he, himself, had all changed their lives the night the bomb went off in the sand.*

MID-PAGE: *As if back then he would have believed he'd end up duking it out with a demon, trying to save the world from damnation.*

END OF PAGE: *But that night, in the dry cold that washed in the second the sun went down over the dunes, he and his boss had walked into a minefield . . . and only one had walked out.*
*The other? Not so much. . . .*
—J.R. Ward—*Crave*

Let's pull apart this opening prologue page to understand why it engages the reader and keeps on re-hooking them.

OPENING SENTENCE: *Some two years after the fact, when Jim Heron was no longer in special ops, he would reflect that Isaac Rothe, Mathias the Fucker, and he, himself, had all changed their lives the night the bomb went off in the sand.* [Surprising Situation, Unique Characters, Danger, Foreshadowing with Warning and Question(s) Raised.]

MID-PAGE: *As if back then he would have believed he'd end up duking it out with a demon, trying to save the world from damnation.* [Surprising Situation and Totally Unexpected, a different Unique Character, Action/Danger – different than what's already been introduced, Foreshadowing with Warning that's again different than what's already been introduced, Surprising or Shocking Dialogue – internal, and Question(s) Raised.]

END-OF-PAGE: *But that night, in the dry cold that washed in the second the sun went down over the dunes, he and his boss had walked into a minefield . . . and only one had walked out.* [Another Surprising Situation and Totally Unexpected, Question(s) Raised.]
*The other? Not so much. . . .*[More Foreshadowing with Warning and Question(s) Raised.]

A very powerful opening to a paranormal romantic suspense, which promises the reader – the paranormal reader, the suspense reader and the romance reader – a hold-on-to-their-hats fast and compelling read.

**NOTE:** Always treat a prologue's hooks with the same care and intention as you do the hooks in the opening chapter. And, if using a prologue, make sure you don't ignore your hooks in that opening chapter page, too.

## PART 3: OPENING A CHAPTER

The reason you want to pay particular attention to the openings of your chapters is because they are a natural place to set a book down, second only to the ending of the last chapter. Most readers these days read last thing in the day, right before turning out the light and sleeping. This predisposes a person to look for a natural point where the story can be set down. If they do, the longer it takes them to return to the story, the easier it is to forget about that novel and start a different one. We've all done this — being unable or unwilling to pick up a book because once we stepped away from the story there were not enough reasons for us to return. That's why you're learning about hooks: reasons for engagement that will intrigue a reader enough to return to your story as soon as they can.

We'll be examining several novels to show that a good writer doesn't leave it to chance as to whether the reader will continue to read or not. These writers do not stop using hooks by creating only a strong opening line or opening page in a novel. They follow up the promise to the reader they made there — that this is an engaging novel that you'll want to keep reading — and they do this by continually creating compelling lines through the use of strategic hook placement.

Here's an example from a historical romance where the author writes for both romance readers and readers of historical novels. This means she juggles the pacing and expectations of both targeted readers.

OPENING LINE: *Don't believe the stories you have heard about me.*

END OF FIRST CHAPTER: *Africa. The very word conjured a spell for me, and I took a long drag from my cigarette, surprised to find my fingers trembling.*

*"All right," I said slowly. "I'll go to Africa."*

END OF THIRD CHAPTER: *"You've already made the betting book at the club," he told me, holding me fast with those remarkable eyes.*

*"Have I, indeed? And what are the terms?"*

*"Fifty pounds to whoever names the man who beds you first," he stated flatly. . .*

*I rose and went to the door, turning back just as I reached it. I gave him a slow, purposeful look, taking him in from battered boots to filthy, unkempt hair.*

*"Tell me, who did you put your money on?"*

*He stretched his legs out to cross them at the ankle. He folded his arms, behind his head and gave me a slow grin. "Why, myself, of course."*

—Deanna Raybourn—*A Spear of Summer Grass*

Now let's pull apart the hooks the author used to draw the reader from the first sentence to the end of the first chapter and on to the end of the third chapter, where she raises a strong story question that will take the rest of the novel to answer.

OPENING LINE: *Don't believe the stories you have heard about me.* [Surprising or Shocking Dialogue (internal), Foreshadowing without Warning (first person POV internal) and Question(s) Raised Hooks here, very appropriate for the two genres this author is writing for—those who don't want to inhale a story at a rapid speed, but savor and enjoy bite by bite.]

END OF FIRST CHAPTER: *Africa. The very word conjured a spell for me, and I took a long drag from my cigarette, surprised to find my fingers trembling.*

*"All right," I said slowly. "I'll go to Africa."* [Overpowering Emotion—for the POV character as shown by her visceral reaction, the beat between her thinking the word—Africa—and her response; Question(s) Raised; Foreshadowing without Warning (this decision will impact the course of the story) and a Surprising Situation (based on the reader knowing at this point that this character came into this interview determined to change nothing in her world to please others.)]

END OF THIRD CHAPTER: *"You've already made the betting book at the club," he told me, holding me fast with those remarkable eyes.*

*"Have I, indeed? And what are the terms?"*

*"Fifty pounds to whoever names the man who beds you first," he stated flatly. . .*

*I rose and went to the door, turning back just as I reached it. I gave him a slow, purposeful look, taking him in from battered boots to filthy, unkempt hair.*

*"Tell me, who did you put your money on?"*

*He stretched his legs out to cross them at the ankle. He folded his arms, behind his head and gave me a slow grin. "Why, myself, of course."* [Because this is three chapters in, the reader already knows the POV character has arrived in Africa and has met a stranger, a very attractive stranger, while waiting to speak to the governor of the country. Here the author builds to the Surprising or Shocking Dialogue Hook last line by adding in a Surprising Situation Hook—that total strangers are making such a risqué bet on this woman; Foreshadowing without Warning that this meeting will play out over the course of the story; Question(s) Raised and the Totally Unexpected—definitely to the POV character but also to the reader.]

The next example also comes from a historical romance but one with a mystery/suspense element. Pay attention to how quickly the author establishes the historical tone as well as the suspense layer and how she engages, or hooks the reader, and leads her deeper into the story, but at a gentle pace. The novel is not meant to be pure historical or pure suspense — the focus, the reason the core readers are reading, is for the romance. This is the first sentence in the story.

> *The heel of one of her high-button boots skidded across the stream of blood that seeped out from under the door.*
> — Amanda Quick — *The Mystery Woman*

In this sentence above there's a Surprising Situation Hook, Question(s) Raised Hook, the hint of Action/Danger (based on a stream of blood) and the Foreshadowing with Warning Hook. The need to engage mystery/suspense readers requires more hooks than if the author was writing only to historical romance readers.

Let's look at how an urban fantasy novelist uses hooks at the opening of his second chapter to quickly re-engage the reader and raise story questions that push the average reader to continue reading in order to discover the answers.

But let's assume the author wrote a quick initial draft and only later returned, looking for an opportunity to add hooks to the key locations in his manuscript.

ROUGH DRAFT: *The bar we were going to was known to be dangerous. You meet people there but it's still dangerous.*

Pretty straight forward with a possible Foreshadowing with Warning Hook along the lines of there might be trouble happening as a result of the location but it's not very compelling. Let's see how the author, Simon R. Green, approached this chapter opening.

> *Strangefellows is the kind of a bar where no one gives a damn what your name is, and the regulars go armed. It's a*

*good place to meet people, and an even better place to get*
*conned, robbed, and killed.*
—Simon R. Green—*Agents of Light and Darkness*

Now we have a chapter first sentence opening that builds to the hooks in the second sentence. The first draws you into the second and bam—you are hooked with Question(s) Raised, much clearer Foreshadowing with Warning that something is about to happen, the Action/Danger Hook, and a Surprising or Shocking Dialogue Hook (third person internal). At this point, the readers might be thinking to themselves, 'I'll just read another page or two to see what happens to these characters in this kind of place', and they keep reading. That's the power of strong hooks in key locations.

Here's another first line opening, deeper into another urban fantasy story. The deeper you are into a story, the more you have to build on what the reader already knows and make sure your hooks re-engage the reader.

Let's assume the author, Marjorie M. Liu, crafted a less than stellar opening sentence to this chapter. After all, it's Chapter 12 of a book with 18 chapters, and she ended the last chapter with the protagonist getting hit by a bus, which raises very strong story questions. At this point, in the story the reader knows the protagonist is magically protected during the day by demons inked onto her skin and have seen a few occasions where she survived being beat up or shot at. Some writers might be tempted to get lazy here and write something like this:

ROUGH DRAFT: *It really hurt. The bus I mean, in spite of my being protected by the demons who resided on my skin.*

If this was the first time the readers were made aware of the character's protective guardians, there would be some hooks present, but it's a well-known detail by this point in the story.

So let's look at how Liu keeps the reader engaged by layering in new information that contains strong hooks.

> *I had never been hit by anything larger than a dune*
> *buggy — and that was under extenuating circumstances*
> *involving a runaway donkey, a one-legged zombie with a shot*
> *gun, and the unfortunate arrival of a freak sandstorm.*
> —Marjorie M. Liu — *The Iron Hunt*

This line contains the Action/Danger Hook, a Surprising Situation, Surprising or Shocking Dialogue (first person internal) and Question(s) Raised Hooks, which compels the average reader to not only read a few more sentences to find out more of what happened to the protagonist as a result of the bus disaster, but also because it's easier and easier to root for such a unique character that keeps revealing more and more of her world in such a way.

Do not get lazy as a writer by working hard on those initial chapter hooks and neglecting the later chapters. Those matter too, if you want a reader to remember your novel as a compelling read all the way through.

Let's examine an opening to a chapter a little deeper into thriller/suspense author Tess Gerritsen's novel. Deep into this series, this being the seventh book featuring Boston PD Detective Jane Rizzoli and Medical Examiner Dr. Maura Isles, the author chose to start chapter one in the POV of an unknown woman that ended on her realizing a stalker has entered her home. The second chapter features Dr. Isles being present at the unwrapping of a mummy from a local museum and, at the end of the chapter, discovering it wasn't ancient remains she was looking at but a more recent death. Here, at the opening of the third chapter, Gerritsen once again re-engages the reader. But before we look at her word choices, let's assume there was an initial draft.

ROUGH DRAFT: *The two detectives entered the morgue after having been called on a suspicious death.*

Not a lot intriguing or engaging in this opening line because, based on the ending of the last chapter, this is what a reader would expect to happen. This approach would leave a reader waiting for something more and whenever that happens it's easy to disengage from the story.

So how did Gerritsen start her third chapter opening?

*"Is it just my imagination," said Detective Barry Frost, "or do you and I catch all the weird ones?"*
— Tess Gerritsen — *The Keepsake*

Here we have Surprising or Shocking Dialogue, Foreshadowing with Warning and Question(s) Raised Hooks. If nothing had happened in the story up to this point — if the reader wasn't curious to find out about the woman who knew a stalker had entered her home, or the identity of the recently unwrapped mummy — this three-hook opening might not be enough to keep a reader moving deeper into the story. But after the surprise of the last two chapter endings, fewer hooks here actually creates a breathing space for the reader.

The next example is the opening of Chapter 2 from a novel about dissolving relationships written by an author known for his dark sense of humor. In the first chapter the two protagonists — Annie and Duncan — have traveled from England to the United States to tour specific locations associated with an obscure musician who disappeared from the public eye twenty years before. Duncan is obsessed with his musical idol's life and abrupt disappearance, and the trip brings home to Annie that maybe this relationship, which, prior to the trip, satisfied her as an okay one and probably the best she could expect, might not be all that great. The couple has now returned to England, but with this chapter opening it will become clear that irrevocable cracks are appearing in the relationship.

Let's assume the author, Nick Hornby, had to work to thread a few hooks into this first sentence in chapter two.

ROUGH DRAFT: *Annie knew the recent trip made her reevaluate her relationship with Duncan.*

This is a straightforward statement of fact, a telling to the reader what the author wants them to know. In a first or rough draft, this can work because it lets the author know the intention behind what they want to show the reader. Some writers might leave this as is, but the best writers revisit their work, especially in the key locations we're examining for hooks, to make sure they create a stronger reason for the reader to keep reading.

Let's look at how Hornby does this at the opening of chapter two, about thirty-two pages into the novel.

*Annie scrolled back through the photo library on her computer and started to wonder whether her whole life had been a waste of time.*
—Nick Hornby—*Juliet, Naked*

The above is a quiet, subtle deep POV layering of hooks that includes Question(s) Raised, Foreshadowing without Warning and for some readers, Overpowering Emotion (not simply emotion but the kind that can create a visceral response of empathy, understanding or strong memories. Since the dissolution of a relationship is something that many readers have felt firsthand, and depending on how raw or recent the event was, this emotion can be stronger for some than others).

The novel is not meant to be fast-paced, but paced more slowly, so that a reader can ponder along with the characters the changes happening in their lives. A three-hook opening to a new chapter is very appropriate to a slower paced novel.

**NOTE:** Chapters leading to the Crisis (midpoint of a story) and the Climax/Black Moment (when all seems lost or unsalvageable near the end of a story) usually require more hooks than the average chapter opening. These locations are where the tension is intentionally increased in a story.

## PART 4: ENDING A CHAPTER

The end of a chapter is one of the most natural places for a reader to set a book down. The average American reader spends less than an hour per session reading and so is predisposed to look for opportunities to stop reading. Paying particular attention to chapter endings and creating strong hooks there will either produce the type of novel a reader can't put down or one that, if they do, they will be drawn to return to as soon as possible.

**NOTE:** Do not layer in too many hooks at the end of every chapter if it's not appropriate to what you are writing. How do you know? Study authors published in the type of story you want to publish to get a good feel for the average number of hooks readers expect.

This first example comes from the sixth book in a mystery series, deep into the story, at the end of chapter 28 of 33 chapters.

> *. . .I bought them from an old lady, a thief in her own right, but a stupid thief who didn't understand their significance. If only she knew what she really had — "*
> *"What?" Tess was past all patience.*
> *"The very things that Edgar Allan Poe may have been killed for, in his final days in Baltimore."*
> —Laura Lippman — *In a Strange City*

In the above mystery, the reader has learned a lot about Baltimore, where the series is set, and about an unusual shooting death linked with Edgar Allen Poe, given it happened at his grave, as well as being introduced to a series of quirky characters, some of whom were avid antique collectors and some who seemed connected but the dots didn't fit. All of this leads to this telling chapter ending that clearly spells out the stakes in tying together the disparate threads. So the hooks here include:

- Surprising or Shocking Dialogue,
- Foreshadowing with Warning,
- Surprising Situation,
- Action/Danger (with the stakes being raised from interest in Baltimore collectibles to collectibles connected with a famous Baltimore resident),
- Question(s) Raised.

Five hooks at the end of a chapter this far into the story sets off the gallop to the Climax or Black Moment. It increases the pacing and re-engages the reader for the final chapters of the novel.

Let's look at the ending of a young adult novel that combines a sci-fi utopian story line with an action-adventure pacing. At this point in the story, the reader has met three teenagers, two of whom are residents of an elite Albuquerque, New Mexico high school, and a third who has no idea about her past, having recently woken up in the arid landscape outside of Albuquerque with amnesia. The three find themselves pulled through a computer to a very different and very dangerous world. At the end of chapter nine, the teens are responding to sounds of a crying child, much against the instincts of Rayen, the teen with amnesia who senses there might be more than simply a child in distress. The trio has come upon a little girl in the middle of a field, but before they can approach her, an enormous walking crocodile-like creature appears. Before we get to the last three lines as written by the author, Micah Caida, let's assume there was an early draft ending of this chapter.

ROUGH DRAFT: *The creature was very frightening but if we didn't act the little girl was at risk.*

This version above basically sums up the situation and spells out the risks if the teens help the child or don't help her. But not only is the telling approach decreasing the tension, the hooks are minimized to Question(s) Raised; Foreshadowing with Warning and Action/Danger.

How did the author, Micah Caida, approach the end of this chapter to ensure readers would turn the page to find out what was going to happen next?

We're in the POV of the main protagonist, Rayen, in this example:

> *Color drained from Gabby's face. She stared open-mouthed at the beast emerging from beneath the ground then squeezed out a whisper. "The child."*
> *A trap. I hated being right.*
> *Just as much as I hated what I had to do next.*
> —Micah Caida—*Time Trap*

Can you see how utilizing these hooks:

- Surprising or Shocking Dialogue,
- a stronger sense of Action/Danger,
- Foreshadowing with Warning,
- Overpowering Emotion (Gabby's response as well as knowing a young child is in danger),
- Totally Unexpected,
- Surprising Situation,
- and strong Question(s) Raised.

The increase of hooks ratchets the story up to the point the reader *must* turn the page to find out what's going to happen next T.he chapter ending went from three hooks to seven hooks, which means if one or two of the hooks did not resonate with a particular reader, there were plenty of other chances to keep them engaged.

The following two examples come from a novel that's the eighth in the mystery series featuring Chief Inspector Armand Gamache and his associate, Inspector Jean-Guy Beauvoir. In the opening of this story, which is predominantly set in a remote and mysterious monastery deep in the woods of Quebec, the readers are introduced to the monks of the secluded order, but with no clear idea why. Then the story shifts to the city of Montreal and Jean-Guy's budding relationship with Inspector Gamache's daughter.

This is a secret relationship, because Jean-Guy is loathe to hurt his superior by being romantically involved with his only daughter, or to risk losing what has only been a dream for a long time—loving Anne Gamache. During the course of a lazy, relaxed morning, Jean-Guy recites a biblical quote to Anne when he receives a call to prepare to leave with her father on a new case. He does not explain the quote's meaning and departs from Anne, who tells him she loves him, even if he can't say the same to her. He's not a man used to emotions or trusting others' emotions. After his departure, Anne reads the referenced quote which creates the end of chapter one.

> *Then Annie sat on the sofa and sipping the now cool café she flipped through the unfamiliar book until she found it.*
> *Matthew 10:36.*
>
> *"And a man's foes," she read out loud, "shall be they of his own household."*
>
> —Louise Penny—*The Beautiful Mystery*

This chapter ends with the following hooks:

- Foreshadowing with Warning,

- Surprising Situation (not the usual quote you'd expect a Chief Inspector to use to describe how he approaches a murder investigation),
- Action/Danger (the mention of foes and the fact Jean-Guy and her father have left on a murder investigation),
- Question(s) Raised.

This series is not the traditional police procedural but more an examination of the human spirit that's slowly uncovered as one investigator — Gamache — looks at the people involved in a crime while his subordinate — Jean-Guy — sees all involved as potential suspects and thus dangerous.

In chapter two, the two investigators are transported to the isolated location with words of warning from their boat captain, making it very clear that no one, absolutely no one, gets past the front door of the monastery. The reader receives a history of the monks and why law enforcement even being called to this location is very unusual. So the focus, up to this point, has been on the journey and the setting. Thus the ending of chapter two must re-engage the reader as to the focus of the story. Let's assume the author, Louise Penny, scribbled a raw draft before revisiting and strengthening.

ROUGH DRAFT: *The Chief Inspector knew there would be no problem about their being allowed access to the monastery as they had been summoned by the Abbot himself.*

This version does include Question(s) Raised but it is also telling, and who called law enforcement is not as strong a story question as why they were summoned. If this had been the ending of chapter two, the average reader could easily have set the book down. So let's see how Penny kept the beautifully evocative tone of the story while threading in a few stronger hooks.

*Chief Inspector Gamache, Jean-Guy Beauvoir and Captain Charbonneau were about to be let in. Their ticket was a dead man.*

— Louise Penny — *The Beautiful Mystery*

Now we have:

- Action/Danger (presence of a dead man, up until this point the reader might have assumed there was a murder victim, given these are homicide investigators, but after the preceding pages of lyrical descriptions focused on the isolation, the world of the monks, the intrusion of this internal thought beings home the Action/Danger Hook),
- Question(s) Raised,
- Foreshadowing with Warning,
- Surprising or Shocking Dialogue (internal third person POV) and the reader is immediately refocused on the mystery elements of the story.

**NOTE:** The difference between a two-hook chapter ending and a four-hook chapter ending can mean the difference between a memorable read and a so-so read.

Let's revisit a historical romance story's opening line that we looked at earlier. Here we're at the end of the first scene in the second chapter. By this time the hero and heroine have met (it is a romance versus a story with a romantic element), a dead body has been discovered and it's clear the individual was killed and that the female protagonist is at risk. What is not clear to the POV character is whether she is at risk from the hero or someone else, which is used to build to this end of scene hook at the end of the second chapter. The character Joshua Gage is the love interest in the novel.

*"Later Miss Lockwood," Joshua Gage said quietly behind her.*

*She could not decide if the words were a threat or a promise.*

— Amanda Quick — *The Mystery Woman*

This end of scene and end of chapter contains the following hooks:

- Action/Danger (since this is a romance novel, it's seen as an emotional form of danger not life threatening),
- Surprising or Shocking Dialogue (third person internal),
- Questions(s) Raised,
- Foreshadowing with Warning.

That's a four-hook ending. If you were a romance reader, ready to set a book aside because it's late and you're tired, would this end of scene/end of chapter compel you to read a little bit more? If it does, the hooks are working.

Now we're moving on to the end of chapter four in this same novel. Up to this point the reader knows that a man named Euston has threatened the heroine and she has little recourse to protect herself given that she is a woman and he's of a higher social status than she is. This ending creates a Surprising Situation to the character when the hero informs her that he's taken care of Euston, creates the Question(s) Raised Hook (what are the ramifications of what's happening and how will this change the relationship between hero and heroine) and Foreshadows that events are changing for all parties involved.

*By morning Euston would be persona non grata in all of the wealthy homes of London. Gossip traveled faster than a flooded river through the gentlemen's clubs of London.*

— Amanda Quick — *The Mystery Woman*

Keep in mind the genre, so a three-hook ending to a chapter at this point of the story keeps the reader turning the pages while the tension is kept to a simmer as opposed to a full boil.

Here's another example, several actually, from the fourth book in an urban fantasy series. In this series this protagonist, Alex Noziak, a witch/shaman, has been sent to the Underworld with two other companions, to help a young teen who's been kidnapped by a powerful demon. The story combines elements of urban fantasy, action adventure, mystery and a thriller so it must keep all these readers engaged.

What's important to note is that the author keeps building in hooks at the end of her chapters, giving her readers a reason to keep reading, all of her readers. Even without knowing what had happened in the story up to these endings, ask yourself if you as a reader, especially if you're a reader of urban fantasy or the paranormal, whether you'd keep on reading? If you would, the hooks are working.

> END OF CHAPTER 8:
> *Where were we that magic didn't work? And what was I going to do now?*
> *No way did I want to risk hurting Benjamin by fighting my way off the bridge. No way.*
> — Mary Buckham — *Invisible Journey*

Action/Danger, Foreshadowing with Warning, Question(s) Raised, Overpowering Emotion Hooks.

> END OF CHAPTER 9:
> *He just turned and started walking which, given the length of his legs, meant I had to double-time for us to keep up. But I did.*
> *I hoped it wasn't the last bad decision in a long line of iffy ones I'd made lately.*

—Mary Buckham—*Invisible Journey*

Surprising or Shocking Dialogue, Question(s) Raised, Foreshadowing with Warning Hooks.

### END OF CHAPTER 19:

*I screamed. And screamed. And screamed, as heat blasted through me – acid etching my blood, firing every nerve into hyper-sensitive.*

*And between one harsh, pain-washed breath and the next, I woke up.*

*Then wished I hadn't.*

—Mary Buckham—*Invisible Journey*

Surprising or Shocking Dialogue (internal), Question(s) Raised, Foreshadowing with Warning, Action/Danger, Surprising Situation, Overpowering Emotion Hooks.

### END OF CHAPTER 21:

*We stood in the middle of an island. All around us the sand gave way to what looked like a river – a rolling, seething river of fire. I'd seen pictures of magma but they paled in comparison to this. Easily two hundred yards wide on all sides, the fire oozed along – oranges and reds and yellows twisting and tumbling together.*

*But that wasn't the worst part. Within the river were body parts – heads and arms and hands – all twisting and straining.*

*But no sound. Open mouths caught in mid-scream, but nothing audible was there.*

*"Look at the edges," Mandy whispered next to me, chewing her lower lip.*

*I wanted to ask what edges. Instead I followed the direction of her gaze. Like a sand castle built too close to an ocean's brutal waves, the island silently, relentlessly eroded as the river ate away the fragile sand.*

*Soon it'd sink into that river. . . .*

—Mary Buckham—*Invisible Journey*

Surprising or Shocking Dialogue, Question(s) Raised, Foreshadowing with Warning, Action/Danger, Surprising Situation, Totally Unexpected Hooks.

END OF CHAPTER 24:
*"Which way?" Mandy's voice sounded like she was screaming in the noiseless jungle. Which she wasn't, but up against quiet this thick, it came across that way.*

*Kelly pointed but said nothing.*

*I didn't either as I stepped forward, waiting for the boogieman to pop out from behind every over-sized leaf, every thick trunk, every twisted, splayed fern.*

*My mistake was I wasn't looking behind us.*

—Mary Buckham—*Invisible Journey*

Surprising or Shocking Dialogue, Question(s) Raised, Foreshadowing with Warning, Surprising Situation, Totally Unexpected, Action/Danger Hooks.

END OF CHAPTER 40:
*Step after hesitant step, we skidded down a pebbly slope, the whispering wails increasing, the suffocating heat increasing, the annoying sweat rolling out of our pores. By the time the walls squeezed in so close I bruised my arms and elbows every third step, I was sure this place couldn't get worse.*

*I was wrong.*

—Mary Buckham—*Invisible Journey*

Surprising or Shocking Dialogue, Question(s) Raised, Foreshadowing with Warning, Action/Danger Hooks.

The author compelled the reader to turn that page at the end of one chapter to read even a little further into the next chapter, where more hooks were threaded through. The number of hooks in the later chapter ending examples above are based on the thriller, action-adventure elements of the story as the story moves toward the midpoint and the climax of the story. If the story had been straight urban fantasy, the author might have decreased some of the hooks, but not many because those novels are also considered fast-paced.

**NOTE:** Regardless of what you write, do not ignore your end of chapter hooks.

Now let's examine how thriller writer Lee Child ends several chapters in a row. In chapter one, the reader is introduced to the protagonist—Jack Reacher—who in this particular story finds himself in a new duty station as a Military Police Major investigating the unexpected and suspicious death of a General near the base.

The first chapter focuses on the mystery elements of the story—a dead general is found at a pay-by-the-hour motel in suspicious circumstances and the crime scene is laid out in some detail. The author doesn't leave the ending of this chapter without re-engaging the reader. How? Like this:

*"Depends what else was in the briefcase," I said.*

—Lee Child—*The Enemy (end of 1st chapter)*

Bam! Not only does the investigator have a high-ranking officer dead, one who had no business being in the area where he died, but Child makes sure there are Foreshadowing with Warning, a Surprising Situation, strong Question(s) Raised and the Totally Unexpected Hooks. Which compels the reader to read at least one more chapter. In this kind of suspense novel the chapters are kept shorter to increase the pacing so that the decision to read just a little further is easier to make, especially with the strategic placement of hooks.

In the second chapter, the protagonist and his assistant have traveled to the home of the deceased's wife to see what she might know about why her husband was found where he was. This is what happens at the end of this second chapter:

> *Off to the right was a den or a study. Its door was open. I could see a desk and a chair and dark wood bookcases, I took a cautious step. Moved a little more.*
> *I saw a dead woman on the hallway floor.*
> — Lee Child — *The Enemy* (end of 2nd chapter)

Now we have Totally Unexpected, Surprising Situation, Action/Danger, Foreshadowing with Warning (that there's more at play here with both the general and now his wife, who the protagonist had been seeking, being found murdered) and Question(s) Raised Hooks. A five-hook chapter ending used to keep the reader engaged. Thus far the focus has been on the mystery elements of the story — more than one suspicious death and why.

Chapter three continues with the investigation, but at the end of chapter four, there's a shift in the story line to a secondary plot line that uses dialogue at the end to build to a killer hook and raise new story questions. The whole focus up to this point has been the death investigation and the world of the U.S. Army. At the end of this chapter we see how Child layers the story by bringing in a secondary plot which is going to cause complications for the protagonist when the character returns a phone call from his brother, Joe. There had been messages from Joe through each of the preceding chapters, but here the protagonist, Jack, deals with responding to his only sibling with whom he hasn't spoken in three years.

> *"Hey, Joe," I said.*
> *"Jack?"*
> *"What?"*
> *"I got a call."*

*"Who from?"*
*"Mom's doctor," he said.*
*"About what?"*
*"She's dying."*
— Lee Child — *The Enemy (End of fourth chapter)*

What the author does so brilliantly here is create:

- Surprising or Shocking Dialogue Hook (builds up to the last line),
- Foreshadowing with Warning,
- Question(s) Raised,
- Surprising Situation,
- Totally Unexpected Hook.

This five-hook ending easily leads the reader to continue into the fifth chapter in the novel.

For some readers, there could also be the Overpowering Emotion Hook, which is even stronger for those who have dealt with the death of a remaining parent.

If the reader was inclined to set the novel down, they might now be enticed to read just into the beginning of the next chapter to see what the news means to the character. Child remains on the bestseller lists because he'll make sure that next chapter opening is threaded with hooks to keep the reader engaged.

This next example is the end of the first chapter of a young adult novel by Pittacus Lore. We've examined the opening sentence to this book earlier, as well as the hooks used at the end of the first paragraph. Now we're going to examine how Lore re-engages the reader at the end of a chapter that lasts only four pages.

The length helps keep the pace flowing through a chapter that's mostly introspection and back story. The more narrative, the slower the pace of a story can be, so we're paying particular attention to how Lore picks up the tension at the end of this paragraph, which induces the reader to keep reading.

The set up to this ending is that the POV character has discovered online a young man named John Smith who might be a Lorien, a being from another planet, like herself. He came to public attention through his involvement with a school being destroyed and several students killed. She's been trying to get to a computer to learn more about him but keeps running into obstacles.

Before we look at the author's words, let's assume he had to work on building in his hooks.

FIRST DRAFT: *I want to find this missing boy called John Smith because I feel he might be important.*

Maybe a Question(s) Raised Hook here and a hint of Foreshadowing without Warning Hook, but the reader is being told, which creates a passive reading experience.

SECOND DRAFT: *I'm afraid this boy named John Smith is important and I'm afraid for him at the same time.*

A stronger Foreshadowing with Warning Hook here and a Question(s) Raised Hook so no additional hooks than in the last version, even as we have a little more emotion on the page. Not the Overpowering Emotion Hook, just emotion. Now let's look at how Lore leads the reader through the last paragraph, building hooks throughout.

> *Perhaps John Smith, if that's his real name, is merely a boy with a grudge who was pushed too far. But I don't think that's the case. My heart races whenever his picture appears on my screen. I'm gripped with a profound desperation that I can't quite explain. I can feel it in my bones that he's one of us. And I know, somehow, that I must find him.*
> — Pittacus Lore — *The Power of Six*

Pulling the example above apart can show us how Lore builds his hooks and how he makes sure that he uses multiple hooks so those readers who respond to one type of hook over another might still be engaged. Notice also that Lore understands his target audience—young adult readers—and does not overwhelm them with too many hooks.

*Perhaps John Smith, if that's his real name, is merely a boy with a grudge who was pushed too far.* [Question(s) Raised Hook plus a hint of the Action/Danger Hook, but not a strong hook yet, more a hint.] *But I don't think that's the case.* [Foreshadowing without Warning and different Question(s) Raised Hooks.] *My heart races whenever his picture appears on my screen. I'm gripped with a profound desperation that I can't quite explain.* [These last two sentences include the Overpowering Emotion Hook, both viscerally and through internalization—heart races, gripped, profound desperation—to clearly indicate what the POV character is feeling and how strong the emotions are.] *I can feel it in my bones that he's one of us.* [Surprising Situation, except the reader might have guessed this by this point. Here the POV character is making it more a statement of certainty and Question(s) Raised.] *And I know, somehow, that I must find him.* [Stronger Foreshadowing with Warning Hook here both in motivation for her next actions and a hint of what she plans to do next. Plus a Question(s) Raised Hook—will she go after him? What's going to happen next? Is he really one of them?]

**NOTE:** Scene and Chapter ending hooks often build toward that final line with other hooks so that the last hooks are enhanced for the strongest scene and chapter endings.

The next examples come from another urban fantasy novel and are used to show that the author is a New York Times author because she rarely ends a chapter without recommitting the reader to the story through the strategic use of powerful hooks. Without going into any detail about what's been happening up to the end of chapter four in the novel, which is where we'll pick up our first example, see if you as a reader, are hooked enough to want to find out even just a little more?

> END OF CHAPTER 4:
> *I gave them a hard look. Walked to the door. Opened it.*
> *And found a demon waiting on the other side.*
> — Marjorie M. Liu — *The Iron Hunt*

Surprising Situation, Totally Unexpected, Danger and Question(s) Raised
Hooks.

> END OF CHAPTER 8:
> *But my legs wobbled. My heart thundered.*
> *I was scared. Really scared.*
> *Just not for me.*
> — Marjorie M. Liu — *The Iron Hunt*

Overpowering Emotion, Foreshadowing with Warning, Action/Danger, Question(s) Raised Hooks.

> END OF CHAPTER 11:
> *I heard the roar of a large engine. I turned, and the sun*
> *blinded my eyes. Hands touched my back.*
> *Someone pushed.*
> *And a bus hit me.*
> — Marjorie M. Liu — *The Iron Hunt*

Danger, Totally Unexpected, a Surprising Situation, Foreshadowing with Warning, and Question(s) Raised Hooks.

As you can see with the previous examples, the author keeps raising story questions with her hooks and knows the ends of chapters play an important role in doing just that.

The next example is from a Gothic Romance, which opens in the historical context of the eighteen hundreds in England. Readers of these novels expect a hint more mystery and danger to the romance with almost a melodramatic approach, which you'll see at the end of chapter one. The chapter opens with the female protagonist being made aware that after the death of her father, for whom she'd been care-taking, now, as a single woman and not yet married, she's placing a burden on her sister and brother-in-law, especially after she turns down the offer of marriage from a suitable, if ever so boring, suitor. So the protagonist has made a decision to visit a school chum far removed from the constraints of England.

The reader wants a sense of danger, but not too much, a sense of mystery, but more romance than dead bodies or threats, and is open to a slower pacing because the intention is the enjoyment of the history and the growing romance that contains a hint of risk. Let's see how the author, Deanna Raybourn, keeps all these elements in play and re-engages the reader at the end of the first chapter.

*"That is kind, Charles. And I promise to send word if I need you. But what could possibly happen to me in Transylvania?"*
—Deanna Raybourn—*The Dead Travel Fast*

Notice the strategic use of the following hooks:

- Foreshadowing with Warning (since most readers associate the location mentioned as being the home of vampires),
- Action/Danger (for the same reason as the last hook),
- Surprising or Shocking Dialogue,
- Question(s) Raised.

The reason the Surprising Situation or Totally Unexpected Hooks do not apply here is because the reader has already been informed of her destination. So a four-hook ending—

which is about as tense a chapter ending as the average reader wants for a Gothic Romance.

**NOTE:** Always keep in mind your core reading audience and their expectations for the number of hooks while remembering that regardless of what you write, the key placement locations of hooks will remain the same.

The next example is from an older mystery series about a middle-aged woman who wants to do something more with her life, so she volunteers to work for the CIA. She's initially slated to be a courier, which was considered a relatively safe job, but as the series progresses the protagonist, Mrs. Pollifax, finds herself in more and more unusual situations. This would be considered an amateur sleuth series because Mrs. Pollifax is not trained to be a spy or deal with international skullduggery, but manages with her own skill sets to get herself, and others, out of trouble.

This genre is meant for a lighter read, which means less tension on the page so hooks that create Foreshadowing with and without Warning, Question(s) Raised or Surprising Situations Hooks are more often utilized than Action/Danger, Evocative or Totally Unexpected Hooks. However, every once in a while, especially as you're leading the reader toward the first turning point of the story (One-fourth to one-third of the way into the novel), crisis point of the story (midpoint) or climax (near the end), stronger hooks can be used because they raise more questions and increase tension.

This example comes at the end of chapter six of twenty-one chapters, so near the first turning point, which shows the reader the simple assignment for this character is about to change. Mrs. Pollifax has arrived at her destination and this is after she's gone to sleep on the first night of a new assignment.

*A moment later she realized that not only was the door open but that someone else was in her room with her.*
— Dorothy Gilman — *A Palm for Mrs. Pollifax*

What hooks has the author raised here?

- Action/Danger (especially to a woman alone in a hotel room),
- Surprising Situation (to the POV character as well as the reader),
- Foreshadowing with Warning,
- Totally Unexpected (to the POV character and the reader, too),
- Question(s) Raised.

So a five-hook chapter ending. Compare the above number of hooks to the ending of chapter four in the same story:

*It was time for her to get to work, she realized, and time to forget her impulsive and abortive call on Hafez.*
—Dorothy Gilman—*A Palm for Mrs. Pollifax*

This chapter ending contains two hooks, with one not being that strong—Question(s) Raised and there's a hint of Foreshadowing without Warning that something might be about to happen as a result of her deciding to get to work, but it's nowhere near the number of hooks as in chapter six. Nor should every chapter ending have four or five or more hooks IN THIS TYPE OF STORY.

Here's another example of ending a chapter with a two-hook ending from the same author. Set up to this ending is that the protagonist, Mrs. Pollifax, is traveling with a young girl companion, Debby, in Bulgaria. Their car brakes have been tampered with and both have survived a dangerous car crash. Mrs. Pollifax must reach their destination to meet with an undercover agent and has just discovered that the only transportation available is a motorbike. So these two sentences end the chapter.

*"Oh beautiful," cried Debby ecstatically. "I know how to drive a motorcycle, I ride one lots of times at home."*

*It was in this way that Mrs. Pollifax and Debby roared into Tarnovo on a motorcycle with Debby at the handlebars, the luggage roped to the rear and Mrs. Pollifax squashed between them, one hand inside of Debby's belt, the other clinging to her hat.*

— Dorothy Gilman — *The Elusive Mrs. Pollifax*

Above we have a two-hook ending — a Surprising Situation Hook and Question(s) Raised (what's going to happen next) Hook. This again raises an issue to be aware of in a series story, such as a mystery series or fantasy series, any series where some of your readers may be familiar with the protagonist and main characters. Knowing the type of response to a situation a POV character has, or has had in the past, can decrease the power of hooks, or increase them depending on the situation.

In this particular series, to the series reader, this end of chapter hook might also include Foreshadowing with or without Warning because this reader knows/expects something major to happen right around the corner, but for the moment there's not an imminent level of threat. The average amateur sleuth reader would not necessarily find this a Totally Unexpected Hook because this is the type of situation you often find the Mrs. Pollifax character involved with, but to a new-to-the-series reader this could be seen as a Totally Unexpected Hook.

Even with the only one- to two-hook chapter ending employed in the last example, the author leaves the reader on a fun, light note, which is often expected in an amateur sleuth novel, so target reader expectations are met and satisfied, while keeping them engaged in the story.

Remember that hooks are subjective. Make it easy for your reader to respond to the hook by using more than one in key locations in your story. If two hooks are average for your type of story, aim for two or three hooks, that way you're not creating too many hooks (increasing the tension too much) or too few in case one of your hooks does not work on a reader.

Next we'll look at the ending of chapter three in a young adult novel. The opening of the story started with a one-hook opening, which can be appropriate in a genre where the pacing expectations are not grab-them-by-the-throat-and-don't-let-go.

Up to this point in the story, we're aware the protagonist, a girl named Ever, has survived a terrible car wreck in which her parents and only sister were killed. So the reader has a lot of emotional empathy with this character. We also know she's been relocated to a new school and is hanging out with two other kids seen as misfits by others in the school environment. A very handsome young boy of the same age, named Damen, has just arrived at the school and has been paired with Ever in her English class. Ever is very attracted, but is fighting that attraction even if the reader isn't sure why.

The other fact we know is that Ever is very reclusive because, ever since the accident, she can read other people's auras, hear their thoughts, and this constant barrage of unwanted information is overwhelming.

Let's build toward the ending sentence of the third chapter, a key chapter for many readers as to whether they will continue with the book or set it down and move on to something else more interesting.

FIRST DRAFT: *It's funny that I can't read Damen's aura.*

There's a Question(s) Raised Hook and a hint of possible Foreshadowing without Warning Hook, but it's a little on the vague side. Some readers might find a Unique Character Hook if they think of reading auras as unusual for a person.

SECOND DRAFT: *I wonder why I can't read Damen's aura? I hadn't been able to read his thoughts either. Interesting.*

In these initial versions, the hooks are broken into two sentences with two hooks each, but then the writer waters down those hooks by making it clear the issues raised are not a big concern to the POV character. If that's the case, why should it matter to the reader? All issues raised have thus been effectively neutered.

Let's turn to how the author, Alyson Noël, approached the ending of this important chapter:

> *I mean, how can I explain that ever since the accident, the only people whose thoughts I can't hear, whose lives I can't know, and whose auras I can't see, are already dead?*
> — Alyson Noël — *Evermore*

Now we'll pull apart this ending sentence to learn which hooks the author uses to build to this third chapter in such a way that it compels the reader to keep reading, just a little more, to find out what's going on.

*I mean, how can I explain that ever since the accident,* [Overpowering Emotion—we know she's lost everyone and while the emotion might not be as strong as the first time we've learned this information, it still can tug on a person's emotions. Particularly a teen reader who might often think of their lives, the people they love, as always being just as they are] *the only people whose thoughts I can't hear,* [First beat here. This is not a hook as much as building to a hook. Think of this as the first downward stroke on a drum building to a climactic ending] *whose lives I can't know* [Second beat which creates tension], *and whose auras I can't see* [Third beat which means something is about to happen], *are already dead?* [And the final crescendo of these beats builds to this last phrase, which contains the most hooks.]

The hooks present include:

- Surprising Situation,

- Unique Character (the average reader would not expect this to be the reason the girl Ever wants to NOT be attracted to Damen),
- Foreshadowing with Warning (this twists what's about to unfold in the story),
- Surprising or Shocking Dialogue (first person internal dialogue that the reader did not expect to hear from the girl),
- A Totally Unexpected Hook (in part because of the ramifications),
- Question(s) Raised.

## PART 5: OPENING AND ENDING OF SCENES

The ends of scenes, like the ends of chapters, are a natural place for a reader to set a book down unless you, as the author, compel them to read further to answer questions you raised by using powerful hooks.

A scene is a unit of your story that occurs at a specific location and time that moves your story forward by creating change.

In some novels — suspense, thrillers, action-adventure, westerns — you can find one scene per chapter; pacing that increases tension. In many novels you can find more scenes as the story builds to the first turning or plot point (about one-fourth to one-third of the way into a novel when a decision is made and action taken that will change the course of the story for the protagonist or protagonists), the Crisis point of the story (midpoint) and the Climax or Black Moment (almost the end of the book). Using a single scene in shorter chapters is a way to increase pacing as the author builds to these key turning points in a story, regardless of the type of novel.

The point for a writer to remember is, as you write toward the key scenes mentioned above, it's important to increase your hooks as you open and close these scenes. This builds your tension and increases your pacing. It's also important to utilize hooks at the opening and ending of chapters, especially longer ones, which tend to slow a story's pacing.

**NOTE:** In novels that have longer chapters, and more scenes per chapter, the need to include hooks at the end of the scenes is as important as it is at the end of chapters. The hooks give the reader more incentive to read just a little more.

Let's examine an end of scene example from a novel with strong humor elements that crosses so many genres it's hard to label or define, and thus, in a big box store would be filed under general fiction. It's a relationship novel but on several levels—relationships spawned between fan and idol, between a man and a woman as their staid relationship becomes very rocky, between a man and a woman via the internet and across continents. It's often described as dark humor, male lit.

**NOTE:** The reason it's important to get a reasonable handle on the type of story and the hooks used in that kind of story is to bring home the concept that some hooks can work more effectively in certain types of stories.

A little background leading up to this scene: A British couple—Anne and Duncan—have traveled to the United States to trace key locations associated with a reclusive rock star twenty years after this musician walked out of a concert and effectively disappeared. Duncan is part of a small but fanatical group of fans, connected via the internet, who share a cult-like obsession about theories concerning why the star disappeared. Duncan considers himself an authority on the minutia of this star's brief period of fame.

At this point of the story the reader knows the couple has visited a number of important, if mundane, locations and now they are looking at a toilet used by the star on the last evening before his disappearance.

Let's assume our author had to build in humor, as well as other hooks, to create the end of scene example we'll be examining.

ROUGH DRAFT: *Duncan was so fascinated by the star's toilet episode I thought we might never get away.*

Since the scene started with a focus on the fact that the POV character, Annie, and her love interest, Duncan, had come thousands of miles to see this toilet, at the end of the scene the reference to his fascination is no longer a Surprising Situation Hook or a Question(s) Raised Hook.

It's as if once you've told one potty joke, which might surprise your listener, the next twenty do not have the same impact.

So let's see how Nick Hornby approached the end of his novel's first scene:

> *Duncan took one last look and shook his head. "If toilets could talk, eh?"*
>
> *Annie was glad this one couldn't. Duncan would have wanted to chat to it all night.*
>
> — Nick Hornby — *Juliet, Naked*

End of scene hooks are like end of chapter hooks. The author can build up to them, layering them from the information already imparted to the reader, and create a hook or hooks that are intended to keep the reader willing to read at least into the next scene. So let's pull apart this end of scene to see what Hornby did to re-engage the reader with his hooks. Keep in mind this novel is not a fast-paced, race-to-the-end story, but a slowly unfolding tale focusing on several relationships, including the one between Duncan and Annie that is beginning to unravel.

Here's a breakdown of the hooks used: *Duncan took one last look and shook his head. "If toilets could talk, eh?"* (Surprising or Shocking Dialogue, Surprising Situation, Question(s) Raised.)

*Annie was glad this one couldn't. Duncan would have wanted to chat to it all night.* (Surprising or Shocking Dialogue from Annie — third person internal; Foreshadowing without Warning — that the behavior of Duncan is starting to annoy his partner; Question(s) Raised — how long can Duncan keep finding such mundane trivia exciting, and will this pilgrimage be the last straw for the relationship?)

**NOTE:** Humor can effectively be a hook, but because it is so subjective, you can hit, or miss, with this hook.

Here's another end of scene example in this same novel. At this point, Duncan and Annie have traveled to San Francisco where the musician's former lover now lives. This woman—Juliet—inspired the most famous of the musician's songs as well as the name of Hornby's book. Duncan is on his own in visiting Juliet's house, or walking past it, as Annie is already pulling away from her partner's obsessive fandom.

This scene is about eighteen pages into the story and ends the fifth scene in the book. By this point a lot of writers will assume the reader is engaged in the story—and will go along for the ride—so they forget, or get lazy, about continuing to raise story questions via hooks. The best authors don't—not if they want a long career as a published author who continues to sell books and create strong fans.

> *There was no doubt he'd have been clearer-headed if he'd stopped somewhere near the BART station for a drink and a visit to the restroom. But he'd been thirsty and in need of a toilet before, and had always resisted the temptation to break into a stranger's house.*

—Nick Hornby—*Juliet, Naked*

The end of scene hooks used above include:

- Surprising Situation,
- Foreshadowing without Warning (that a decision and action is about to be made and taken that can change the course of the story but not in an OMG way),
- Surprising or Shocking Dialogue (internal),
- Totally Unexpected (not what the average reader might consider or what this character would do based on what the reader has learned about him so far in the story),

- Question(s) Raised (will he break into her house? What will happen if he does?).

This is a five-hook end of scene at a place in the story that the reader, if reading at night, would most logically set the book down. But by the strategic use of multiple hooks right here, the reader is compelled to read just one more scene or another chapter, where Hornby will add in more subtle but effective hooks.

This next example comes from a mystery series set in Boston and opens the third chapter. Since chapter openings are often scene openings, make sure you study both in looking at how many and what types of hooks are used. If a reader can visually see that the scene is short, it's often easier for them to commit to reading it as opposed to a longer chapter. If reading on an e-Reader, think in terms of the time it takes to read a scene or chapter. The longer it takes to read, the more the use of hooks can keep a reader engaged and moving through the scene or the chapter.

This next example is a short scene opening a new chapter, and yet the author does not ignore the use of powerful hooks in the opening and ending of this scene. This use keeps the reader from an excuse to set the book down, whether in paper or e-Reader format.

*The phone call came at three the next morning.*
*"You remember me?" A woman's voice.*
*"What?" I was still half-asleep. I checked the caller ID: PRIVATE NUMBER.*
*"You found her once. Find her again."*
*"Who is this?"*
*Her words slushed through the phone line. "You owe me."*
*"Sleep it off," I said. "I'm hanging up."*
*"You owe me." She hung up.*

— Dennis Lehane — *Moonlight Mile*

Let's dissect this last passage to pull out the hooks.

*The phone call came at three the next morning.* [Surprising Situation—to the POV character given the time; Question(s) Raised and for some readers Foreshadowing with Warning as most people do not receive calls at this hour unless something bad has happened.]

*"You remember me?" A woman's voice.* [Surprising or Shocking Dialogue and more Question(s) Raised.]

*"What?" I was still half-asleep. I checked the caller ID: PRIVATE NUMBER.*

*"You found her once. Find her again."* [Foreshadowing with Warning that what's happened in the past is going to create events in the current story; Question(s) Raised.]

*"Who is this?"*

*Her words slushed through the phone line. "You owe me."*

*"Sleep it off," I said. "I'm hanging up."*

*"You owe me." She hung up.* [Different Foreshadowing with Warning than above; new Question(s) Raised and more Surprising or Shocking Dialogue.]

Can you see how the author did not simply open and end with a few hooks, even in this short scene, but he continued to thread hooks in throughout to lead the reader into the next longer scene?

Here's an example from the ending of a scene roughly fifty pages into a historical Gothic Romance. By this point in the story the protagonist, a young woman named Theodora Lestrange, has arrived in Transylvania, at the isolated castle of her best friend's fiancé, a man both mysterious and compelling. Theodora is attracted to him but knows she should not be. She has had little contact with him until this scene when he makes an effort to be more of a charming host instead of an aloof stranger.

Since end of chapter and scene hooks can be built upon, I'm including the last two sentences for context. The man and potential love interest (even if he's engaged to the protagonist's best friend) is the first one speaking.

> *"Letters — on such a fine day, when we might walk together? Oh, no, Miss Lestrange. I will begin your education upon the subject of Transylvania, and you will find I am an excellent tutor."*
>
> *He offered me his arm then, and as I took it, I thought for some uncountable reason of Eve and the very little persuasion it took for the serpent to prevail.*
>
> — Deanna Raybourn — *The Dead Travel Fast*

In this example, the hooks present are Foreshadowing without Warning (as the reader can sense that the change in the relationship between these two matters to how the story plays out), Surprising or Shocking Dialogue (for the POV character to create the association of the serpent in the Garden of Eden with this man she's attracted to can be shocking to her, and to the reader) and a Question(s) Raised. That's a three-hook ending to the scene.

What if the author hadn't bothered with the hooks here and stopped her writing with, *". . . you will find I am an excellent tutor,"* or *"He offered me his arm and I took it."* No hooks at all, which would mean that fifty pages into the story, near the beginning of the third chapter, at a natural place to put the book down for the night, the reader would have no reason to turn the page. Instead, Raybourn compels the reader to read just a little more to find out what happens next with this couple.

Here's another example from a contemporary literary novel. In the first chapter the reader is made aware of the fact that a young woman has been arrested and jailed on suspicion of murdering her dying mother. This act has shocked the community where the girl grew up and she and her family are well-known. The last paragraph leads up to the combination of hooks we'll examine, but before we do that, we'll look at what the author might have written.

ROUGH DRAFT: *I didn't kill my mother. I was innocent.*

Because the reader already knows of the situation these two statements of fact from the POV character are what one would expect a young woman jailed for matricide might say, so no hooks here. No questions created to keep the reader wanting to find out more. So how did the author, Anna Quindlen, create stronger end of chapter hooks?

> *No matter what the police and the district attorney said, no matter what the papers wrote, no matter what people believed then and still believe, these years later, the truth is that I did not kill my mother. I only wished I had.*
> — Anna Quindlen — *One True Thing*

Let's look deeper at this previous example and take it apart to see what hooks are present in these two sentences:

*No matter what the police and the district attorney said,* [Notice the use of anaphora, repetition of a word or phrase at the beginning of successive clauses that builds to the shocking internal dialogue of the next sentence. By repeating the same message three times, the reader strongly understands the important point that the character is innocent, which again builds up to the last thought being in contrast to all these opinions.] *no matter what the papers wrote, no matter what people believed then and still believe, these years later, the truth is that I did not kill my mother.* [Bold statement of fact.] *I only wished I had.* [The build-up of innocence to this about face of wanting to have killed her mother creates the hooks of Surprising or Shocking Dialogue (internal), Question(s) Raised, a Surprising Situation, and the Totally Unexpected. Four strong hooks that compel the reader to turn the page to find out what happens next.].

One of the reasons the end of the first chapter is such an important place to re-engage the reader strongly is that most readers, once they have read two to three chapters into a story, will commit to reading the whole story. If they've read the whole story and like it at the end, they will be more disposed to tell another reader or buy your next book. Well-placed hooks at the end of the first chapter lead the reader into those all important second and third chapters.

**NOTE:** Hooks alone cannot make or break your novel, but they can go a long way to making a reader want more of your story.

Here's the ending of a scene from a different type of novel, a private eye mystery. When writing a series based on the same protagonist, the author is balancing what the returning reader knows about the series against the new-to-the-series reader who must be brought up to speed. In the opening of this novel the protagonist, Alex McKnight, is rebuilding his home which had been torched by a killer in the previous book in the series.

Up to this point, the reader knows McKnight's father built the home, and the rebuilding of the log structure is a labor of love, as well as a testament to a past uneasy father-son relationship. Since the story is set in northern Michigan, building a log cabin by hand with snow just around the corner is a foolhardy endeavor, but McKnight is determined to try, struggling by doing it alone—until the local barman, Jackie, gives some advice to the character. The average writer might finish the scene on that note. Advice given—full stop. Like this:

ROUGH DRAFT: *Jackie said, "You should ask him to help you."*
*"No. I don't want to."*

But Hamilton takes the next step by threading in some hooks right here.

> *Hell, maybe Jackie was right. There was one man who could really help me.*
> *But I'd be damned if I was going to ask him.*
> —Steve Hamilton—*Blood Is The Sky*

This is the ending of the fourth scene in the book, eight pages into the story, and with these few lines the reader has new story questions via the introduction of a new character (not a unique one because we don't have enough information on who this person is yet), but a Question(s) Raised Hook is applied, a Foreshadowing without Warning Hook is revealed and a Surprising or Shocking Dialogue Hook occurs because the reader has no idea why McKnight feels so strongly about this unknown new person. The Surprising Situation Hook might resonate with a new-to-the-series reader, but to the returning reader, this might not be surprising.

**NOTE:** Scene and chapter endings in series can have more or less hooks depending on what the reader already knows about the character or reoccurring information.

Let's look at another set of end of scene hooks. This is from an urban fantasy story. This is the end of the first scene in the novella.

**NOTE:** If you have a scene ending before you reach the end of your first chapter, treat that scene hook as importantly as you would hooks at the end of your first chapter.

The lead up to the end of this scene is that the reader has just realized that the POV character shuns being noticed, though we don't have all the details behind why she behaves this way. We also know she is the date of a very wealthy, very powerful man who, for the first time in five years, has appeared at a function with a woman on his arm, her.

But the author does not leave the reader focused on the POV character enjoying her date with an attractive and wealthy man. Instead the last line of the scene reads:

> And that, as my mother had always said, was a good way to get dead, and fast.
> — Marjorie M. Liu — *Armor of Roses*

What hooks are present here?

- Action/Danger — anytime it's clear a person could be killed can be seen as a dangerous situation,
- Surprising Situation — how many of us are given this kind of advice from our mother? And/or a Surprising Situation Hook because of the fact the POV character feels threatened by simply being on a date.
- Foreshadowing with Warning — since this issue is raised, the reader expects the possibility of the POV character being in trouble as a result of her date,
- Surprising or Shocking Dialogue — if you have *never* been warned about dying simply because you had a date then this hook applies,
- Question(s) Raised — is something going to happen to the character because of her being seen on a date with this particular man?

A point needs to be made clear here, regarding the Surprising or Shocking Dialogue Hook. If your mother ever warned you about behavior which could injure or kill you — drunk driving, running around with a wild crowd, doing drugs, jumping off a bridge to go swimming, etc., — then these types of warnings in dialogue would not be surprising or shocking. They are all examples of conversations the average reader might have had, or heard others have, with their mothers. But that's not what's being discussed in this short story. The issue is whether the POV character is drawing attention to herself because of her date; someone who otherwise, in a different story and situation, could be seen as quite a catch. But not in this story, which is why the Surprising or Shocking Dialogue Hook applies, until the reader knows more about the man in question.

**NOTE:** If the topic under discussion is one that the average reader might be familiar with, using that topic in an expected situation will not create as strong a hook as using the hook in an unexpected situation.

This last example ends the first scene in the third chapter of a mystery novel. Most readers are committed to a story by the third chapter or, if they're wavering, the third chapter is usually where a reader will make their decision as to keep going or find another novel. If you, as a writer, are submitting three sample chapters to an editor or agent, this is also a very important point to lure those specific readers into wanting more of the work, and hooks are a valuable tool to do just that.

Let's look at how mystery author, Louise Penny, keeps a reader engaged here with the end of her first scene in the third chapter. In an earlier example we learned the protagonist, Chief Inspector Gamache, and his assistant have arrived at a remote monastery, called to investigate a murder, an unheard of situation for the monks. Only the two officers will conduct the investigation to minimize the impact of strangers being amongst the monks, but it also means the two outsiders will be living with a potential murderer until the case is solved. Let's see how Penny will use that information, already known to the reader, by presenting it in a new way at the end of this scene, but we'll assume there was a rough draft crafted initially.

*FIRST DRAFT:* Jean-Guy did not like the fact that his superior agreed to only a minimal crime scene investigative group at this isolated location.

This approach might contain an element of Foreshadowing with Warning Hook but it's more a plain summation of what's been set up already. So how did Penny approach this end of scene to keep the reader wanting to turn the pages?

> *The door closed behind them with a soft, snug thud. The monk brought up the large key and placed it in a large lock, and turned.*
> *They were locked in.*
> — Louise Penny — *The Beautiful Mystery*

By slowly building to this scene ending, the hooks are enhanced. Beat one is the audio sound of the door closing. Beat two is the visual of this huge key inserted into the lock and engaging it. Then the final statement brings home the final beat — the characters are committed to being locked in with a potential killer or killers. The hooks here include Overpowering Emotion (implied fear for many readers built to this point because of the situation that had been hinted at already but is now driven home); Question(s) Raised and Foreshadowing with Warning.

If the author had summed up the situation telling rather than showing the scene ending, the scene itself would not have been as powerful.

*ROUGH DRAFT: Now the two of them were going to be locked inside with a possible killer.*

In a different kind of novel, by a different writer, this might be used, but it would not have held the sense of finality, of events being put into motion by this very telling sequence of small but irrevocable actions, that is a strong element of Penny's author's voice.

Readers tend to remember, and thus discuss with other readers, the books that kept them turning the pages long after they expected to set the book down. By paying attention to your hook placement, especially at the end of scenes and chapters, where it's all too easy to stop reading, you can make your book stand out for readers.

## PART 6: END OF BOOK

Exit lines are an oft forgotten element in the pacing of a novel. The reason is most writers are just happy the story is over. They've tidied up all the plot and subplot issues. Answered all the story questions and ended on an all's-well-that-ends-well note. Shouldn't that be enough?

No. Not if you want your reader to hunger for your next book, and especially not if you are writing a series book with an overarching story line.

**NOTE:** Some series books can also be stand-alone novels. The protagonist or main characters can return in the next book, but there's no plot thread that unites several stories — the search for something missing, an unresolved relationship or relationships, the resolution of a multi-book external element (save the planet, find/stop an archenemy, solve a problem/challenge).

Writing a stand-alone or single title book, ending your novel with all the story threads resolved, and the promise to the reader fulfilled, can entice the reader to want to read more of your work. It can be that simple — ending too abruptly, leaving huge story questions unresolved or, if resolved, having the solution coming out of left field, all can result in frustration and disappointment for a reader. Do this and it'll make it more challenging to convince readers to come back time and time again to read your work.

Writing a series of stories that contain an unresolved story question creates a built-in hook to re-engage the reader for the next book in the series. That's where the power of hooks comes into play. Remember that at their core, hooks raise questions in a reader's mind. Resolve the issues pertinent to the current story in a strong and satisfactory way but don't forget to hook the reader for your next book.

Here's an example from an amateur sleuth mystery novel with an overarching relationship. The mystery plot is resolved in every novel, but the relationship between the protagonist and two very different men helps drive the series sales and keeps fans returning to find out what will happen between the protagonist and two men who attract her at the same time.

> *He stepped softly into the doorway to my bedroom and knocked softly on the jamb. "Are you awake?"*
>
> *"I am now. You scared the hell out of me."*
>
> *It was Ranger.*
>
> *"I want to see you," he said. "Do you have a nightlight?"*
>
> *"In the bathroom."*
>
> *He got the light from the bathroom and plugged it into a baseboard outlet in my bedroom. It didn't give off much light, but it was enough to see him clearly.*
>
> *"So?" I said, mentally cracking my knuckles. "What's going on? Is DeChooch okay?"*
>
> *Ranger removed his gun belt and dropped it on the floor. "DeChooch is fine, but we have unfinished business."*
>
> —Janet Evanovich — *Seven Up*

Here we have:

- Foreshadowing with Warning,
- Action/Danger (in an emotional sense),
- Surprising or Shocking Dialogue,
- Surprising Situation,
- Totally Unexpected (that Ranger is finally forcing a relationship decision),
- Question(s) Raised.

A six-hook ending that, if omitted, would have left the series readers a little flat although the mystery elements of the story were resolved.

For those not aware of Janet Evanovich's Stephanie Plum series, Evanovich wove a deft dilemma for her NJ bounty hunter, Stephanie Plum, in the guise of two different guys, both of whom she wanted, both of whom wanted her, and both of whom she described as "scaring the hell out of her".

So each book in the series brought the main character—Stephanie—that much closer to making a hard choice between Joe Morelli and Ranger. Thus in the seventh book in the series, *Seven Up*, Evanovich leaves the reader with a very strong story question—what is happening between Stephanie and Ranger? Evanovich played this sexual tension and continuing story question by ending book seven with the hook of one man having showed up in her bedroom.

Evanovich herself credits her largest pre-sales numbers ever—as book eight was coming to market—to ending book seven on such a great hook.

Mystery author Linda Fairstein also uses the hook of a relationship between her protagonist, an assistant DA, and a NYPD homicide detective. Theirs has been a friendship with an implied subtext—could be more than friendship, but through several books one or the other of them was always involved with someone else. In the novel, *Entombed*, this changed as the male character lost the woman he was going to ask to marry him. This in itself raises a great story hook—what's going to happen to this secondary character after receiving such a blow. Then there's the relationship between the primary character—Manhattan Assistant DA Alexandra Cooper and the detective Mike Chapman.

If Fairstein did not have an overarching story question uniting the books in her series, she might have ended the novel with a simple, all's-well-and-done ending. Something like this:

ROUGH DRAFT. *We'd solved the murder and felt good about it. Another win for the NYPD and me. Time to head home for a glass of wine, a hot bath, and a good book.*

No hooks here, just a tidy wrap up that would make it easy for the reader to set the book down and go to sleep. Nothing to raise questions or make them look for the next book in the series as a must-read. So let's see how the author approached her ending. Mike is the detective who just learned his fiancée had been killed in a freak accident, Alex is the female District Attorney who has always been just out of Mike's reach, with the two of them never willing to turn their professional relationship into something more, and Mercer is Mike's best friend and NYPD partner:

> *I started through the doorway to go after Mike. There was something else I wanted to tell him. I had a need to make some kind of physical contact with him as badly as I wanted him to embrace me.*
>
> *"We've got work to do, Alex," Mercer said, clamping a strong hand on my shoulder to hold me in place.*
>
> *I looked up at him, ready to plead my case, but he gave no ground. I turned away from the flashing lights, let him close the door behind us, and walked back to sit in the armchair, surrounded by Poe's dark birds.*
>
> *Mercer pulled up a stool opposite me and stroked my head until I lifted my eyes to look at him. "Let the man go, Alex. Just let him go."*

—Linda Fairstein—*Entombed*

Now we have the following hooks:

- Overpowering Emotion (based on knowing the detective just lost the woman he loved and his best friend, Mercer, realizing the last thing Mike needed was the other love of his life to see him as an emotional basket case),

- Foreshadowing without Warning,
- Surprising or Shocking Dialogue,
- Question(s) Raised Hook.

This is a mystery series, not a romance series, and yet the hook of will-they, won't-they, is still played up. Not with every book, but as one of several story questions raised along with other questions, such as will the primary character stay a DA, will a killer return, will personal healing happen?

Relationships are not the only hook that can be raised at the end of a book, even if it is a good one. Other story questions can set up a follow up book.

In the following thriller novel by author Tami Hoag, the author sets up the kidnapping of a young boy and the hunt for him as the framework for a thriller story set in a small Minnesota town. At the end of the story, the boy is found, which ties up the primary plot line, but the killer is not apprehended, leaving a strong story question suggesting that the abduction and killing of children is not yet over. See how she includes Foreshadowing with Warning, Action/Danger, Surprising or Shocking Dialogue (internal), and Question(s) Raised Hooks in a very subtle way. At this point, the reader knows from the POV of the killer that he's not finished, especially with this particular child and family. By ending in the POV thoughts of the mother of the child, in contrast to what the reader knows, hooks are included and story questions raised for the next novel.

*He could have been lost forever, vanished into a shadow world, as many children were every year, never to be seen again, leaving behind only questions and heartbreak for the people who loved them. For reasons known only to the dark mind of his abductor, Josh had been allowed to cross back out of the shadows. That was all that counted. The truth, justice, revenge, were distant and abstract thoughts for Hannah. Their*

*world had been shattered, their lives irrevocably altered, but*
*Josh was home. That was all that really mattered.*
  *Josh was home. Their lives could begin again.*
—Tami Hoag—*Night Sins*

Though Hoag uses the words—their lives could begin again—the subtext of the last several pages of her story is not to take anything for granted. Your loved ones. Security. Or the assumption that a killer will not strike again. All stunning hooks for readers of thrillers and suspense.

Leaving a story ending on a hook is paramount if you are writing a series, or connected books.

Prologues, or a portion of a chapter of the next book by the same author, are often used to create story hooks to pick up that next book by the same author. The best authors don't let the next book sell itself. They make sure a reader is intellectually and emotionally satisfied with the current story, and that some story questions are already raised for the next story.

In the last third of one novel, you start giving more page space to a secondary character or plot line that will spin off into another novel. The more you can invest a reader in wanting to know more about all of your characters, the easier it is for you as an author to sell connected books, and for your readers to anticipate your next book eagerly.

Do not think only in terms of books that are related by characters, although it is an effective hook in many Nora Roberts books. Roberts is famous for her trilogies—three sisters, three brothers, three witches—that then spin off into multi-generational sagas. She is no fool. She knows if a reader gets hooked into one story line, they expect to find out what happens to others in the 'family' and thus future sales are built into the mix.

Think also in terms of place—a locale—small Southern town, or an island off the coast of Nova Scotia, or the eccentric characters from a future world. Or an event—related stories impacted by a historic event or a current event—adults who all experienced a traumatic experience as children, etc.. Each might have their own story, and thus their own book, if hooks are woven into your current story.

So keep in mind: if you want an open-ended series, of any kind, create open-ended last pages or paragraphs that build to open-ended last lines. On the other hand, if you are writing stand-alone books, last lines must give the sense of closure and release, breaking the spell you've woven as an author in such a way that the reader will pick up your next book just to re-experience that thematic completeness you've accomplished.

How do you do that? Return to your first lines. To the theme and questions raised there. Make sure you've addressed both as you end your story. Take the time to get your last line just right. Make it a line your readers remember and you will hook them into picking up your next novel.

Compelling characters, strong writing, a grasp of the craft elements of pacing, point of view, dialogue and plotting— they are the backbone of your novel. But once you've mastered them, understanding and using hooks can take a good book and make it stronger, make it harder to put down, and make it easier for the reader to continue to read.

## PART 7: CREATING MULTIPLE HOOKS

Many writers who are first exposed to the concept of hooks can erroneously make two assumptions: the first is to assume you only need one hook to open your story (though in some stories that can be enough, if it's a strong one), but the second assumption is more problematic. That's to assume that to use multiple hooks in the opening of a novel, or scene opening, or a chapter, means that the sentence must become long and unwieldy. But that's not the case. Short can work just as well and contain multiple hooks at the same time.

Look at the following example from a paranormal romance novel that has eight of the 10 Universal Hooks!

> *"Kill the baby."*
> –Sherrilyn Kenyon — *Acheron*

Three words, eight hooks — Action/Danger, Overpowering Emotion (the thought of a baby about to be killed will elicit this hook in most readers), a Surprising Situation (especially for a romance novel), the Totally Unexpected (given it's a romance novel), Question(s) Raised, Surprising or Shocking Dialogue, Unique Character (especially the person who is issuing the order) and Foreshadowing with Warning (that this action will have repercussions in the story) — and the author has created a very powerful opening line. The only two hooks that are missing are the Humor and Evocative Hooks, neither which would have been appropriate given the sentence.

The more hooks a single line contains, the more tension you'll have on the page, and the more tension, the faster your pacing will be.

For the rough draft, you might find yourself cramming in every hook you can possibly use because you've researched the NYT authors and the debut authors with six-figure contracts and noticed how many hooks they use in their genre. Next thing you know, you're throwing blood and gore into a Women's Fiction story because you want the Action/Danger Hook, or flowery, poetic language into a police procedural opening to gain a hook usually found in literary novels.

I've stated this already, but will state it again because it's a very important point. Read what you plan to write and analyze which hooks are the most common for your type of story. Research how many hooks are usually used and where hooks are normally found.

**NOTE:** Always research the intensity or tension level created by your genre and write hooks that fit this level of reader expectation.

Let's look at an amateur sleuth mystery novel set in an international location to see how one author combines multiple hooks while keeping his opening sentence tight.

Before we get to the example, let's assume the author wrote several drafts before he homed in on his opening.

ROUGH DRAFT: *I was chained up in a Cambodia prison cell and no one knew I was here.*

The reader is told about the situation and a Question(s) Raised Hook is here—why does no one know he's there—but because we know nothing about this POV character, it's natural for the reader to withhold their empathy until they're given a reason to root for this protagonist. After all, this character might deserve to be in prison.

So an opening line with a weak Question(s) Raised Hook not only leaves the reader waiting to engage, they might also be confused as to what kind of mystery this is. It could come across as pretty gritty and brutal when the opposite is true.

This particular mystery series, written by Colin Cotterill, features Dr. Siri Paibourn, who is a wry, and daily defiant official coroner of Laos in the mid-1970s. Each book is chock full of cultural and historical details of a country struggling in the aftermath of the Vietnam War, through the point of view of a man who never gives up his zest for life or belief in the humanity of most of his fellow men. Let's see how Cotterill uses this opening story line to remind his series readers about his protagonist, as well as hook his new readers in an engaging opening sentence.

> *I celebrate the dawn of my seventy-fourth birthday handcuffed to a lead pipe.*
> *— Colin Cotterill — Love Songs from a Shallow Grave*

Since most readers would not expect to be handcuffed to anything on their birthday, Cotterill uses a Question(s) Raised Hook here, but takes it to the next level by adding in the age element, which moves the internalization to both a Surprising Situation (being handcuffed) and the Totally Unexpected (given the character's age). Plus, this adds in a number of questions, as it's clear this situation is going to have repercussions in the story and the reader must keep reading to find out more about the seventy-four-year-old protagonist and if he survives this opening situation, so the Foreshadowing with Warning Hook is present. Which leads to the Action/Danger Hook. If the reader didn't know his age, just that he was male, there would not necessarily be as strong a sense of danger.

So the Cotterill opening line contains five hooks in this one opening sentence.

**NOTE:** If in doubt, there is no hook.

Now that you know what to look for, if, in your analysis of other novels or stories, you learn that the best authors use two to three hooks in an opening, and debut writers use three to six, then what you'll want to aim for is three to five hooks at a minimum. Too few hooks and your opening will fall flat; too many hooks and it can jar the reader—and not in a good way.

## ASSIGNMENT:

1. Learn from other authors. Copy great opening sentences, or ends of chapters or scene sentences, as these can be the easiest to identify as containing hooks. Then hand-write one hundred great hook sentences. The process of hand-writing slows you down to really absorb what you're seeing.

2. Find eight to twelve books like what you are writing. (Yes, you can use the same books from the first assignment in this book or books already on your bookshelves.) By *like* I mean that your book would be shelved in the same area in a bookstore. Again, make sure some of these books are by debut authors or authors you have never read. Why? Because their hooks must work stronger to entice you into reading more. Once you've selected your books (make sure you haven't read the book yet because you want to be hooked based on that key first line, not by what you know happens on page three) look at just the opening line. (If it's a short line or in dialogue, read until there's a natural stop.) Write the line down so you're not analyzing this line in context with what comes next in the story. Then compare these 8-12 lines. Look for which hooks are used most often now that you've learned the ten most common hooks. Ask yourself how many hooks are the norm. Ask, too, if you'd keep reading based on just this line.

3. Dissect killer hook lines. See what happens if you rewrite them. Do they become stronger or weaker?

4. Identify your own strengths and opportunities as a writer. Do you fall into certain types of hooks by default, avoid others because they are more challenging to write?

5. Focus on your beginnings and ends of scenes and chapters. It can be too daunting to consciously think about each and every sentence you write in a full-length novel, or even a shorter novella or short story. However, you can pour energy into every sentence in the opening and closing of paragraphs that begin or end a scene or chapter. Make improvements here, after you've worked on your killer opening line, and you'll make your manuscript stand out in a crowded marketplace.

6. Study headlines that grab your attention. Not the subject of the headline but how the subject is presented or not presented. What causes you to slow down, pause or click through to read more? What are copywriters if not masters of understanding and using hooks? Headlines won't be complete sentences, but they do create an opportunity to focus closely on what grabs your attention, and therefore how copywriters do so with tight, focused and powerful words (when they work). Also, study when a headline doesn't work for you and play at how to change it up (without adding tons of additional words) until it does hook you.

**RECAP:**

Hooks are invaluable tools to create powerful writing. The more you study and learn about the 10 Universal Hooks, and those hooks you tend to gravitate toward writing, the easier it will be to apply them to your future work. Do not limit yourself to what you currently use as hooks, but be willing to try some new ones. Expect this to feel awkward and stiff initially, as we often feel when trying any new skill, whether it's learning to ride a bike, drive a car or use a new-to-us writing technique. It's only with practice that you will get better, and your writing will improve, too.

## PART 8: MOST COMMON QUESTIONS ABOUT HOOKS

**Q:** Can your sentence have more than one hook?

**A:** Yes, most opening sentences, in particular, do. Depending on the genre or sub-genre you are writing, and the amount of tension you want and need on the page, you'll need to add or decrease the number of hooks.

**Q:** How do I know how many hooks are appropriate in the key places you mention for what I'm writing?

**A:** By studying other novels in the genre you're writing. Especially the more recent debut authors, as the number and types of hooks used ten or twenty years ago can change, and well-known authors can sell novels based on name recognition alone vs. their need to engage and re-engage the reader.

**Q:** What if my novel crosses many genres? How do I focus on what hooks work best?

**A:** Determine the main focus of your story. Is it the mystery or the romance or the western element, etc.? Think in terms of the reader who wants to read what you're writing and what attracts them most and then study and use hooks for those readers first. If you don't know who your strongest readership might be, ask early readers—critique partners, friends, beta readers—who they think would love your book most.

**Q:** How do I learn more about hooks?

**A:** Read books, especially those that have kept you up late at night reading when you wanted to go to sleep. Read them once for enjoyment then reread to examine the key placement of hooks on the page to see what types of hooks were used and how many at these key points. The more you see hooks in action, the easier it is for you to see in your own work which hooks to apply and where.

**Q:** I don't like all the kinds of hooks. Is that a problem for me as a writer?

**A:** No. Once you discover the types of hooks your readers respond to based on what you're seeing in the genre you're writing, you can focus on them. There is a problem if you love only one or two kinds of hooks only, such as the Evocative Hook, but are trying to write to a genre that tends NOT to love the Evocative Hook as much as you might. Once you start writing for publication, you must think about your reader more than your own preferences.

**Q:** Are placement of the hooks affected when the reader is using an e-reader? Do the pages fall the same way?

**A:** Yes. If the writer is writing on a word document (standard page formatting), and approaches their hook placement to that media, the hooks will be embedded where they need to be on e-Readers.

# BIBLIOGRAPHY

Ashner, Jules. *Whacked*. New York. Weinstein Books. 2009. Print.

Barr, Nevada. *Deep South*. New York. Berkley. 2001. Reissue Print.

Belkin, Lisa. First, *Do No Harm: The Dramatic Story of Real Doctors and Patients Making Impossible Choices at a Big-City Hospital*. New York. Fawcett. 1994. Print.

Berg, Elizabeth. *Open House*. New York. Random House. 2000. Print.

Briggs, Patricia. *Moon Called*. New York. Ace. 2010. Print.

Buckham, Mary. *Invisible Journey*. Cantwell Publishing. 2013. Print.

Buckham, Mary. *Invisible Magic*. Cantwell Publishing. 2013. Print.

Caida, Micah. *Time Trap*. Atlanta. Silverhawk Press. 2014. Print.

Carmichael, Kathy. *Hot Flash*. MacGowan Press. Tampa. Re-issue 2015. digital.

Child, Lee. *The Enemy*. New York. Delacorte Press. 2004. Print.

Child, Lee. *The Hard Way*. New York. Random House. 2006. Print.

Child, Lee. *Gone Tomorrow*. New York. Bantam Dell. 2009. Print.

Cleve, Chris. *Little Bee*. New York. Simon & Schuster. 2009. Reprint.

Cohn, Rachel. *Cupcake*. New York. Simon and Schuster. 2008. Print.

Cornwell, Bernard. *Agincourt*. New York. Harper Collins. 2009. Reprint.

Conroy, Pat. *South of Broad*. New York. Dial Press. 2009. Reprint.

Cotterill, Colin. *Love Songs From a Shallow Grave*. New York. Soho Crime. 2011. Print.

Craig, Christie. *Divorced, Desperate and Delicious*. New York. Lovespell. 2011. Digital.

Crumley, James. *The Last Good Kiss*. New York. Vintage Contemporaries. 1988. Print.

DeMille, Nelson. *The Lion's Game*. New York. Grand Central Publishing. 2000. Print.

Diamant, Anita. *The Red Tent*. New York. St. Martin's Press. 2010. Reissue Print.

Dunnett, Dorothy. *The Disorderly Knight*. New York. Random House. 2010. Reprint.

Dunnett, Dorothy. *The Ringed Castle*. New York. Random House. 2010. Reprint.

Eugenides, Jeffrey. *The Virgin Suicides*. New York. Farrar, Straus and Giroux. 2010. Reprint.

Evanovich, Janet. *Seven Up*. New York. St. Martin's Press. 2010. Print.

Follett, Ken. Jackdaws. New York. Penguin. 2002. Print.

Forsyth, Frederick. The Cobra. New York. Penguin. 2010. Print.

Gardiner, Meg. Mission Canyon. New York. Penguin. 2008. Print.

Gardner, Lisa. *Touch & Go*. New York. Penguin Group. 2013. Print.

Gerritsen, Tess. *The Keepsake*. New York. Ballantine Books. 2009. Print.

Gilman, Dorothy. *A Palm for Mrs. Pollifax*. New York. Fawcett. 1973. Print.

Gilman, Dorothy. *The Elusive Mrs. Pollifax*. New York. Fawcett. 1971. Print.

Green, John. *The Fault In Our Stars*. New York. Penguin Group. 2012. Print.

Green, Simon R. *Agents of Light and Darkness*. New York. Berkley. 2003. Print.

Grunwald, Lisa. *The Irresistible Henry House*. New York. Random House. 2010. Print.

Hamilton, Steve. *Blood is the Sky*. New York. St. Martin's. 2003. Print.

Hanff Korelitz, Jean. *Admission*. New York. Grand Central Publishing. 2009. Print.

Harris, Charlaine. Dead Over Heels. New York. Simon & Schuster. 1996. Print.

Hoag, Tami. *Night Sins*. New York. Bantam. 2003. Print.

Hornby, Nick. *Juliet, Naked*. New York. Penguin. 2009. Print.

James, P.D. *The Private Patient*. New York. Vintage. 2008. Print.

Katzenbach, John. *The Madman's Tale*. New York. Ballantine Books. 2004. Print.

Kenyon, Sherrilyn. *Acheron*. New York. St. Martin's Press. 2010. Print.

Kenyon, Sherrilyn & Love, Dianna. *Whispered Lies*. New York. Pocket Books. 2009. Reprint.

Koontz, Dean. *Lightning*. New York. Berkley. 2003. Print.

Krentz, Jayne Ann. *Copper Beach*. New York. Penguin. 2012. Print.

Le Carré, John. *A Most Wanted Man*. New York. Scribner. 2008. Print.

Lee, Y. S. *A Spy in the House*. Sommerville, MA. Candlewick. 2010. Reprint.

Lehane, Dennis. *Moonlight Mile*. Harper Collins. New York. 2010. Print.

Lippman, Laura. *In a Strange City*. Avon Books. New York. 2001. Print.

Liu, Marjorie M. *Armor of Roses*. Anthology: *Inked*. New York. Berkley. 2010. Print.

Liu, Marjorie M. *The Iron Hunt*. New York. Berkley. 2008. Print.

MacHale, D.J.*The Soldiers of Halla*. New York. Simon and Schuster. 2009. Digital.

Mantel, Hilary. *Beyond Black*. New York. Henry Holt and Co. 2006. Reprint.

Martin, George R.R. *A Game of Thrones*. New York. Bantam Books. 2011. Print.

McKillip, Patricia A. *The Sorceress and the Cygnet*. New York. Berkley. 1991. Print.

Monk, Devon. *Dead Iron*. New York. NAL. 2011. Print.

Mosley, Walter. *Fear Itself*. New York. Time Warner. 2003. Print.

Noël, Alyson. *Evermore*. New York. St. Martin's. 2009. Print.

Page, Sharon. *The Club*. New York. Dell. 2009. Print.

Penny, Louise. *The Beautiful Mystery*. New York. St. Martin's Press. 2012. Print.

Perry, Anne. *A Sudden Fearful Death*. New York. Ballantine Books. 1993. Print.

Picoult, Jodi. *My Sister's Keeper*. New York. Atria Books. 2004. Print.

Picoult, Jodi. Songs of the Humpback Whale. New York: Washington Square Press. 1992. Print.

Pitticus, Lore. *The Power of Six*. New York. Harper Collins. 2011. Reprint.

Pratchett, Terry. *Carpe Jugulum*. New York. Harper Collins. 1998. Print.

Quick, Amanda. *The Mystery Woman*. New York. Jove Books. 2013. Print.

Quindlen, Anna. *One True Thing*. New York. Random House LLC. 2010. Reprint.

Ramirez, Misa. *Hasta La Vista, Lola!* New York. Minotaur Books. 2010. Print.

Raybourn, Deanna. *A Spear of Summer Grass*. Ontario. MIRA. 2013. Print.

Raybourn, Deanna. *Silent on the Moor*. Ontario. MIRA. 2012. Print.

Raybourn, Deanna. *The Dead Travel Fast*. New York. Mira. 2010. Print.

Roberts, Nora. *Black Hills*. New York. Jove. 2009. Reprint.

Rollins, James. *The Judas Strain*. New York. Harper Collins. 2009. Reprint.

Scalzi, John. *Zoe's Tale*. New York. Tor. 2008. Reprint.

Stabenow, Dana. *A Deeper Sleep*. New York. St. Martin's Press. 2006. Print.

Walls, Jeanette. *Half Broke Horses*. New York. Scribner. 2009. Reprint edition.

Walls, Jeanette. *The Glass Castle*. New York. Scribner. 2005. Reprint.

Ward, J. R. *Crave*. Penguin. New York. 2010. Print.

Wentworth, Patricia. *Brading Collection*. New York. Perennial. 1992. Print.

Westerfeld, Scott. *Uglies*. New York. Simon Pulse. 2011. Print.

Wilde, Lori. *Sweet Surrender*. Harlequin Blaze. Toronto, Ontario. 2010. Print.

Witting Albert, Susan. *Indigo Dying*. New York. Berkley Book. 2004. Print.

Did You Like Writing Active Hooks: The Complete How-to Guide on Kindle? Let the world know by posting a review. You = Awesome. Me = Grateful.

I also love hearing from fellow writers and readers! Find me on Goodreads or Facebook or Twitter!

Want to dig deeper into the power of Hooks to engage readers and keep them turning the page?
Hooks help guide the reader deeper and deeper into your book.
You can enroll in any of my online classes on the 10 Universal Hooks or get the whole bundle. Work at your own pace, anywhere, anytime. Listen to my lectures with slides. Learn from all new examples not included in the WRITING ACTIVE HOOKS books. Try the exercises and take the quizzes to master hooks in YOUR writing.
*Click here to join the class now:* http://bit.ly/1YrvflK

Ready to take on new writing challenges? Join me one Wednesday a month for a live writing webinar. Every month I tackle a different aspect for writers.
It's your chance to dig into new aspects of writing. You can pick topics that interests you one at a time, or you can register for six months of webinars all at once.
Click here to see the topics and learn more:
http://bit.ly/2u5Cgiz

Want to Read my Urban Fantasy Novels?
"Not since Kate Daniels and Mercy Thompson have I fallen in love with a female character like I have with Alex Noziak."
~Urban Girl Reader.

Click here to grab *INVISIBE MAGIC*, the first book in the series: http://amzn.to/YFgJIU

Be the First to Find Out When My Next Writing Craft Book or Class Comes Out.
I'm always working on the next big thing. Get a publication alert by signing up for my newsletter.
At MaryBuckhamOnWriting.com

Questions? Comments?
Help make the next edition of this book even better. If you've found a pesky typo in this book, here's your chance to let me know. Have a writing craft issue you'd like me to cover in the next books in this series, let me know. Email suggestions to: Assistant@MaryBuckham.com

A few lesser-known facts about me:
I love to read and analyze fiction. I've been known to stay up all night to finish a new novel, devouring first and then re-reading to analyze. I love teaching others about ways to improve their own fiction because first and foremost I am a writer — like you!

I'm a USA Today Bestselling author who has fan girl moments at every writer's conference I attend.
There's not a type of fiction that I don't love (except horror, if it's done really well it can scare the willies out of me and then I get nothing done for days! So I moderate my horror consumption).

I love being an author of both fiction and non-fiction work. Love writing. Love talking about writing. And I love hearing from readers. Email me, anytime, and I'll get back to you as soon as I can.

All the best,

Mary Buckham

Printed in Great Britain
by Amazon